Shakespeare *the Papist*

Shakespeare *the Papist*

Peter Milward, S.J.

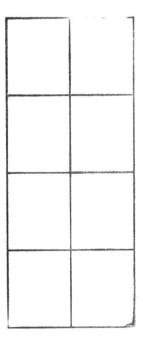

Sapientia Press
of Ave Maria University

08 05

Requests for permission to make copies of any part of the work should be directed to:

Sapientia Press
of Ave Maria University
5050 Ave Maria Blvd.
Ave Maria, FL 34142
888-343-8607

Cover Design: Eloise Anagnost

Printed in the United States of America.

Library of Congress Control Number: 2005900804

ISBN-13: 978-1-932589-21-4

Table of Contents

Introduction

"He died a papist." These words written about William Shakespeare, who died in 1616, are found among notes left by an Anglican divine, Richard Davies, who was for a time rector of Sapperton in Gloucestershire in the latter half of the seventeenth century. They are still preserved among the treasures of his college of Corpus Christi, Oxford. He was thus living at a time and in a place sufficiently close to the actual scene of the poet's death for us to accept him as a credible mouthpiece of local tradition. His profession as an Anglican divine, moreover, removes him from any suspicion of religious bias, such as might have attached to a Catholic priest making a similar claim for the poet. Consequently, most of Shakespeare's biographers, apart from a few confirmed skeptics, accept the words, if with some reluctance. Many of them hastily add, however, that even if Shakespeare died a Papist, it is unlikely, given the untoward circumstances of his age, that he would have lived as one or written as one.

On the other hand, in recent years a surprising number of studies have appeared, dealing with various aspects of the dramatist's religious background and early formation, whether at Stratford or (according to a theory that is drawing widespread interest) Lancashire. No less surprising is the fact that they incline to the view that if Shakespeare died a Papist, he also was brought up as one. In such matters, of course, where records are scant and fragmentary, there can be little absolute certainty. But what evidence we have amounts to some degree of probability, pointing to the likelihood that Shakespeare was up till the time of his dramatic career a Catholic—with a Catholic father, John Shakespeare, presiding over his formative years and a Catholic daughter, Susanna Hall, comforting him in his declining years at Stratford. At least, both of them were listed for one year apiece in the "recusancy returns" for not attending the services at the local Anglican church.

Now what, it may be asked, of the period in between the Papist beginning and the Papist end? What of Shakespeare's dramatic career? Can we say of any of his plays that have come down to us, thanks in no small measure to the Anglican editors of the First Folio of 1623, Shakespeare's fellow actors, John Hemings and Henry Condell—can we say of them that they betray Catholic sympathies on the part of the dramatist? Few even among Catholic scholars are prepared to affirm that they do, however much they would like to think so. Only the great Catholic Victorian thinker John Henry Newman, in one of the essays included in his *Idea of a University* (1873), ventured the opinion that Shakespeare "has so little of a Protestant about him that Catholics have been able, without extravagance, to claim him as their own". One such Catholic was, no doubt, his colleague the Shakespearian scholar Richard Simpson, whose detailed notes on *The Religion of Shakespeare* were put together and published in 1899 by a priest of Newman's Oratory, Henry Sebastian Bowden. After him mention may also be made of that other great Catholic thinker of the twentieth century, G. K. Chesterton. In his book *Chaucer* (1932), in a chapter on "Chaucer and the Renaissance", he observes, "That Shakespeare was a Catholic is a thing that every Catholic feels by every sort of convergent common sense to be true." Such general assertions, however, can hardly be expected to carry any weight with an academic community which is ever on its guard against any manifestation of religious bias.

Now, therefore, at the present stage of Shakespeare studies, it is all the more necessary to turn from the few biographical data concerning the dramatist and what they may tell us of his religion to the plays themselves as constituting his literary and dramatic heritage to after ages. Nor is it enough to survey the plays in general, pausing briefly at occasional signs in them of a religious interest. Rather, we have to question the plays one after another, so far as possible in their chronological order of composition, to what extent they reveal a Catholic cast of mind or Catholic sympathies. At the same time, we have to remember how dangerous it would have been for the dramatist to betray Catholic sympathies at all openly. He was writing at a time of intense anti-Catholic persecution, which was at its height during the period when he was most active in the production of his plays, roughly from 1590 to 1610. And among the members of his audience there would have been not a few spies and informers ready to report him to the authorities for any lapses of loyalty to the existing regime. Like Edgar and Kent in *King Lear*, he could never feel safe in leaving off his disguise. He could express his true feelings (supposing them to have been Catholic) only at a remove from his seeming words, while leaving himself with a convenient excuse in case of accusation.

Unfortunately for my present purpose, however, this same disguise would be effective not only among Shakespeare's Elizabethan contemporaries but also among modern

Shakespeare scholars. However many implications I may find in the plays pointing to deep Catholic sympathies, I still have to face the response of "Not proven" as well from Catholic as from agnostic critics. All I can do in this book is to go through the plays in a way no Shakespeare scholar has (to the best of my knowledge) ever done, and to show how far the hypothesis that Shakespeare was a Catholic (at least, at heart) may be substantiated from the text of each play. This is a process that, I might add, culminates in the two plays which we know were produced, shortly after they were printed in quarto form, for recusant audiences in the north of England during the winter of 1609–10, namely *King Lear* and *Pericles*.

All I require of my readers at this point is that they approach my discussion of Shakespeare's plays with an open mind and without preconception. I do not claim to offer them a rigid scientific proof for all my assertions, most of which (I admit) call for such qualifications as "probable" or at least "possible". What I do claim is that they all fit together according to that species of proof which John Henry Newman in his *Grammar of Assent* (1870) terms a "convergence of probabilities" (echoed by Chesterton in his above-quoted words). To attain such an insight it is not required of any reader that he should be himself a Catholic or even sympathetic to Catholicism. Not a few scholars who have pursued this investigation and come out in favour of the Catholic interpretation—notably J. H. De Groot in his book on *The Shakespeares and "The Old Faith"* (1946)—have set out from a Protestant or agnostic position. All that is required of readers is, I would say, what Coleridge calls a "willing suspension of disbelief", involving the patience to peruse all I have to present by way of a hypothesis, without making up their minds on the matter till they have heard it to the end.

A Note on Nomenclature

"CATHOLIC"—not "Roman Catholic"—is the term used to denote members of the Catholic (or "universal") Church of the Latin West, and to differentiate them from members of the Orthodox (or "right-minded") Church of the Greek East, especially from the time of the Great Schism from the eleventh century onwards. It included all Englishmen up till the time of the sixteenth-century Reformation. As for "Roman Catholic", it is a term that has only recently acquired currency in contradistinction with those Anglicans who also claim to be "Catholic", under the other name of "Anglo-Catholic". Neither term is to be found in writings of the sixteenth century.

"Papist" is a term often used of English Catholics from the reign of Henry VIII onwards. They still recognized the supremacy of the Pope as vicar of Christ and head of the universal Church, against the claim made by Henry VIII and his successors (except Mary Tudor) to be supreme head (or "governor" in the case of Elizabeth I) of the Church of England. The term was mainly used by Protestants against the Catholics, not by the Catholics themselves. Shakespeare uses it only once, in *All's Well That Ends Well*, in the mouth of the clown Lavache, who is at once criticized by the

Countess for being "a foul-mouthed and calumnious knave" (I iii.57).

"Recusant" (from the Latin *recusare*) is the technical term used by Elizabethan officials for those Catholics who refused to attend the new "heretical" services of the Anglican Church, despite the increasingly severe penalties involved. On the other hand, those Catholics who conformed outwardly, while remaining Catholics at heart, were termed "Church Papists". There is no evidence that Shakespeare was himself a recusant, though both his father John Shakespeare in 1592 and his daughter Susanna Hall in 1606 were named in the "recusancy returns" for those years.

"Protestant" is the normal term for those who associated themselves in some way with the "reforms" introduced by Martin Luther from 1517 onwards, especially as a result of the Diet of Speyer in 1529, when the reform party presented a *Protestatio* against the Catholic majority. Such reforms were prohibited but circulated in England under Henry VIII (with the connivance of Thomas Cromwell and Thomas Cranmer), then openly accepted by the government under Edward VI, but again prohibited under Mary Tudor, till they were finally accepted and imposed on all Englishmen under Elizabeth I. From then onwards the Church of England, for all its minor differences, was recognized as one of the "reformed" Churches in union with those on the continent, and Elizabeth with her government invariably supported the Protestant cause in those countries against the Catholics. Shakespeare, however, never uses the term.

"Puritan" is the term used by both Papists and Protestants from the mid-1560s onwards for those more radical Protestants in England who aimed at a form of church government and "discipline" modeled on the pattern of Calvin's Church in Geneva. At first they stood out for their refusal to accept the prescribed vestments for liturgical ceremonies or to admit the right of the bishops to impose their use, though they recognized Queen Elizabeth as "governor" of the Church of England and accepted the thirty-nine articles of that Church. They themselves did not use the term till the early seventeenth century, but Shakespeare uses it with some frequency (seven times) in his plays.

"Anglican" is not a term commonly used in Elizabethan documents, except in the Latin form of *Ecclesia Anglicana*, as when it appears in the title of John Jewel's celebrated *Apologia Ecclesiae Anglicanae* (1562). This is translated not as "Anglican Church" but as "Church of England" in its two translations (one by Lady Anne Bacon, mother of Sir Francis) of 1562 and 1564. The other term, "Episcopalian", comes much later, chiefly with reference to the Church in America, but "the Episcopal party" is used in England at the time of the Puritan rebellion in the mid-seventeenth century.

chapter 1
Shakespeare's Papist Background

IN THE HISTORY of Shakespearian scholarship it has long been the received wisdom to lay emphasis on the plays themselves, without paying overmuch attention to their historical context—according to Shakespeare's own principle, "The play's the thing." In any case, the plays themselves seem to direct our attention beyond the narrow confines of the age in which they were composed, to lands beyond the seas in a world of romance, or to ages in the history of England long before the dramatist or any member of his audience was born. Such is the impression put into memorable words by Shakespeare's friend and rival, Ben Jonson, in his eulogy prefixed to the First Folio of 1623, to the effect that the author was writing "not for an age but for all time".

Still, once the scholars of the eighteenth century got down to the task of preparing critical editions of the plays, they found it necessary to establish the precise text, in view of the many variant readings among the quartos and the First Folio. The dramatist himself seems to have been blissfully unconcerned about the transmission of his plays to posterity, in contrast to the care he evidently took over the printing of his two long poems, *Venus and Adonis* and *The*

Rape of Lucrece, which he dedicated in 1593 and 1594 to his noble patron, the young Earl of Southampton. A similar care we find taken by Ben Jonson over the printing not only of his poems but also of his plays. Why, we wonder, despite the evident interest in literary fame expressed in his sonnets, did Shakespeare adopt such a cavalier attitude towards his plays, and even towards those very sonnets?

Then, following the lead of the great Edmund Malone, the scholars went on to explore the precise date of composition of the plays, as well as of their publication. The probable order they came up with turned out to be very different from that in which they had been arranged in 1623 by the editors of the First Folio—though the latter were two of Shakespeare's fellow actors in the King's Men. Again, following the lead of Richard Farmer, in his *Essay on the Learning of Shakespeare* (1767), they began to search for the various literary sources on which the dramatist had based the plots of his plays—not content with Dryden's easy assumption, in his *Essay on Dramatic Poesie* (1668), that Shakespeare "needed not the spectacles of books to read Nature, he looked inwards and found her there". Nor were they content with the more obvious sources in Holinshed's *Chronicles* (for the English history plays) and North's *Plutarch* (for the Roman plays). But they went on, especially during the Victorian age, with the activities of the Shakespeare Society and the New Shakespeare Society, to rummage through the writings of classical, mediaeval, and Renaissance authors, as well as Tudor translations of the Bible, for echoes and influences of all kinds over and above the major sources.

As for the historical context in which the dramatist lived and wrote his plays, that they were mostly content to leave in the hands of professional historians. Sadly, however, they overlooked the fact that those historians might be as little interested in the plays of Shakespeare as they themselves were in the detailed events of the age. This is why a professional historian of the Elizabethan age such as A. L. Rowse could write a biography of Shakespeare (1963) replete at once with scorn for the literary scholars who had preceded him in this task and with self-satisfaction as an expert on that period. Yet for all his self-professed expertise, Rowse was ill-equipped to deal with the religious background, considering his undisguised contempt for the religious controversies that formed no small part of it.

In this respect, however, Rowse was in sympathy with not a few Shakespeare scholars, who went so far as to project their prejudices into the mind of the dramatist himself. At least, they could have appealed to several significant utterances in the plays, where the dramatist, though mainly silent on the religious issues of his day, seems to imply a loathing for all religious controversy. These utterances may not have an undeniable relevance to such controversy, but their significance may be gauged by their irrelevance to the dramatic context, or what T. S. Eliot might have called their lack of an "objective correlative". One is where Mercutio in the turning point of *Romeo and Juliet* calls down "a plague o' both your houses" (III i.96)—considering that the conflict between the houses of Montague and Capulet might well sound in Elizabethan ears as an echo of that between the Catholics and the Protestants and that one prominent Catholic house happened to be that of Viscount Montague. Another is where Helena in the contemporary comedy of *A Midsummer Night's Dream* exclaims against the "devilish-holy fray" in which "truth kills truth" (III ii.129), with a probable reference to the fray not so much between her competing lovers as between the controversialists of the age. A third is where the licentious Lucio early on in *Measure for*

Measure maintains, oddly out of context, that "grace is grace despite of all controversy" (I ii.26).

When we turn from the plays to the controversies, we may notice that, contrary to Rowse's unhistorical prejudice, they were for the most part by no means merely academic, inspired by an *odium theologicum* between rival sects. Rather, they arose out of a historical situation created by Henry VIII largely for personal reasons and coming to a crescendo under Elizabeth I. It came to be interpreted by Elizabethan Catholics as a full-scale persecution, though covered up by Elizabeth's ministers in terms of an "execution of justice" against traitors. In their eyes it was a situation comparable to that enacted against the early Christians by the Roman emperors.

The full awareness of this persecution was first given formal expression in print by the Jesuit Robert Persons on the basis of his experience of a year's ministry among the afflicted Catholics of England. In the summer of 1580 he had returned to his native land with his fellow Jesuit Edmund Campion, but in the following year Campion had been arrested, imprisoned, and tortured with the rack in the Tower of London, arraigned with others in Westminster Hall, and sentenced to death as a traitor. This sentence had, moreover, been carried out at Tyburn (near today's Marble Arch) with all its gory requirements of dismemberment in sight of a large crowd. Persons himself had had to take refuge on the continent from the imminent danger in England; when he heard the details of his friend's death, he could contain himself no longer but gave vent to his indignation, before the year was out, in a small book published in Latin at Rouen under the title *De Persecutione Anglicana Epistola* (1581). Two more editions in Latin were published the following year at Rome and Ingolstadt, with French and English translations at the same time. In this way it was Persons's aim to spread an awareness of the current persecution against the English Catholics through all the Catholic countries of Europe, and particularly in the courts of kings who might put political pressure on Elizabeth's government to desist from such bloody measures.

Persons's accusation was taken up in two more books compiled in Latin from a variety of documentary sources including his epistle. One was published in 1583 by another English Jesuit, John Gibbons, under the title *Concertatio Ecclesiae Catholicae in Anglia*, and the other in 1589, a larger compilation under the same title by the secular priest John Bridgewater. This outcry prompted the all-powerful Lord Burghley, in whom the Catholics recognized their principal opponent, to maintain what he called in a book of that title, *The Execution of Justice in England,* an official but anonymous publication of 1583, against "traitors and enemies of the realm, without any persecution of them for questions of religion". The book was also immediately published in Latin and French translations. The author was in turn challenged by the chief representative of the English Catholics, the president of the English college (or seminary) at Rheims, Dr. William Allen, in his dignified *True, Sincere and Modest Defence of the English Catholics* the following year. Against Burghley he specially emphasized the fact that the Catholics and their priests were suffering not for any political activities with which they might be charged, but for their faith. His book was also translated into Latin and published under a title similar to that used by Persons, *Ad Persecutores Anglos.*

From the beginning of her reign Elizabeth and her ministers had proceeded with caution in urging a religious policy that had been decided by only a small majority—achieved in the absence of the imprisoned Catholic bishops from Mary's reign—at her first Parliament in 1559. Subsequently, however, with the arrival in her realm of the Catholic Queen of Scots, Mary Stuart, in 1568, with the rising of the northern earls in support of her and the Catholic cause in 1569, with the excommunication of Elizabeth by Pope Pius V in 1570, and with the Ridolphi Plot resulting in the execution of the Duke of Norfolk in 1572, the screw was increasingly turned on the Catholics, now that they could be shown as traitors, not martyrs. From then onwards it became increasingly difficult no less for the wise than for the simple to distinguish the religious from the political cause, surrounded as they were by what Shakespeare calls "the seeming truth which cunning times put on/ to entrap the wisest" (*The Merchant of Venice* III ii.100). So to more and more Catholics, especially among the laity, it seemed that the only way out of their intolerable afflictions was the forceful method of invasion from one or other of the Catholic powers on the continent, whether France or Spain. Such a conclusion, however, increasingly played into the hands of their enemies at home.

From 1574 onwards, the priests who had been ordained at the seminary at Douai (before its removal to Rheims in 1578) began returning to England—not, it was emphasized, for any political purpose, but to bring the comforts of their religion to their fellow Catholics. All the same, they became a special object of pursuit by the English authorities through a network of spies, which had already been organized by Lord Burghley with the able assistance of Sir Francis Walsingham since 1569, in connection with the Ridolphi Plot. Once they were caught, the priests might expect the fate of cruel torture on the rack, forcing them to come out with confessions concerning their friends and associates, then of execution by being hanged, but drawn down while alive and cut up into quarters before an often bloodthirsty crowd. The first of them to suffer in this barbarous way was a former friend and pupil of Campion's at St. John's College, Oxford, Cuthbert Mayne, who was put to death in Cornwall in 1577. From then onwards one such instance led to another, till a crescendo was reached with Campion's execution in 1581, and that led to a whole literature on the subject from either side, culminating in the above-mentioned epistle of Robert Persons on *The Persecution of Catholics in England*—to give its English title, published in 1582. Yet in the case of Campion and Persons, their persecutors were able to point by way of self-justification to a papal-approved but ill-advised and ill-conceived expedition to Ireland in 1579, when the papal nuncio accompanying the small army had been the noted Catholic controversialist from Louvain, Nicholas Sanders.

All these events have to be kept in mind—though they are rarely mentioned by Shakespeare scholars—when considering the dramatist's religious and political background. For they were all happening while he was growing to maturity in the seeming backwater of Stratford-upon-Avon and probably, as a growing number of scholars are coming to agree, in Lancashire. In particular, when Campion and Persons arrived on the shores of England in the summer of 1580, Shakespeare was already a young man of sixteen, and, if we accept the so-called "Shakeshafte theory", he was on the point of leaving Stratford for the more secure haven of English Catholics in Lancashire. Was the young Shakespeare then, one may ask, a Catholic? The answer to this question is partly (the other part, at home in Stratford, remains to be considered) bound up with this theory, which, though first proposed some seventy years ago, now flourishes among Shakespeare scholars as never before. It is based on the mention of a certain "William Shakeshafte" in the will of a large Catholic landowner in mid-Lancashire, Alexander Houghton, which he drew up in the August of 1581. This William is commended, with another young man, Fulke Gwillom, either to Alexander's brother Thomas or to his friend Sir Thomas Hesketh, in connection with musical instruments and play-clothes for amateur theatricals. In addition to this will, a wealth of circumstantial evidence has been adduced, notably in recent times by E. A. J. Honigmann in a book entitled *Shakespeare, the 'Lost Years'* (1986), indicating that this young man named Shakeshafte may well have been the young Shakespeare. This, moreover, implies that, in order to belong in those dangerous times to a Catholic gentleman's household, whether as player or, especially, as tutor (disguised as a player), he must have been regarded as a loyal Catholic.

In that case, it may be asked, what was the young William Shakespeare, of Stratford-upon-Avon in Warwickshire, doing at such a time in such a remote county of England as Lancashire? To answer this question, we have to return to his family background and religious upbringing back in Stratford. As for his father, John Shakespeare was evidently a firm Catholic, even to the extent of being regarded as a recusant for his refusal to attend the services of the Church of England. For we find his name listed in the official recusancy returns for 1592, when in response to a royal proclamation of 1591 against Jesuits and seminary priests a special search was being made for Catholic recusants. On that occasion, it is true, he pleaded fear of "process for debt" as his reason for not attending church at the prescribed times, but we know that this was a typical subterfuge made by Catholics for evading the law.

In any case, John's recusancy is confirmed by a copy of a certain "Spiritual Testament" composed by the saintly

Archbishop of Milan, Charles Borromeo, for the use of afflicted English Catholics as a means of affirming their desire to die in the Catholic faith, when (as was most likely) they might be deprived of spiritual assistance in the hour of death. Copies of this testament had evidently been handed by Borromeo to Campion and Persons when they stayed with him on their journey from Rome to England in 1580. Then in the course of their journeys through the counties they in turn distributed it among English Catholics, to such effect that they had to write to Milan for more. A copy of this testament, made out in the name of John Shakespeare, was discovered hidden in the rafters of his house in Henley Street by workmen engaged on repairs in the mid-eighteenth century. For a time its authenticity was called in doubt, notably by Edmund Malone (who had at first accepted it), since that was an age of Shakespearian forgeries. But other versions of the same testament in other languages came to light in the early twentieth century, so that today it is generally regarded as genuine.

Now, it may further be asked, how could John Shakespeare have come by his copy of the testament? Can it be shown that he had some connection with Campion or Persons, and that he might have met one or the other of them during their journeys through the English Midlands in the summer and autumn of 1580? This might seem to be a hard matter to prove, since both men were naturally reticent about the places where they had stayed and the persons who had provided them with shelter. For their benefactors would have been subject to penalties almost as severe as those meted out to the priests—as we know from the cases of not a few of the "English martyrs" of that period. Campion himself reports to his superior general in Rome, "The enemy have so many eyes, so many tongues, so many scouts and crafts." Yet in a certain Lansdowne MS in the British Library there is a document drawn up in Burghley's handwriting, giving the responses made by Campion during his interrogation (under torture on the rack) in the Tower. Among the persons specified as having given him hospitality is Sir William Catesby, a relative of the Ardens, who had two houses in the region of Stratford, one at Lapworth in the Forest of Arden some ten miles to the north of Stratford, and the other at Ashby St. Leger on the border of Warwickshire and Northamptonshire. In either case, it would have been an easy ride for John and/or his son William to meet the renowned Campion and to receive a copy of the Spiritual Testament.

Yet another question is how much the young William or his father would have known about Edmund Campion or Robert Persons in such a provincial backwater as Stratford. Well, for a backwater, it is surprising how many of the schoolmasters at Stratford Grammar School during this period had connections with both Oxford and Lancashire. Many of them, including two who would have taught the young William there in his boyhood, Simon Hunt (1571–75) and John Cottam (1579–82), came from Lancashire, and all of them had Oxford degrees. The intervening one, Thomas Jenkins, was not from Lancashire, but he had been a colleague of Campion's as fellow of St. John's College, Oxford, in the 1560s. As for John Cottam, he was both neighbour to Alexander Houghton near Preston and brother to the seminary priest Thomas Cottam. The latter came over to England about the same time as Campion but was arrested soon after his arrival, and after long imprisonment he was arraigned with Campion and others in Westminster Hall, though his execution was delayed till May 1582. Before he died, he was admitted into the Society of Jesus. As for

Simon Hunt, he left Stratford in 1575 in company with one of his pupils, Robert Dibdale of Shottery, for Allen's seminary then at Douai, went on by himself to Rome, and was there admitted into the Society of Jesus. From all or any of these masters, particularly Thomas Jenkins, William may have heard about Campion, while on his part Campion may have heard from either Simon Hunt or Thomas Cottam of the recusant's son, the young and talented William, before arriving in England. Cottam in particular came to England with a letter from Robert Dibdale for his family in Shottery, but it remained undelivered and thus has been preserved in the state archives.

Speaking of letters, it may have been from John Cottam that William received a letter of introduction to Alexander Houghton, who was one of several Catholic gentlemen in Lancashire on the lookout for reliable Catholic tutors for their children. Such tutors might also be employed, according to the humanistic ideal of the age and the practice of Jesuit colleges abroad, as producers (and authors) of plays to be presented by their young charges for the entertainment of the household at such seasons as Christmas and Shrovetide (preceding Lent). The idea of such an introduction may well have come up in the course of a conversation with Campion at Catesby's house, when William might also have learnt of Campion's plans to visit the county of Lancashire in the early spring of 1581. The suggestion has even been made, by the author of *The Annotator* (1954), Alan Keen, that William may have already received some of his early schooling at Douai, maybe in company with Robert Dibdale. There is, however, no convincing evidence in support of this intriguing suggestion, apart from the signs of precocious talent in Shakespeare even from his earliest plays, besides the odd mention in *The Taming of the*

Shrew (II i.79) of "a young scholar, that has been long studying at Rheims", the very city to which Allen had moved his seminary in 1578.

Anyhow, assuming that the young William shortly made his way to Alexander Houghton's residence at Lea Hall, near Preston, we know from the above-mentioned Lansdowne MS that Campion confessed (under torture) not only to having spent the spring of 1581 in Lancashire, but also to having stayed part of the time at the home of Alexander's half-brother Richard at Park Hall, Charnock Richard (though this may have been Burghley's written conjecture). To that house he probably brought the books he needed for the completion of his Latin treatise *Rationes Decem*, which was printed at the secret printing press at Stonor Park in Oxfordshire and distributed on the benches of St. Mary's church, Oxford. In this case, we have the interesting situation of both the young William Shakespeare and the mature Jesuit Edmund Campion dwelling at the same time under the same family auspices in the same region of Lancashire, after having probably met each other in Warwickshire the previous summer. Then, what would have been more natural than for William, with his passion for drama, to have asked Campion about the Latin plays which the other had composed for his students at the Jesuit college at Prague, before being sent on the English mission? Thus Campion would have enjoyed the dignity of being Shakespeare's first tutor in the art of dramaturgy. Then on his side, it would have been no less natural for Campion to invite William to make the *Spiritual Exercises* of St. Ignatius Loyola, which Jesuits such as Campion aimed at giving to promising young men such as William. For here and there in the plays one comes upon interesting echoes of various places in these Exercises, such as the dramatist could have heard only from the lips of a Jesuit, seeing that the book of Exercises had not been issued for the general public—it had rather been intended as a guide for the giver of the Exercises—nor had it yet been translated into English.

As for William's wife, Anne Hathaway, whom he presumably met and married in 1582, the year after his presumed meeting with Campion, she was not only his senior by seven years but also a neighbour of the Dibdales in the village of Shottery and also, it seems, of the young man mentioned with William Shakeshafte in Alexander Houghton's will, Fulke Gwillom. It is thus conceivable that William was first introduced to Anne by Fulke on their return to Stratford after Alexander's death later on in 1581. All we know about the wedding is based on the evidence of their application for a licence to marry without the foregoing banns in late November 1582. In that application Anne's surname is misspelt as "Whateley", after having been spelt as "Hathwey" only a few entries before, and her residence is identified not as Shottery but as the nearby village of Temple Grafton. The latter place is no doubt mentioned as the church of the bride, at which the wedding was to be performed—or perhaps had already been performed. It is also interesting that the priest in charge of this village church is known, from a contemporary Puritan *Survey of the Ministry* for Warwickshire (1593), to have been an old Marian priest named Sir John Frith. So we may imagine William and Anne as having previously celebrated a "pre-contract" of marriage in a Catholic ceremony before this priest at Temple Grafton, rather like Claudio and Juliet in *Measure for Measure*, and then, when Anne's pregnancy became obvious, hastily arranging for a marriage licence at the bishop's registry in Worcester—though we have no record of their wedding at the Trinity church in Stratford. If all this is to be rejected as mere imagination, it is at least the kind of imagination commonly allowed to biographers of the bard.

Then, as for Shakespeare's mother, Mary Arden, the case for her Catholicism is stronger, if still circumstantial. We know that her father, Robert Arden, died in 1556 during the reign of Mary Tudor, leaving a markedly Catholic will, in which he bequeathed his soul "to Almighty God and to Our Blessed Lady, Saint Mary," and his land in Wilmcote to his youngest daughter Mary. We also know that the head of the Arden family in Warwickshire, Edward Arden of Park Hall, near Birmingham, suffered the extreme penalty of death for his supposed complicity in the Somerville Plot of 1583, Somerville being a relative of his by marriage. Nothing was proved against him, but it was clearly a trumped-up charge brought against him by his enemy, the powerful Earl of Leicester, who was envious of the other's prestige in the county—with a pedigree going back to Saxon times. The prosecution of the case was entrusted to the local magistrate, the "Puritan" Sir Thomas Lucy, a former pupil of the martyrologist John Foxe, and famous for his part in driving the young William (for his deer-poaching) from his home in Stratford. Among his victims may have been Mary Arden, both as cousin to Edward Arden and as wife to the suspected recusant John Shakespeare. This may well have been the occasion for the latter's hiding of his Spiritual Testament in the rafters of his Henley Street house. Thus we may see Mary Arden with her husband John and William's wife Anne all pointing in their several ways, from their several perspectives, to the Catholic allegiance of William himself—at least up till the beginning of his dramatic career.

Now we come to the main question to which all these biographical data have been leading up. Even granted, allowing for the many loopholes in this evidence, that the young

William Shakespeare had been brought up as a Catholic, to what extent is it relevant to his subsequent plays? Why are there so few signs of his Catholic formation in them? It may, of course, be maintained that, considering the known facts of the persecution of Catholics during the reigns of both Elizabeth I and James I—a persecution that came to its climax between 1588 (the year of the Spanish Armada) and 1605 (the year of the Gunpowder Plot)—he could hardly have left any signs of his Catholicism such as to convince an agnostic Shakespearian scholar of modern times. For those signs would also have been such as to convince a "suborned informer" of his own time, of whose danger he shows an awareness in Sonnet 125. If he had learnt anything from his recusant father in Stratford, or his recusant patrons in Lancashire, or Jesuit priests such as Campion, it was the lesson (he puts into the mouth of Iago) of not wearing "my heart upon my sleeve/ for daws to peck at" (*Othello* I i.64). To this lesson he significantly subjoins the words "I am not what I am", which he puts into the mouth not only of a villain such as Iago but also of the innocent Edgar in *King Lear.* In the latter context, Edgar is pursued, like the hunted priests in the Elizabethan age, by proclamations and intelligence of his whereabouts, forcing him to adopt the expedient of disguise so that, as he declares, "Edgar I nothing am" (II iii.21). Shakespeare, too, it may be said, was obliged to adopt a corresponding form of disguise in his plays, written as they were for performance on the stage and subject to the possibility of suborned informers (such as his fellow dramatist Anthony Munday) being among his audience. But then, it may be objected, how can a present-day scholar penetrate such a disguise that had to be so carefully hidden even from the Catholics in his audience? And what then is the point of his trying to do so? May he not justly incur the protest Shakespeare puts into Hamlet's mouth when defying Rosencrantz and Guildenstern to pluck out the heart of his mystery (III ii.389)? Surely one has need of the utmost caution in this matter.

Yes, I agree one has need of the utmost caution, though hardly for the same reasons as Shakespeare, if a committed Catholic, had need of it. Times have changed, and there are no suborned informers among my readers, who might accuse me of what I am doing and have me led off to prison, with the prospect of torture and execution. I will, however, have to face a jury of unconvinced and agnostic scholars, who are all too ready to pick holes in my reasoning and to deliver the verdict of "Not proven". In any case, there is no need in these days of my being at all shy about trying to pluck out the heart of Shakespeare's mystery. This is what Shakespeare scholars today are doing all the time. Surely it is one aim of Shakespeare scholarship to draw as close as possible to the secret of his dramatic genius, to sound the full depths of meaning in his plays, to explore the height and depth, the length and breadth of his achievement, to inquire why he wrote the plays he did, what determined his choice of plots and words, and what he put into them not only on their surface, where they are apparent to any spectator or scholar, but even in their hidden depths.

For this reason, moreover, there can be no question of my looking for any overt or concealed Catholic propaganda in the plays, as if he might have been writing them in order to win over any Protestant or uncommitted Catholic members of his audience to the Catholic cause. Such an aim, if recognizable to any member of his audience, Catholic or not, would have been self-defeating, as being no less recognizable to any suborned informer. Even if such an aim would have been recognized only by Catholic members of his audience, it was precisely out of such Catholics, once they had come to betray their faith, that the English government chose their informers as being for that reason more subservient to their purpose. In such a way Campion had been betrayed at Lyford Grange in 1581 by one George Eliot, posing as a zealous Catholic. And in such a way Shakespeare, too, might be betrayed by a fellow dramatist such as Anthony Munday, who had entered upon his literary career with a detailed exposition of what he called *The English Roman Life* (1582) and two other books in denunciation of Campion himself.

Rather, what I am proposing is that, if Shakespeare was still a fully committed Catholic and had even made an election under the guidance of Campion, resulting in a decision to embrace the career not of a priest but of a dramatist, for the purpose of presenting the Catholic cause aright "to the yet unknowing world" (*Hamlet* V ii.393), then he had somehow to do so in his plays, however deviously and with whatever indirections. He had to be like Hamlet, spying upon his enemies, even while being spied upon by them, striving to keep one step ahead of their devices by means of other no less ingenious devices of his own. His was the dangerous sport "to have the ingener/ hoist with his own petar" (*Hamlet* III iv.206) and "to pay with falsehood false exacting" (*Measure for Measure* III ii.303). It may not necessarily have been a deliberate device of his ingenuity, since, as Hamlet comes to learn, "our indiscretion sometimes serves us well,/ when our deep plots do pall" (V ii.8). In other words, when men devise one way of proceeding, as with the deep plots of Allen and Persons, God has a way of disposing otherwise. And then men have to adapt their short-sighted proposals to the all-seeing disposition of divine providence.

Indeed, I would go so far as to submit that, if Shakespeare was at once a committed Catholic and a dramatic genius, he would have had no need to make any deliberate insertion of a Catholic meaning into his plays. He would have been unable to keep it out of them, just as he was unable to prevent his character of Falstaff from running away with him. It would have been as if the idea, the inspiration, no less than the character, takes over. Then, it may be added, the more he came to follow his dramatic inspiration in his mature plays, the less power he would have had in himself to suppress the "divine spirit" springing up from the depths of his soul and insisting on utterance. Rather, he would have had to devise means of remaining faithful to that spirit while qualifying the utterance by what would have been acceptable to a largely Protestant audience. It may well be for this reason that we come upon so many expressions in the plays of the need to suppress one's feelings, even at the expense of a broken heart. Such, for instance, is Hamlet's cry, "But break, my heart, for I must hold my tongue!" (I ii.159). Such is the cry of the poor queen of Richard II, "Oh, I am press'd to death through want of speaking!" (III iv.72)—with reference to the *peine forte et dure* inflicted on those who refused to plead guilty or not guilty, such as the Catholic widow of York, Margaret Clitherow, who suffered this cruel death for sheltering Catholic priests in 1586. Then, like Duke Vincentio in *Measure for Measure*, it may also be said of the dramatist behind the duke that his "givings out" were "of an infinite distance from his true-meant design" (I iv.54). Or, like Lennox in *Macbeth* speaking to another lord while uncertain how far that other is to be trusted, the dramatist, too, may have aimed in his speeches at evoking thoughts that could "interpret further" (III vi.1). Or, like the clown Launce in *Two Gentlemen of Verona*, he may even have been defying his audience in claiming, "Thou shalt never get such a secret from me but by a parable" (II v.40). For the dramatist, no less than his character of Fluellen in *Henry V*, was a master in the art of "seeing figures in all things" (IV vii.35) and of making riddling use of them for a hidden meaning of his own. Or again, he might well have been making his own the despairing cry of the Lady Constance in *King John*, "Oh that my tongue were in the thunder's mouth!/ Then with a passion would I shake the world" (III iv.38). Such, I may add, is the spirit which, according to St. Paul, intercedes for the faithful with "sighs too deep for words" or (in another translation) "unutterable groans" (Romans viii.26).

These outbursts, I admit, may prove nothing outside their dramatic contexts, at least from the viewpoint of an unsympathetic critic. Nor do I claim they prove anything in the strict sense of proof. Yet there is a strange similarity among them, pointing beyond their immediate context to something deep in the heart of the dramatist. As Claudius says of Hamlet, "There's something in his soul/ o'er which his melancholy sits on brood" (III i.173). They may be imagined as rays of sunlight, emitted from an unseen centre too bright to behold towards a shining circumference. Taken separately, they may not "prove" that Shakespeare was a Catholic or anything but a great dramatist. But taken together, they point to the possibility, or rather the probability, that the plays in which they severally occur may have a new, unsuspected Catholic significance.

Now it is time for me to pass from these preliminary, biographical considerations to my proposed investigation of the plays one by one, taking them, so far as possible, in their chronological order of composition. Then we may perhaps come to see them all in their totality as leading up to the conclusion which agrees with the old tradition, recorded by the Anglican Richard Davies, that Shakespeare "died a papist". Or rather, it is my aim in these pages to justify this tradition in the light of the preceding plays, and to show that the dramatist not only died but also lived and wrote as a Papist. And for this I may adduce the testimony of another, more contemporary witness, the Protestant John Speed, who in his *History of Great Britain* (1611) associated the Jesuit Robert Persons with the dramatist of *Henry IV* (both Parts) as "the papist and his poet", with reference to the parody of a Protestant in the character of Sir John Falstaff. Nor am I content to make the claim that Shakespeare was a Papist in the mere matter of religious allegiance. Rather, I claim that the deep meaning of all his plays, as of his dramatic genius, derives both from his hidden heart and from the equally hidden faith of Catholic England.

chapter 2
Papist Apprentice

Titus Andronicus

AS WITH SO MUCH else in Shakespeare, the way he came to learn the art of drama remains a mystery. This mystery is all the more opaque for those who accept the common opinion—going back to the legend of his deer-poaching in Charlecote Park—that the young Shakespeare left Stratford for London in the mid-1580s. For those, however, who follow the Shakeshafte theory, that he made his way not directly to London but indirectly via Lancashire, the mystery begins to dissipate, leaving a probable explanation of what has been termed "the compositional genetics" of Shakespeare's first plays and his early attempts at dramaturgy. According to that theory, the young William, adopting the local variant of his surname as Shakeshafte, would have gone as tutor to the recusant family of Alexander Houghton in 1580, through the recommendation of the Stratford schoolmaster, John Cottam. But in Alexander's will William's position as tutor, being illegal, was covered up as a player, and as such he was recommended to the recusant neighbour Sir Thomas Hesketh, who (we know) kept a company of players. On Alexander's death late in 1581, however (with the arrest and execution of Edmund Campion earlier in the same year), instead of taking advantage of that recommendation, William would have returned to Stratford, to keep out of the impending danger to recusants in Lancashire. Back home he soon found a wife in Anne Hathaway, who gave him his three children, Susanna in 1583 and the twins Hamnet and Judith in 1585. Then for his livelihood in the field of drama, he may well have pursued Alexander Houghton's recommendation and returned to Lancashire, to join Hesketh's players; then on the death of Sir Thomas in 1588 he may have transferred to the larger group of local players under the patronage of Lord Strange, son and heir to the Earl of Derby. With them, moreover, he would have found an ideal opening to the London stage, since Strange's Men performed not only for local audiences but also for the more lucrative London stage. This is all admittedly no more than probable, though there are also some interesting indications of Shakespeare's early connection with the Hesketh residence at Rufford Hall to the south of Preston. But what is certain is Shakespeare's connection with Strange's Men in their recorded performance of two of his early plays, *Titus Andronicus* and *Henry VI* (presumably Part I), for Philip Henslowe at the Rose Theatre on the South Bank of the Thames in the spring of 1592.

Beginning then with *Titus Andronicus*—what a strange play, we may wonder, for this young dramatist to have presented possibly as his first piece of drama for the London stage! What on earth could have induced him to set out on his dramatic career in the great city with such a gruesome revenge play? And from a Catholic point of view, what on earth could have prompted him to dip his hands in so many bloody scenes as appear in the play?

In answer to these questions, which are rarely asked by commentators on the play, it has first to be remembered that Shakespeare was as yet an apprentice in dramaturgy. He was probably not yet his own master, but he no doubt had to follow the advice and direction of others, such as the manager of the Rose Theatre. It has also to be remembered that those were the years when the revenge play was in fashion, owing to Thomas Kyd's box-office success with *The Spanish Tragedy* from 1589 onwards. At that time there also existed an early play of *Hamlet*, which is mentioned by Thomas Nashe in 1589 in a context that includes an implied reference to Kyd himself as author—though some have attributed the authorship to Shakespeare, who had but recently named his son Hamnet in 1585. Thirdly, there is a tradition, mentioned by the Restoration dramatist Edward Ravenscroft, that *Titus Andronicus* was not originally Shakespeare's play, "but brought by some private author to be acted, and he only gave some master touches to one or two of the principal parts or characters". Certainly, the plot of the play is a strange one to have come even from the juvenile pen of Shakespeare. Yet the language of the play is undoubtedly full of Shakespearian words and turns of phrase such as we come upon in his mature work.

As for a possible Catholic dimension of the play, it may be discerned not so much in spite of as because of its many gory scenes. For example, when we hear Lucius reporting to his father Titus in the opening scene that their Gothic captive "Alarbus' limbs are lopp'd" (I i.143), it sounds like a grisly echo of the common spectacle of the fate endured by Catholic "traitors", such as Edmund Campion, at Tyburn. In their cases hanging was usually followed by drawing the victim down while still alive and lopping his limbs into quarters, before the body parts were thrown into a basket for summary disposal. Such in this play is the fate not only of Alarbus, son of the Gothic queen Tamora, but also of

Lavinia, sister of Lucius and daughter of Titus, according to the revenge plotted by Tamora with the advice of the villain Aaron. The same slangy word "lopp'd" is again used by Marcus Andronicus, Titus's brother, on seeing his niece's pitiful condition, when he asks her, "What stern ungentle hands/ have lopp'd and hew'd and made thy body bare/ of her two branches?" (II iv.16). The branches are her two hands, which have been cut off, as has her tongue. This parallel fate shared by Alarbus the Goth and the Roman Lavinia may perhaps be interpreted as that shared (in the contemporary imagination) by Elizabethan Protestants under the Spanish Inquisition, according to what Lucius calls "our Roman rites" (I i.143), and (in reality) by English Catholics in their own country. But in the play the emphasis is on the long-drawn-out sufferings of Lavinia rather than on the preceding instantaneous sacrifice of Alarbus in the first scene. Her sufferings are, moreover, explicitly described in terms of martyrdom, as when Titus laments that she has no "tongue to tell me who hath martyred thee" (III i.108).

Then, towards the end of the play, we come upon the single case in all Shakespeare's plays of the use of the derogatory epithet "popish" (V i.76). This epithet, like the related "Papist" (which is also used only once, in *All's Well That Ends Well*, I iii.58), was commonly used by Protestants as a term of abuse against Catholics in that age, as in the title of Robert Crowley's Puritan *Discourse against the outward apparel and ministering garments of the popish church* (1566). This is interpreted by some recent scholars as a sign of the dramatist's disaffection towards his former religion, as when he also says of heresies in *A Midsummer Night's Dream*, that they "are hated most of those they did deceive" (II ii.140). But this is taking Shakespeare's use of the epithet out of its dramatic context. For here the word is put into the mouth of the villain Aaron, who uses it as an incentive for Lucius to keep the oath required of him. "Yet for I know," he says, "thou art religious/ and hast a thing within thee called conscience,/ with twenty popish tricks and ceremonies." Here, it may be noticed, the epithet "popish"—for all its derogatory implications such as would have appealed to Protestant members of the audience, while serving as a sop to suborned informers—has a favourable meaning in relation to Lucius's religious conscience, which must incline him to the keeping of an oath. In it, moreover, we may find the additional implication that the Roman Andronici, Titus and Marcus, Lucius and Lavinia, are somehow on the Catholic side, at least in the dramatist's mind, while the Goths under their queen Tamora are somehow Protestant. Then, we may add, if Tamora stands for Queen Elizabeth, for whom does Aaron the Moor stand, if not for "the black earl" of Leicester, Elizabeth's notorious favourite? And then their revenge might be comparable to that taken by the Protestant government against the Catholics for the previous sufferings of the Protestants under Queen Mary.

As for the use of the word "conscience" in this context, it could be associated in the dramatist's mind partly with St. Ignatius's advice of a daily "examen of conscience" in the book of *Spiritual Exercises*, partly with those Catholic exiles who from the outset of Elizabeth's reign were prompted by their "conscience" to quit their native land and to seek refuge on the continent. Such is the burden of a plaintive poem composed by the former head of the wealthy Houghton family, the elder brother of Alexander, Thomas Houghton, while in exile at Douai (or Rheims). It was perhaps the unsuccessful rising of the northern earls in 1569 that led Thomas in the same year, shortly after the completion of his new residence at Houghton Tower, to follow his friend and mentor William Allen. His poem begins, "At Houghton Tower, which is a bower/ Of sports and lordly pleasure", and each stanza ends with the refrain, "To keep my conscience." Such was also a theme running through the minds of all Catholic recusants from the time of their great precursor, Sir Thomas More, who was one of the first to suffer "for conscience' sake" under Elizabeth's terrible father Henry VIII.

Finally, mention may be made of an echo in this play of another fateful event which occurred in the reign of Henry VIII, but whose tangible memory persisted through the reign of Elizabeth I, and even till today. It is where in the last act a Goth brings Aaron and his child before Lucius, pleading that he found the child crying beneath the wall of "a ruinous monastery" (V i.21). In the pagan setting of *Titus Andronicus*, whose "Roman rites" include human sacrifice, such a monastery must be anachronistic. But its ruinous condition was only too familiar to Shakespeare and his Elizabethan audience, living as they did so soon after the destruction of all the monasteries in the realm between 1536 and 1540. The dramatist himself might even have been thinking of a particular monastery familiar to him from the Forest of Arden, the ruined Wroxhall Abbey near Rowington, where there had been two nuns in pre-Reformation times named Shakespeare—one of them with the religious name of Isabella, which the dramatist chose for his novice-heroine in *Measure for Measure.*

The Three Parts of *Henry VI*

Turning now to the other Shakespearian play attributed to Strange's Men in 1592 under the title of "Harey the vj", which seems to be *Henry VI* Part I, what evidence may we find in it of a Catholic interest? To begin with, it would only be natural for a Catholic Englishman in the Elizabethan age to look back with nostalgia to the Middle Ages, when the English were all Catholics—apart from the relatively few Lollards. No doubt, in the course of that history there were many tragedies, as what history is there free from tragedy? No doubt, too, there had been many scandals in the English Church, not to mention the long decline of ecclesiastical and monastic life since the Black Death in the mid-fourteenth century. Shakespeare's own plays of mediaeval English history are also full of tragic material, and two of them, *Richard III* and *Richard II*, have the word "tragedy" in their full titles. All these particular tragedies would have been interpreted by the Catholic reader or spectator as events leading up to and culminating in the disastrous reigns of Henry VIII, Edward VI, and Elizabeth I, when the disasters were inseparably bound up with the religious changes presented under the name of "reformation", followed by "persecution".

This interest in the past was fostered among Elizabethan readers by the chronicles of such authors as Edward Hall, with his account of *The Union of the Two Noble and Illustrious Families of Lancaster and York* (1548), and Raphael Holinshed, with his *Chronicles of England, Scotland and Ireland* (1577, enlarged 1587). It was the former chronicle of fifteenth-century English history that was, according to Alan Keen in *The Annotator* (1954), annotated by the young Shakespeare, presumably under Hesketh auspices at Rufford Hall. These annotations betray an attitude of English patriotism and loyalty to the "old faith", despite the Protestant bias of the author. The main source of the history plays and some of the tragedies, however, is the less biased chronicle of Holinshed (in the 1587 edition). Both chronicles provided the dramatist with abundant material for his plays through which he might convey to members of his audience, whether Catholic or Protestant, a nostalgia for the Catholic past of England under cover of promoting their patriotism, while avoiding the possible accusations of an informer.

Moreover, by instructing the members of his audience in their English heritage, he might have entertained hopes of undoing the impact of radical Protestantism with its inbuilt tendency, as Dryden puts it in *Absalom and Achitophel*, "nothing to build and all things to destroy". Such, for example, is the tendency attributed by the Gentleman in *Hamlet* to the rioting Laertes, who behaves "as the world were now but to begin,/ antiquity forgot, custom not known" (IV v.103). Such, too, is the tendency attributed by the Servant in *Timon of Athens* to those "that under hot ardent zeal would set whole realms on fire" (III ii.33). The latter are identified by Dr. Johnson in his notes on the play with the Elizabethan Puritans who, he observes, "were then set upon a project of new modeling the ecclesiastical and civil government according to Scripture models and examples". Thus with his history plays (in which he is regarded by some scholars as setting the fashion rather than following it), Shakespeare may be seen as counteracting the above-mentioned tendency in radical Protestantism (or Puritanism) partly by reminding his Elizabethan audiences of their rich cultural heritage, partly by using (in Eliot's words) "these fragments" of English history to "shore against" the ruins of his dear country left by the insatiate lust and greed of Henry VIII.

From these general considerations we may turn to the three Parts of *Henry VI* with their ongoing presentation of the calamitous Wars of the Roses, asking to what extent Shakespeare's treatment of English history in them reveals some Catholic sympathy, without betraying him to an informer in his audience. First, it has to be remembered, as with *Titus Andronicus*, that the dramatist was at this time still an apprentice and not yet his own master in the choice and composition of his plays. This may explain why in the three plays, as John Dover Wilson has shown in detail in his three editions of them for the Cambridge Shakespeare, there appear so many echoes from plays written by the contemporary "university wits". The young Shakespeare was evidently borrowing from them, as he borrows from all kinds of sources in all his plays, and thus evoking Greene's notorious denunciation of him to his fellow "wits", in *A Groatsworth of Wit* (1592), as "an upstart crow, beautified with our feathers", who is "in his own conceit the only Shake-scene in a country". Or he may have been entrusted by the manager of the Rose with the task of improving or completing plays already written by those "wits"—which would only have augmented their indignation at seeing this newcomer to the London stage preferred before themselves. As yet the name of Shakespeare had appeared on no title page of his printed plays, and it was not unusual in those days for drama to be the combined work of several authors, even without their understanding and consent. Nor may we except Shakespeare from this custom, despite the unwillingness of not a few scholars to do so—at least until he became the recognized dramatist for the newly formed Chamberlain's Men in 1594.

As for the subject matter of these three plays, we may distinguish three points of special interest in them from a Catholic viewpoint. One is the civil conflict between the Houses of Lancaster and York, when seen as reflecting the similar religious conflict in Elizabethan England. For the latter conflict was not just on the level of religious opinion, but it entered deeply into almost every department of life, even to the extent of dividing families within themselves. Thus we find Gloucester complaining at the outset of *King Lear*, "Love cools, friendship falls off, brothers divide . . . and the bond cracked between son and father" (I ii.118). Such is also the conflict depicted in *Titus Andronicus*, first between Titus and the Goths, then between the subsequent candidates for imperial power, Saturninus and Bassianus, when Titus foolishly casts his vote in favour of the former, only to find him plotting with Tamora and Aaron against him. (One may be reminded of the way King Philip of Spain gave his initial support to Queen Elizabeth, in the vain hope of marrying her in succession to her half-sister Mary, only to find himself rejected by her and even treated as her enemy for his Catholic religion.) Such, too, is the conflict between the Houses of Montague and Capulet in *Romeo and Juliet*, where the family names come, it is true, from the source material, but at least one of them would have been associated in the dramatist's mind with the Catholic Viscount Montague, Anthony Browne, whose daughter Mary was the mother of Shakespeare's patron, the young Earl of Southampton.

A second point is a Lancastrian bias discernible in these plays in opposition to the Yorkists. True, the Lancastrians have an admitted blood guilt from the time of the first Lancastrian ruler, Henry IV, who confesses his responsibility for the murder of Richard II by Sir Pierce Exton, and the same guilt is recalled by his son Henry V on the eve of Agincourt. Still, we cannot call Henry IV a usurper, as not a few critics regard him, seeing that the deposition of Richard II in Westminster Hall took place according to due process of law and was accepted, if reluctantly, by Richard himself. As for Henry VI, though he is depicted in the three plays that bear his name as a weak, ineffectual ruler, according to the sources, he stands out as the one man of peace among his quarreling nobles, a man of prayer whose mind, as Queen Margaret scornfully says of him, "is bent on holiness,/ to number Ave-Maries on his beads" (Part II, I iii.58). It is too easily assumed that the dramatist agrees with the queen, but that queen is hardly an object of his approval, considering the way she is defied by Richard of York as "she-wolf of France" with "a tiger's heart wrapp'd in a woman's hide" (Part III, I iv.137)—words notoriously applied by Robert Greene to Shakespeare himself in his *Groatsworth of Wit*. On the other hand, the real usurpers are shown as the trouble-making Richard of York with his three sons, Edward, George, and Richard. The climax of their usurpation comes with the younger Richard, who steps to the English throne over the successive corpses of Henry VI, Edward IV, his brother George, and the two little princes, sons of Edward IV. This Lancastrian bias may have come to the young Shakespeare from his years in Lancashire, as being the last bastion of the "old faith" in an increasingly Protestant England. Yet he would have known that the great county of York on the other side of the Pennines was hardly less retentive of its old Catholic allegiance, and among its families Edmund Campion found hardly less support on his journey through England in the autumn of 1580 than among the families of Lancashire in the spring of 1581.

A third point of special interest may be noted in a certain continuity between these three plays and *Titus Andronicus*, both in their gory battle scenes and in their specific use of the verb "lop" with grim reference not (in its normal usage) to the branches of a tree but to the limbs of a human body. From the two such uses of this verb already noticed in *Titus Andronicus*, we find an echoing use of it in each of the three Parts of *Henry VI* and nowhere else in the plays of Shakespeare (save once in Part I of *Henry IV*, IV i.43). In Part I we hear Joan La Pucelle trying to bribe the fiends who have hitherto been assisting her, by promising even to "lop a member" off her own body (V iii.15). In Part II we hear Queen Margaret exulting over Duke Humphrey in his downfall, as having suffered "two pulls at once,/ his lady banish'd and a limb lopp'd off"—where the limb is metaphorical for his rod of office (II iii.41). More to the point is the appearance of the verb in Part III, where we hear Richard of Gloucester (before he becomes king) recalling how the ruthless Clifford "lopp'd the branch/ in hewing Rutland" (II vi.47).

To what extent, however, Shakespeare was himself responsible for the repetition of this grim image may be doubted, considering the probability of joint authorship in all three plays. The same doubt may be applied to two more problems converging on Part I with regard to the Catholic allegiance of the author. First, there is the unfavourable portrayal of Joan La Pucelle as a religious hypocrite, which might be considered more characteristic of a Protestant than a Catholic pen. In Act I she is shown as devoutly appealing to the aid of "heaven and Our Lady gracious" in her fight to save France from the English enemy (I ii.73). But in Act V, when faced with defeat in battle, she is shown as seeking the help of her "familiar spirits", the fiends, who appear to her but can no longer assist her (V iii.10). In extenuation of this portrayal it might be pleaded that such was the view of her taken by the English even in that Catholic age. But it may be doubted how far an Elizabethan Catholic, however patriotic the annotator of Hall's chronicle seems to have been, would have agreed with his forefathers on this point. So it only remains open to the Catholic commentator today to cast the blame on one of the "university wits", who would have felt no compunction about slandering a pious Catholic peasant girl like Joan—who is today a canonized saint in the Catholic Church.

Secondly, a similar problem arises out of the portrayal of the "good duke", Humphrey of Gloucester (as he is called in Part II, III ii.123), especially in his confrontation with his proud enemy Cardinal Beaufort. From the beginning of Part I we are shown him spurning his ecclesiastical foe with the words "Under my feet I stamp thy cardinal's hat/ in spite of pope or dignities of church" (I iii.49). One may easily imagine how such words would have found responsive echoes in the hearts of Protestant members of the audience, arguing a Protestant viewpoint in their author. Here again, it might seem that the only response of a Catholic commentator would be to attribute these words to one or other of the "university wits", who were mainly anti-Catholic (and Marlowe a government spy). Yet within the same play we come upon a qualifying declaration put into the mouth of Duke Humphrey himself, when in speaking to the cardinal he draws the scholastic distinction, "Thou art reverent/ touching thy spiritual function, not thy life" (III i.49). That would have made his character more acceptable to Catholic members in the audience, as coming from the pen of a Catholic dramatist.

Then, there is the incident of the false miracle depicted in Part II, where one Simpcox claims to have had his blindness healed by a miracle, only to be exposed as a sham by Duke Humphrey (II i). This may be interpreted as a typical case of a Protestant dramatist gloating over the false superstitions of Rome, in the spirit of John Foxe's *Book of Martyrs*. Only it so happens that the source of this story is not Protestant but Catholic, not John Foxe but Sir Thomas More in his *Dialogue* (1528) against the Lutheran William Tyndale. Finally, when the protracted quarrel between the duke and the cardinal ends in Part II with the deaths of both contenders, that of the cardinal is particularly grim, evoking Warwick's comment, "So bad a death argues a monstrous life." But the pious king interposes with the wise comment "Forbear to judge, for we are sinners all" (III iii.30).

Richard III

If any general proof is needed that Shakespeare was not the sole author of all three parts of *Henry VI*, it may be found in the striking contrast between those three plays and their chronological sequel, *Richard III*. In all three Parts of *Henry VI* we are distracted by the chaos not only in the events dramatized but also in the mind of the dramatist (or dramatists). In them we find all in a state of disorder, but once we turn to *Richard III*, we find all reduced to a symmetrical order. In them the dramatist is still an apprentice, tied as it were to the apron-strings of his would-be instructors in the art of dramaturgy. But now at last he emerges as his own master, whom we see as moving from a Gothic confusion to a Renaissance simplicity. Now at last we have no doubt as to his sole authorship, save for some lingering influence of Christopher Marlowe.

This change from the three Parts of *Henry VI* to *Richard III* may also be explained with reference to the historical source. In the latter the dramatist is still following the guidance of Holinshed, while Holinshed is following that of Hall. But both chroniclers are in turn dependent on the masterly, if biased, *History of Richard III* by Sir Thomas More, which was first printed in full in 1557. Evidently More derived his bias from his principal informant, Cardinal Morton, Archbishop of Canterbury and Chancellor of England under Henry VII. Thus we may see Shakespeare following his Catholic predecessor, but through the filter of two Protestant sources, who would have provided him with immunity from possible prosecution for any undue Catholic flavour in his play.

In any case, there is hardly any Catholic flavour either in More's biography or in the subsequent chronicles. Only in Shakespeare's play we may detect it in the chorus of lament over England, which is later taken up in *Macbeth* with reference to Scotland, and which strangely echoes that of not a few recusant authors in the Elizabethan age. The chorus begins with Gloucester's own ironical complaint, "The world is grown so bad!" (I iii.70)—whereas he goes on to do his best to make the world worse. It continues with Edward IV's Queen Elizabeth, who utters a similar complaint, "What a world is this!" (II i.83). Then, there are two unnamed citizens, who forebode "a troublous world" (II iii.9), and an unnamed scrivener, who twice shakes his head in one short speech, first with the sarcastic lament, "Here's a good world the while!" then with an open denunciation, "Bad is the world!" (III vi.10, 13). All this badness we find concentrated in the character of Richard, as he pursues his ambition to be king—even as in *Macbeth* the ills of Scotland are all ascribed to Macbeth's vaulting ambition. The relevance of all this to Shakespeare's England may be seen in the sonnets, especially Sonnet lxvii, in which the poet looks back with nostalgia to "days long since" in contrast to "these last so bad".

As for the one individual responsible for all this badness in England from the Catholic viewpoint of Shakespeare, we may perhaps find it in his characterization of Edward's Queen Elizabeth in relation to her namesake on the English throne in Shakespeare's time. The former queen is twice addressed by her bitter rival, Queen Margaret, as "poor painted queen" (I iii.241) and "poor shadow, painted queen"

(IV iv.83), and she is despised by Richard himself, once he has won her over to his will, as a "relenting fool and shallow, changing woman" (IV iv.432). Needless to say, if the relevance of these uncomplimentary epithets to the reigning Elizabeth I, accustomed as she was to the flattery of her courtiers and other subjects, and insistent as she was on receiving it, had been recognized by any suborned informer, and if he could have proved his accusation against the dramatist, that would have been the end of Shakespeare's dramatic career! Yet the description is quite accurate concerning the latter no less than the former queen, as we may see for ourselves in contemporary accounts of the old queen's lavish use of cosmetics, as well her indecisive character, which was not infrequently the despair of her ministers. It was, moreover, open to the dramatist to show how aptly the words about Edward's queen fit into their dramatic context, on the basis of the chronicle accounts, with no offence meant to the reigning queen. Rather, the nasty application of those words to the latter might well be retorted on the nasty mind of the informer.

The outcome of the play, however, may be interpreted as a ringing vindication of the new, if usurping, dynasty of the Tudors, beginning with the miserly Henry VII. Even the source of Shakespeare's play, More's *History*, is commonly regarded as bare-faced Tudor propaganda relayed to the young More by his patron, the wily Thomas Morton, who had helped to put Henry Tudor on the throne. (On the other hand, More was no simple advocate for the Tudors, considering the way he incurred the enmity of Henry VII in the Parliament of 1504, and the dating of his work on *Richard III* is ascribed to the following decade.) Then, the question may be raised, why may not this apparent approval of the first Tudor be seen as extending to his successors, including Henry VIII and Elizabeth I? In particular, why may we not take the ringing climax to *Richard III*, in Henry's victory over Richard at Bosworth Field, in conjunction with that other ringing climax to the last of the history plays, *Henry VIII*, in Cranmer's prophecy of the forthcoming golden reign of the baby princess Elizabeth? On the other hand, in contrast to Cranmer's prophecy of a time when "God shall be truly known" in a clearly Protestant sense (V v.37), we may note that Henry's victory at Bosworth is celebrated in unmistakably Catholic terms. We hear the ghosts on the eve of battle praying for "good angels" to guard their champion "from the boar's annoy" (meaning Richard), and Henry himself placing his trust not only in "God and our good cause" but also in "the prayers of holy saints and wronged souls" (V iii.139ff). As for Cranmer's prophecy, that will call for fuller discussion when we come to deal with *Henry VIII*. For the present, it may suffice to say that it occurs in a scene commonly attributed by scholars, who accept the collaboration theory of its authorship, not to Shakespeare but to his young collaborator, presumably John Fletcher, who was son to a former bishop of London and successor to Shakespeare as dramatist for the King's Men. Whereas Shakespeare never uses Foxe's *Book of Martyrs* for source material, this is the source used for the scenes relating to Cranmer, which apparently proceed from the pen of Fletcher.

King John

The history play of *King John* is something of a loner, standing apart from the sequence of plays on fifteenth-century English history and their common dependence on the chronicles of Hall and Holinshed. It also stands out as surviving only in the text of the First Folio of 1623, with no previous quarto to its credit and few clues as to its first performance. It calls, however, for comparison with a similar play on the same reign entitled *The Troublesome Reign of King John*, which was published in 1591. Most Shakespeare scholars regard *The Troublesome Reign* as the immediate source of Shakespeare's play, but there are some who argue the other way round, and a few who maintain a common Shakespearian authorship, seeing the later *King John* as a reworking of *The Troublesome Reign*. From a Catholic viewpoint, the play is somewhat baffling in the way it seems to champion the Protestant cause, according to a tradition that goes back to John Bale's early play of *King John* (ca.1558) and John Foxe's *Book of Martyrs* (1563). For them King John was a courageous precursor of Henry VIII both for his defiance of Rome and for his attempted spoliation of the monasteries.

The crucial scene in Shakespeare's play that seems to baffle Catholic commentators is the long opening scene of Act III, where the cardinal legate from Rome, Pandulph, comes in between the two kings, John of England and Philip of France. Whereas he is respectfully greeted by Philip as "the holy legate of the pope", he is roundly defied by John in a long harangue, beginning, "What earthly name to interrogatories can task the free breath of a sacred king?" and ending with contempt for "the pope . . . and his usurp'd authority" (III i.135–60). John also turns on Philip and chides him for his feeble attempts at moderation, in his excess of indignation at "this meddling priest" and "his juggling witchcraft" (163–69). Such speeches must have won the applause of Protestants in the audience, while leaving Catholics uncomfortable in their seats. The whole passage, moreover, we find censored (in the Second Folio of 1632) by the Jesuit William Sankey for the English College at Valladolid, no doubt as inappropriate reading for his English Catholic pupils.

What is more, it seems that the anti-Catholic tone of this speech is reinforced by the dramatic context, in which the principal part is played less by John himself, who is shown as part tyrant, part ditherer, than by the bastard son of Richard the Lion-heart, Philip Faulconbridge. The Bastard is depicted as a stout supporter of John in both his political and his religious positions, as well in his opposition to the Pope as in his readiness to "shake the bags/ of hoarding abbots" (III iii.7). He also stands up for English patriotism, no doubt as engendered by opposition to the Spanish Armada, and in his concluding lines we may detect the tones of the dramatist himself appealing to the hearts of his English audience: "Nought shall make us rue,/ if England to itself do rest but true" (V vii.117). So he is not unreasonably regarded by some commentators as the dramatist's own mouthpiece.

On the other hand, it is important to interpret these speeches more precisely in view of their dramatic context. First, we may note a deep irony in John's defiance of the Pope's "usurp'd authority", considering that he has himself usurped the English throne in violation of the stronger claim of Prince Arthur, son of John's elder brother Geoffrey. So far from glossing over this fact, like the Protestant author of *The Troublesome Reign*, Shakespeare lays stress upon it in the opening scene of his play, in the furtive exchange between John and his mother, Queen Elinor. When John claims "our strong possession and our right" to the English throne, his mother quietly reminds him of "your strong possession much more than your right" (I i.40). Nor is this the only point on which Shakespeare's play differs from *The Troublesome Reign*. Rather, it may be said that so many and so profound are the differences between the two plays that Shakespeare seems to have deliberately gone through the earlier play, consistently toning down its anti-Catholicism in favour of a more balanced, though still not obviously Catholic, interpretation of

English history in the reign of King John. A detailed discussion of these differences has long since been undertaken by a Protestant scholar, John De Groot, in his study on *The Shakespeares and "The Old Faith"*, and so I have no need to repeat all he has said. But what he does say is sufficient to refute those scholars who maintain that Shakespeare's play precedes *The Troublesome Reign*, as well as those others who claim a Shakespearian authorship for both plays.

As for Shakespeare's characterization of the Bastard and his use of him as a mouthpiece for his own ideas, we may notice an evident inconsistency between the noble-minded rejection of "commodity" as "the bias of the world" put into the Bastard's mouth (II i.574) and the readiness of the same Bastard to obey John in going to "shake the bags/ of hoarding abbots" (III iii.7). Rather, we may discern the dramatist's sympathy in Pandulph's dignified protest against the way the Bastard is "ransacking the church" and "offending charity" (III iv.172). Here we see Pandulph no longer as the Machiavellian ecclesiastic portrayed in *The Troublesome Reign*, but as the wise statesman concerned to keep the peace of the Church between the quarreling kings of France and England. On the contrary, it is the Bastard who appears in relation to King John as the original English Machiavellian, Thomas Cromwell, had been to King Henry VIII, both in his unprincipled support of the king and in his proposed spoliation of the abbeys, not to mention his patriotic front, which the dramatist later satirizes in the character of Cloten in *Cymbeline*—a play that may be interpreted in relation to the history play of *Henry VIII*.

This is all, however, secondary to the main thrust of Shakespeare's play, in which the divided Parts of *The Troublesome Reign* are reduced to a more or less coherent unity. His play is dominated by the character not of John himself or even the Bastard, but of little Prince Arthur. The effective, and affecting, centre of the play in this respect, as also to a lesser extent of Part I of *The Troublesome Reign*, is the scene in which Arthur's custodian, Hubert, is preparing to put out the little boy's eyes with red-hot irons (IV i). This important scene, in which the dramatist seems to be pulling out all the stops of his dramatic talent, is connected by some scholars with the death of his own son Hamnet at the age of eleven in 1596. Yet other scholars, notably Lily Campbell in *Shakespeare's Histories* (1947), relate the scene to the judicial murder of Mary Queen of Scots in 1587, when the fond hopes the Catholics had placed in her over the two preceding decades were brought to a tragic end. In particular, there appears a remarkable parallel between John's anger at Hubert's seemingly literal observance of his instructions concerning Arthur and that of Elizabeth, whether real or feigned, at the haste with which her secretary Davison took the death warrant she had just signed for Mary and handed it without delay to the expectant Lord Burghley. The latter had already suffered much from the indecisiveness of his sovereign in such matters, and he did not wish to give her any time to countermand her orders. On this point at least the Bastard's words on the death of Arthur may be interpreted as an authorial comment with reference both to John's usurpation and to Mary's execution: "From forth this morsel of dead royalty,/ the life, the right and truth of all this realm/ is fled to heaven" (IV iii.143). At the same time, he expresses the fear which must have reechoed in the hearts of all Catholic members of his audience, that now "vast confusion"—as it were anticipating the other and greater masterpiece of confusion discovered by Macduff in *Macbeth* II iii.74—awaits his country "and heaven itself doth frown upon the land" (IV iii.159).

chapter 3

Towards a Catholic Comedy

The Comedy of Errors

ONE FEATURE that impresses us in Shakespeare's comedies is the way he looks in almost all of them away from his native England towards lands of romance, especially Italy and other lands of the sunny Mediterranean. Why is this? Is it merely because the dramatist was an incurable romantic? Yet in his parallel plays of English history he comes dangerously close to tragedy. Indeed, many of his history plays would have been classed as tragedies but for the traditional division of comedy, history, and tragedy, following the order of the First Folio. Or is it because the dramatist wished to maintain a balance between the cruel realism of history or tragedy and the soft romance of comedy? Yet even in his romantic comedies there is a notable element of realism and tragedy, often with the prospect of death hanging over the head of one or other of the major characters till almost the end.

From a Catholic viewpoint, the answer to these questions is a simple one. For Shakespeare as a Catholic, the situation in his own country in his own time would have been too grim to face steadily, save in the form of a grotesque satire such as *Titus Andronicus*. Rather, it would have been a relief for him to turn away from "these last (times) so bad", of which he complains in Sonnet lxvii, whether to the mediaeval history of Catholic England or to the lands of romance on the still-Catholic continent. There he could breathe the air of freedom, whereas England would have been to him, as Denmark was to Hamlet, "a prison" (II ii.261). Still, with all his dramatic imagination, exercised over past ages at home or lands of romance abroad, he was never really able to escape from the England of his own time. This appears in his comedies where, for all his skill in conjuring up the lands of Ephesus and Verona, Padua and Navarre, he is almost transparently referring to Elizabethan England. Behind all the paraphernalia and glitter of romance there lurks a dark, threatening, remorseless reality from which he is unable to escape after all.

Now we may turn to what is often regarded as the first of Shakespeare's comedies, *The Comedy of Errors*. And about it we may again ask the question—similar to that which we asked about *Titus Andronicus*: What prompted the young dramatist to choose this particular story from Plautus's *Menaechmi* for the first of his comedies? Of course, we may say that he didn't choose it himself, but it was chosen for him, as being but an apprentice in the art of dramaturgy. Another likely suggestion is that he may have used this Latin text either (as a boy) at his grammar school in Stratford or (as a tutor) during his time as "a schoolmaster in the country" of Lancashire. For it was a text widely used in schools both in England and on the continent during the Renaissance. So when called upon to compose and produce a play for his Lancastrian pupils at Lea Hall, the young Shakespeare/Shakeshafte may well have drawn upon the *Menaechmi* as his starting point not so much for translation as for adaptation.

Next, we may ask, how did the young Shakespeare take this old classical text and adapt it for his Catholic pupils to perform and his Catholic audience to appreciate in remote Lancashire? The first and most obvious change made by Shakespeare to Plautus was in moving the setting of his play from Epidamnum on the Adriatic Sea to Ephesus on the Aegean. Why? No doubt because Ephesus was more familiar to himself and his audience from its presence in the New Testament, both in Acts xix-xx and in St. Paul's letter to the Ephesians. In Acts xix we read the episode of the silversmiths' riot against St. Paul in defence of their great temple of Diana. To their frenzied minds St. Paul seemed to be undermining both the temple and their own livelihood with his Christian teaching, and against him they whipped up the mob to the furious, repeated cry, "Great is Diana of the Ephesians!" We also read of the common practice of exorcisms, spells, and other forms of magic in that city. Then in Ephesians v we read of the ideal of Christian marriage, which St. Paul associates with the mystical marriage between Christ and his Church.

All this would, no doubt, have been no less acceptable to a Protestant than to a Catholic audience. After all, despite their controversies, they were at least more or less united in their acceptance of the Bible, however differently they might interpret its meaning on particular points. But what is characteristic of Shakespeare's treatment of Ephesus and his adaptation of Plautus in *The Comedy of Errors* is, I submit, his Catholic perspective.

First, we are shown the arrival of an aged merchant of Syracuse, Aegeon, in the city of Ephesus. There he is arrested and arraigned before Duke Solinus on a capital charge of treason, for all his protests that he has come with no evil intent but only in search of his long-lost son. What an odd way, we may wonder, for the young Shakespeare to adapt the *Menaechmi* for his first comedy, by beginning it with such a tragic scene! It is not derived from his classical source but imposed upon it by the dramatist for reasons of his own. What could his reasons have been? One reason might have been that, in altering the setting of the play from Epidamnum to Ephesus (though the latter city was known to him and his audience only from the above-mentioned passages in the New Testament), the dramatist was thinking of a city more familiar to himself and his audience, namely London. In the New Testament and in Plautine comedy there is, of course, no question of merchants from one city being punished for treason in another city owing to the mere fact of their land of origin. But in Elizabethan England it was only too common—according to the law of the land—for Catholic priests arriving from the continent, such as Thomas Cottam, to be arrested and charged with treason for no other reason than their priesthood. Such priests had, therefore, to enter the country disguised as soldiers or merchants, and in their letters to the continent, which were subject to interception by government spies, they often spoke of themselves as "merchants"—according to Jesus' parable of the pearl of great price (Matt. xiii.45–46).

Secondly, there is the love story between the newly arrived Antipholus of Syracuse, who has been more fortunate than his hapless father in eluding arrest, and the lovely Luciana. When Antipholus first sets eyes on her, he immediately, according to the old romantic convention, falls in love with her. This love he expresses not just in conventional romantic terms, but with a significant emphasis on "grace". "Less in your knowledge and your grace you show not," he exclaims, "than our earth's wonder, more than earth, divine"

(III ii.31). Also in the same scene he goes on to speak of Luciana's "gentle sovereign grace" (166). Such terminology has been interpreted, as by John Vyvyan in his *Shakespeare and Platonic Beauty* (1961), with reference to Platonic love, such as had become fashionable at Elizabeth's court since its introduction from Ficino's academy at Florence. But the repetition of "grace", both here and in almost all Shakespeare's plays with reference to an ideal heroine, comes to the dramatist not from Plato but from the Christian Middle Ages and originally from the New Testament. There in Luke i.28 the Virgin Mary is addressed by the Angel Gabriel as "full of grace" (in the rendering of the Catholic Rheims Bible, alone among Elizabethan translations). Thus the heroine is presented to us in terms of Our Lady—which reveals more of a Catholic than a Protestant mentality, considering how abhorrent to Protestants was the mediaeval devotion to her. In confirmation of this point, there is an interesting parallel, associated with this very city of Ephesus, between the classical Greek cult of Diana, the great goddess of the Ephesians, and the subsequent Christian cult of the Virgin Mary as Mother of God, or (in Greek) "Theotokos", a title which was solemnly proclaimed at the Council of Ephesus in A.D. 431 and gladly acclaimed by the people. It may be added that, in the Neoplatonic interpretation of the classics and Christianity proposed by Ficino, a similarity was seen between the pagan goddess of chastity and motherhood and Our Lady as Virgin and Mother.

By contrast, when the dramatist draws upon St. Paul's teaching on Christian marriage in Ephesians v for the speeches he puts into the mouth of Luciana's married sister Adriana, there is much that is acceptable to both Catholic and Protestant members of the audience, but little if anything that might betray his Catholic sympathies. When, however, her words are addressed not, as she imagines, to her husband, the other Antipholus of Ephesus, but to his twin brother of Syracuse, the latter's servant Dromio takes it as a sign that "this is the fairy land" in which they are surrounded by "goblins, owls and elvish sprites" (II ii.193). In a subsequent scene his master echoes him, exclaiming, "There's none but witches do inhabit here!" (III ii.162). This comes not from the teaching on marriage in Ephesians v, but from the description of Ephesus as a place of magic and occult practices in Acts xix. Now this aspect of Ephesus has a special relevance to the Catholics in Elizabethan times, especially when we come to the comic-tragic attempts of the conjuror Dr. Pinch to exorcize Antipholus of Ephesus in Act IV. In the late summer of 1584, soon after the execution of Campion with other priests and Jesuits in 1581–82 and Persons's hasty return to the continent, there arrived in England another Jesuit, William Weston, to continue the secret but dangerous Jesuit mission. He subsequently became involved in a strange series of exorcisms in the houses of certain Catholic gentlemen to the North of London, at Hackney and Denham, in 1585–86. These exorcisms were yet more strangely linked, by means of agents provocateurs working for the English government, to events and persons connected with the Babington Plot for the rescue of the romantic champion of the Catholic cause, Mary Queen of Scots. Among the seminary priests assisting Weston in these exorcisms was one of Shakespeare's classmates from Stratford, Robert Dibdale, fresh from his priestly studies at Rheims (whither the seminary of Douai had moved in 1578). The events were recorded in a manuscript "Book of Miracles", which was later discovered in a recusant house by the Anglican authorities and published in 1603 with sarcastic comments by the Bishop of London's chaplain, Samuel Harsnet, under the title *A Declaration of Egregious Popish Impostures*—which Shakespeare went on to use for his characterization of Edgar as a mad beggar in *King Lear*. Already by the time of Shakespeare's presumed arrival in London, these exorcisms had become sufficiently notorious for him to allude to them in his first comedy as matters familiar to all the members of his audience. A contemporary Puritan author, R. Phinch, in his book entitled *The Knowledge and Appearance of the Church* (1590), also refers to them in his general mention of the "false miracles, lying powers and wonders" claimed by the Papists, who produce them (like Joan La Pucelle in *Henry VI* Part I) "by the help of the devil, with their conjurations, charms and divers other false sleights" to deceive the common people. It might, therefore, be assumed that Shakespeare introduces such a popish exorcism into his comedy in order to poke fun at the Catholic priests and their followers, including the Babington plotters—but for the fact that he names the exorcist in his play Dr. Pinch, with apparent reference to this Puritan critic of the Papists, and so he neatly turns the tables on him and his party.

Now we may come at once to the climax of the play, when the sentence of death passed upon Aegeon in the beginning is to be carried out in what is described as "the melancholy vale,/ the place of death and sorry execution,/ behind the ditches of the abbey here" (V i.120). This description is seen by T. W. Baldwin, in his monograph entitled *Shakespeare Adapts a Hanging* (1931), as identical with the location of the Theatre in Shoreditch, where there used to be the nunnery or abbey of Holywell in pre-Reformation times. Here on October 5, 1588, in the aftermath of the defeat of the Spanish Armada, a seminary priest, William Hartley, who had been printer and distributor of Campion's *Rationes Decem* in 1581, was hanged as a traitor, instead of at the customary gallows at Tyburn. His execution, coming as it did shortly after the exorcisms (as a result of which Robert Dibdale had also been executed) and the "discovery" of the Babington Plot in 1586, may well have been in the dramatist's mind in his composition of this play.

Further, it may be noticed that the abbey shown in this scene is not a "ruinous monastery" like that mentioned in *Titus Andronicus* (V i.21), but it is still flourishing as an abbey under the rule of an abbess. She is here introduced as "a virtuous and reverend lady" (V i.134), and she turns out to be none other than Aegeon's long-lost wife. This may remind us of the situation that recurs in Shakespeare's later romance of *Pericles*. Only, there the Catholic abbess seems to revert to pagan times, as priestess of Diana in the temple of Ephesus, where she is finally restored to her long-lost husband Pericles. From all this it may be concluded that the dramatist—for all his seeming dependence on a classical source, and for all his comparative immaturity as an apprentice in dramaturgy—has skillfully contrived to turn this play from first to last into a Catholic comedy.

The Two Gentlemen of Verona

In turning from *The Comedy of Errors* to *The Two Gentlemen of Verona*, we seem to be taking a step backwards, if not in chronological order of composition, at least in dramaturgical skill. Whereas *The Comedy*, despite its juvenile quality as the work of an apprentice, is commonly a success on the stage, this can hardly be said of *The Two Gentlemen*. The latter play is indeed full of good things that could only have come from the pen of Shakespeare, and Dr. Johnson commended it by noting that few plays "have more lines or passages which, singly considered, are eminently beautiful". It was even esteemed by John Vyvyan as a forerunner, in its depiction of "the rose of love", of *Romeo and Juliet.* But its dramatic effect is seriously undermined by a *dénouement* that is almost universally (and justly) condemned. This comes when Valentine assures the suddenly and incredibly repentant Proteus, "All that was mine in Silvia I give thee" (V iv.83), quite disregarding the feelings both of Silvia herself, who has set her heart on him and is there on the scene, and of Proteus's lover Julia, who is also there but in disguise. Yet this is offered, according to mediaeval convention, as the model of an ideal friendship, which may call for such a sacrifice. Parallels for it are found both in Shakespeare's source, the tale of "Felix and Felismena" in Jorge de Montemayor's *Diana Enamorada* (1542), and in the other tale of "Titus and Gisippus" as told by Sir Thomas Elyot in his *Book of the Governor.* Yet surely, we may think, the young Shakespeare—with that gift for realism which he shows already in this early comedy, at least in the subplot between the two clowns, Speed and Launce—must have felt the awkwardness which ordinary people find in Valentine's self-sacrifice. Why, then, did he choose to place it at the very climax of this play? Was he perhaps overridden by the manager of the Rose or the Theatre in keeping to his source material? Or was he, as Dr. Johnson suggests, yielding to an indolence that prompted him to bring an unsatisfactory play to a hasty end? Or was he perhaps in this play, as in others, looking beyond the requirements of strict realism to some layer of symbolic, possibly Catholic, meaning?

There is, in fact, in this play, as to a lesser extent in *The Comedy of Errors*, a discernible layer of Catholic meaning. Basically, the plot is about two friends, Valentine and Proteus, of whom the former is as yet fancy-free but the latter is in love with and loved by the lady Julia. The movement of the plot takes them one by one from Verona to the ducal court at

Milan. On this journey Valentine is the first to set out, so as "to see the wonders of the world abroad" (I i.6), and on his arrival in Milan he soon falls in love with the duke's daughter Silvia. Meanwhile, Proteus is obliged by his father, on the somewhat worldly advice of a cloistered uncle, to be "tried and tutor'd in the world" (I iii.21). So he, too, betakes himself to Milan, where he also falls in love with Silvia. Here is a situation ripe for another comedy of errors, such as may have appealed to the young dramatist, who seems to have made a speciality of this kind of comedy—which he further develops in *A Midsummer Night's Dream* and *Twelfth Night.* In this parallelism, moreover, we may notice implications of further interest from a Catholic point of view.

First, the theme of going on a journey to a distant country for the sake of education—at a time, we may remember, when Italy was not united but divided into different fiefs or principalities, and in particular the cities of Verona and Milan lay in the different territories of Venetia and Lombardy—may recall the need of Catholic gentlemen in the Elizabethan age to send their sons abroad for their education. That need could be met either at the seminary of Rheims (which had moved there from Douai in 1578 and did not return till 1593) or at the Jesuit school of Eu on the north coast of France (which also moved in 1593 to a more permanent place at St. Omers). This was an urgent priority in the minds not only of Catholic gentlemen, but also of the priests on the English mission, not least the Jesuits. In this connection, it is significant that Proteus's father, Antonio, seeks the advice of his unnamed brother "in the cloister", that is, an enclosed monk, though the advice as given in the play seems somewhat worldly for a religious. In the name of his father, moreover, we may note an anticipation of that other Antonio in *The Merchant of Venice*, who is from the outset of the play concerned for his young friend Bassanio and the means of sending him on a journey, though it is not precisely for the sake of education but of wooing and winning the lady Portia.

In fact, once Valentine and Proteus reach Milan, they show themselves no more concerned about their education than Lucentio on his arrival at Padua in *The Taming of the Shrew*. Rather, first the former and then the latter fall in love with the same lady Silvia, just as Bassanio, already in love with the lady Portia, effectively woos and wins her. Though Valentine has first place in Silvia's affections, it is Proteus who woos her with the impressive song, "Who is Silvia? What is she?" Evidently there is a mystery in the identity of Silvia, which Proteus goes on to disclose in his subsequent words, "Holy, fair, and wise is she", with the reason, "The heaven such grace did lend her,/ that she might admired be" (IV ii.42). This mention of "grace", as lent by heaven, may take us back to the speech of the admiring Antipholus of Syracuse addressed to the divine Luciana in *The Comedy of Errors*, as well as forwards to so many other plays whose heroines are described by their lovers in terms of divine grace. It may also raise our minds—as we have noted in dealing with the earlier comedy—up to the heavenly ideal not so much of Platonic Beauty (according to the suggestion of John Vyvyan) as of Our Lady. In other words, the two friends may be seen as traveling, in a symbolic sense, in search of the same religious ideal expressed in terms appropriate to the Virgin Mary as venerated by Catholics, though embodied in an individual heroine.

On the realistic level, of course, it is not surprising if the Duke of Milan, like Brabantio in *Othello*, is angry at Valentine's clandestine love for his daughter. Yet his anger is comically, and significantly, made known to Valentine by the announcement of his servant Launce: "Sir, there is a proclamation that you are vanished"—which Proteus corrects to "That thou art banished" (III i.217). In this we may note an anticipation of Romeo's banishment, but with the addition of a sinister implication in the term "proclamation", reminding an Elizabethan audience of the royal proclamations that were issued from time to time against Jesuits and seminary priests. For those priests banishment was a common enough penalty and a merciful alternative to execution as a traitor at Tyburn. It is also significant that the means adopted by Silvia for following Valentine into banishment, under the pretence of "holy confession" at "Friar Patrick's cell" (IV iii.43), is oddly similar to that adopted by Juliet for making her way to Romeo at Friar Laurence's cell. Subsequently, on his arrival in the forest outside Milan, with its evocation of the other Forest of Arden, Valentine makes the seemingly commonplace remark "Leave not the mansion so long tenantless,/ lest, growing ruinous, the building fall" (V iv.8). Yet in such words the dramatist may have been thinking, as more explicitly in Titus *Andronicus* (V i.21), of a "ruinous monastery" such as that of Wroxhall in his own Forest of Arden. And so, even in the romantic setting of Renaissance Italy, he may be pointing to the tragic background of Elizabethan England. But like Duke Vincentio in *Measure for Measure*, he has to hide his "true-meant design", and that is not to be elicited from him, any more than from Launce, "but by a parable" (II iv.41), namely the play as a whole.

Then there remains the question about the other heroine of this play, Julia. What, if anything, may be said about her from the Catholic viewpoint? To begin with, when she tells her maid Lucetta about her plan to follow Proteus to Milan, she uses the vivid image of a river, in which scholars have recognized a reference to the current of the river Avon as it flows under Clopton Bridge past Stratford. "The current that with gentle murmur glides," she observes, "thou know'st, being stopp'd, impatiently doth rage" (II vii.25). This is the consideration that prompts her not only to follow her lover but also to adopt male disguise for safety's sake. In this way she is predecessor to so many of Shakespeare's heroines, such as Portia and Jessica, Rosalind and Viola, who have recourse to the same expedient, even while admitting, like Viola, that it is "a wickedness" (*Twelfth Night*, II ii.28). This consideration might also be applied, as it is more clearly applied by Friar Francis in *Much Ado About Nothing* (IV i.220), to the difference made in the lives of English Catholics by the accession of Elizabeth I in 1558 on the death of her half-sister Mary. Before, their practice of religion had been smooth enough, like "the current that with gentle murmur glides", but then they had failed to "prize it to the worth". Now, however, "being lack'd and lost", like the current that is stopped, they have learnt to "rack the value". So Julia on her journey to Milan in the footsteps of Proteus also compares herself to "a true devoted pilgrim" (II vii.9)—not only like the heroes in *Romeo and Juliet* and *The Merchant of Venice*, but also like Helena in her pursuit of Bertram in *All's Well That Ends Well*. So she applies the same image to the river as flowing with changing moods on "his pilgrimage" to the sea. Unlike Silvia, however, Julia is not described in explicit terms of "grace", but at least Proteus before his enforced departure for Milan utters the significant sigh, "O heavenly Julia!" (I iii.50).

The Taming of the Shrew

Among the plays of Shakespeare's apprenticeship in the art of dramaturgy, there seems to be less of a problem regarding

The Taming of the Shrew. There are, of course, some trivial problems: its possible relationship to *The Taming of a Shrew* (where the difference is more than just that of a definite article in the one and an indefinite article in the other), the silence of Francis Meres about it in his 1598 enumeration of existing plays by Shakespeare, and the seeming affront to modern feminists with which the play ends. As for the first of these problems, it may be said that there seems to be no compelling reason why Shakespeare may not have written both plays, the one as a reworking of the other. As for the second, there is a common opinion identifying *The Taming of the Shrew*, which is not in Meres's list, with the unidentified *Love's Labour's Won*, which is. In that case, it would appear that these two early comedies are seen by Meres as forming a pair. Anyhow, leaving aside these problems for editors of the play, it may be observed that this is surely the most popular of Shakespeare's early plays, with the possible exception of *Richard III*. It also raises the question, which is ever at the back of my mind in my present discussion of all the plays, and which was (I submit) ever at the back of Shakespeare's mind, where may we find a Catholic dimension in it? Were shrews, to put it somewhat flippantly, so common among Catholic families in Elizabethan England that they needed instruction in taming them?

Here, however, as we have noticed in dealing with the history of *Richard III*, there is no great problem once we turn from the play and its subject matter to its dramatic source. This has been traced, with some probability, to the great Catholic champion of the early Tudor period, Sir Thomas More. In addition to his reputation for humanism and legal expertise, as well as his defence of the rights of conscience and the sanctity of marriage, More was known as a twice-married family man. The story both of his first marriage with

Jane Colt (of Essex) and his second with Alice Middleton (of Warwickshire) is said to be implied in the colloquy of his friend Erasmus, "The Properties of Shrewd Wives and Honest Wives", which was first published in English translation in 1557. Not that it is identified as the principal source of the play, but it is offered by Richard Hosley (in an article for the *Huntington Library Quarterly*, 1964) as a contributing influence. In More's early life we read of how he tested his vocation to the monastic life with the Carthusians at the London Charterhouse, but he came to the conclusion that his was rather a vocation to married life in the world—rather like our conjectured outcome of the *Spiritual Exercises* of St. Ignatius when made by the young Shakespeare in Lancashire under the direction of Edmund Campion. So he went on a visit to a friend of his father's in the county of Essex, one John Colt, who had three daughters of marriageable age. Though he was more attracted to the second daughter, More chose the elder out of pity for her. Whether she was a shrew or not, we do not know, but she seems to have been a submissive wife to him. As for More's second wife, Alice, she does seem to have been a shrew, for all the assertions of modern female authors to the contrary, and she was even compared by More's contemporaries to the classical shrew, Socrates' wife Xanthippe. Anyhow, the hypothesis of More's influence on Shakespeare's play, by way of Erasmus, finds some confirmation in the clear echo of More's words to his son-in-law William Roper on leaving his Chelsea home for Lambeth Palace, at the summons of the commissioners for the Oath of Supremacy: "Son Roper, I thank Our Lord, the field is won." Such are almost the words spoken by Petruchio's friend Hortensio when congratulating him on his success in taming the shrewish Katharina, "Petruchio, go thy ways, the field is won!" (IV v.23)

When we turn from Petruchio's wooing of the shrew Katharina to the other wooing by various suitors of her milder sister Bianca, we come upon another interesting echo of a Catholic source. This has reference not to the life of Sir Thomas More but to the location of William Allen's seminary, now no longer at Douai but at Rheims (till 1593). When Lucentio seeks to woo Bianca, he has to come to her in disguise, like the priests returning to England on their spiritual mission to the Catholics. So he persuades the dotard Gremio to introduce him to Bianca's father, Baptista, as "this young scholar that has long been studying at Rheims" (II i.79). Here it may be noted that, in her reaction to the two tutors who come to her as suitors in disguise, Bianca states her preference for the old-fashioned ways of Lucentio to the new-fangled music of Hortensio, with the words, "Old fashions please me best, I am not so nice/ to change true rules for odd inventions" (III i.81). This may be interpreted, along the present lines, though here it may seem in a somewhat farfetched manner, as a preference of the "old faith" to the "odd inventions" of the reformers.

Two more passages may be adduced as serving to link this play with the undercurrent of Catholic meaning noted in the two previous comedies. First, on his arrival in Padua, Petruchio professes it as his aim, like that of the two gentlemen of Verona, "to seek (his) fortunes further than at home,/ where small experience grows" and to "come abroad to see the world" (I ii.51). In this respect, he may be compared (as we have noted of the other comedies) to those other young men sent abroad to the continental seminaries for their Catholic education. Secondly, on learning from the old pedant that he has just come from Mantua, the astute Tranio pretends that " 'tis death for anyone in Mantua/ to come to Padua" (IV ii.81), as it were recalling the situation in *The Comedy of Errors* between Syracuse and Ephesus. He therefore persuades the pedant to masquerade as Lucentio's father, Vincentio, in order to deceive Baptista into accepting Lucentio as his son-in-law. This may also indirectly refer to Elizabethan England, particularly London, concerning seminary priests arriving there from Rheims. But that may seem too farfetched, and I would hesitate to emphasize the point.

Also deserving of note is "the old priest at St. Luke's church" (IV iv.88), who is persuaded by Lucentio's other servant, Biondello, to perform the wedding ceremony between Lucentio and Bianca. He may be seen as anticipating the "old religious men" in *As You Like It*, who may correspond to the old priests from Marian times, such as the old Sir John Frith, who was suffered to eke out his ministry at the little church of Temple Grafton on the outskirts of the Forest of Arden. It is this Sir John who may have presided (as we have noted) over the secret wedding of the young William Shakespeare and the older Anne Hathaway "of Temple Grafton" (as she is described in the official records at the diocesan registry of Worcester).

Love's Labour's Lost

The ostensible background to the companion comedy of *The Taming of the Shrew*—assuming that it is to be identified with Meres's *Love's Labour's Won*—namely, *Love's Labour's Lost,* is the religious strife in France between the Catholics and the Huguenots. The setting is Navarre, the little kingdom of the Huguenot leader Henry of Bourbon, who became the first Bourbon king of France in 1589 but was accepted by the Parisians as their king only on his conversion to the Catholic faith—when he is said to have made the cynical remark, "Paris is worth a Mass." That strife is, however, hardly felt at all in Shakespeare's play. It begins with the king's fanciful proposal to turn his court into "a little academe" (I i.13), recalling the actual academies patronized at that time in France not only by Henry of Navarre at his capital in Nérac but also by the king himself, Henry III, at his palace in Paris. To the king in his play Shakespeare gives the name of Ferdinand, that of his noble patron, Ferdinando Stanley, Lord Strange, who became fifth earl of Derby in 1593, only to die the following year of a mysterious poisoning. Some suspicion of murder attached to Elizabeth's Machiavellian minister Lord Burghley, who was not above resorting to such tactics, especially when his victim had some claim to the succession on the queen's death. This claim was being advanced by the Jesuit Robert Persons in his highly seditious *Conference about the Next Succession* (not published till 1595), though the earl himself had affirmed his Protestant allegiance. Among the lords at the court of Navarre two, Berowne and Longaville, are evidently to be identified with two of the Huguenot commanders, Biron and de Longueville, but the third, Dumaine, echoes the name of the Catholic leader, the Duke de Mayenne. Thus they form a strangely ecumenical gathering, four centuries before their time! It is also as though they anticipate Henry of Navarre's conversion to Catholicism, not just for motives of political convenience, as implied in his saying about Paris being worth a Mass, but rather as this was mediated for him by the Catholic representative, Jacques Davy du Perron, the Cardinal Bishop of Evreux. As for the Princess of France, she would correspond to the Huguenot wife of Henry of Navarre, Marguerite of Valois.

The ideal of a Platonic academy seems to have been introduced into France by no less a lady than the queen of Henry II and thereafter the all-powerful queen mother, Catherine de' Medici. She herself sought to maintain a diplomatic balance between the opposing Catholic and Huguenot parties, while herself remaining a Catholic. And so, of the two academies that principally flourished at the time in France, one was Catholic, at the royal palace, having been founded by a poet of the Pléiade, Anthony de Baif, in 1570, and the other was the Huguenot academy in Navarre. The latter was promoted partly by the king's Huguenot adviser, Philippe du Plessis-Mornay, who came to be regarded as the pope of the French Huguenots, partly by the other Huguenot author, Pierre de la Primaudaye, whose book *L'Acádemie Française* (1577, tr. Eng. 1586) provided Shakespeare with much background information on the subject of his play, except that his setting is Anjou, not Navarre.

Now what, it may be asked, is the religious implication in all this background reference to the Huguenot kingdom of Navarre and the Huguenot-Platonic ideal of a courtly academy for Shakespeare's comedy? Does it betray, as some have maintained, a preference for the Protestant over the Papist side of the religious controversies no less in France than in England? Or may it not be seen as indicating a subtle preference for the Papist side? First, within the play itself we notice a strong element of satire against such a courtly academy, particularly as it involves the repudiation of female company for the space of three years. But then, it may also be asked, may not this satire be applied no less to the Catholic ideal of monastic life, which includes the vow of chastity, with complete abstention from marriage and family life? In other plays, however, the dramatist expresses his veneration for this ideal, as in *Measure for Measure*, in the words of the licentious Lucio to the young postulant Isabella, "I hold you as a thing ensky'd and sainted,/ by your renouncement an immortal spirit" (I iv.34), and in *A Midsummer Night's*

Dream, in the praise of Theseus for those who "master so their blood,/ to undergo such maiden pilgrimage" (I i.74). Such a religious life has to be prompted by a sincerely spiritual motive, in view of the kingdom of heaven, in contrast to the motive proposed by the King of Navarre in this play, where he looks for merely earthly fame. It may also be added that there was at this time another academy in London, presided over by Lord Burghley (as Master of the lucrative Court of Wards) for his noble wards, among whom was Shakespeare's other patron, the young Earl of Southampton. At the same time, the dramatist may have been looking back from his contemporary Protestant academies in Navarre and London, which were exclusively for males of the nobility, to the Catholic academy run by Sir Thomas More for his household in London, among whom there were as many women as men—an academy that won the high praise of Erasmus.

From this complex political and religious background we may turn to the theme of romantic love that would seem, if only from its title, to dominate the main plot of this play. Here again we may notice the above-mentioned emphasis on divine grace, this time in relation to the Princess of France, who oddly remains unnamed, in contrast to her three ladies. From the outset she is introduced to the young lords of Navarre by the *enfant terrible* Berowne, who describes her as "a maid of grace and complete majesty" (I i.135)—where the words "maid" and "grace" both seem to point to the maiden of Nazareth who is hailed by the angel (in the Rheims version of Luke i.28) as "full of grace". This description is subsequently reaffirmed by the courtier Lord Boyet, in urging her to be "as prodigal of all dear grace as Nature was in making graces dear" (II i.9). Then she herself reinforces this reference when, in answer to the king's protest, "Hear me, dear lady, I have sworn an oath," she responds with the pun, "Our Lady help my lord! He'll be forsworn" (II i.97).

All this apparent Catholic reference early on in the play, however, may seem to be counterbalanced by a Protestant implication when, in answer to the flattery of the forester, "Nothing but fair is that which you inherit," the Princess exclaims, "See, see! My beauty will be saved by merit. O heresy in fair, fit for these days!" (IV i.21). The implied heresy consists in what the Protestants from Luther's time onwards regarded as the Catholic heresy that salvation was due to the merit of good works. But this was never the official teaching of the Catholic Church. Whereas Luther maintained the thesis of "faith alone" as required for salvation, according to his interpretation of St. Paul's words "The just man shall live by faith" (Rom. i.17, quoting Hab. ii.4), the Catholics never taught that the just shall live (only) by good deeds. That is rather the heresy of Pelagius, as opposed to the Catholic teaching, upheld at the Council of Trent in its Decree on Justification (1547), that for good works to have any merit or saving efficacy they need to be grounded on faith and prompted by grace. So there is nothing really anti-Catholic in the words of the Princess, though they may superficially tell against the Catholics, and though her historical counterpart may be the Huguenot Marguerite de Valois.

In the following scene, however, there seems to be an implicit slap in the face for the notorious Jesuit pamphleteer Robert Persons. This has been detected in the riddling conversation between the pedant Holofernes and his toady Sir Nathaniel. From the simple words of greeting addressed by Jacquenetta to Sir Nathaniel, "Give you good morrow, master parson!", Holofernes takes occasion to engage in a bout of heavy punning: "Master parson, quasi pers-on. An if one should be pierced, which is the one?" (IV ii.85). Subsequently, on Nathaniel's mention of "a certain Father", he interposes with further punning, "Sir, tell me not of the Father, I do fear colourable colours" (IV ii.157). In the former exchange commentators note the evident reference to Thomas Nashe's recent book *Pierce Penniless* (1592), considering that Nashe is commonly identified with Don Armado's witty page Moth, while Nashe's ponderous opponent Dr. Gabriel Harvey of Cambridge University is likewise identified with Holofernes—and Harvey's brother, the parson Richard Harvey, with Sir Nathaniel. On the other hand, there is no reason why in his characters Shakespeare may not have been aiming at two contemporaries in one passage. So "pers-on" following on "parson" might well refer no less to Father Persons (who spelt his own name with an e, whereas his enemies wrote it with an a, so as to imply the false rumour that he was the bastard son of a parson) than to *Pierce Penniless*, or rather to both at once. The Jesuit reference, moreover, seems to be confirmed by Nathaniel's subsequent mention of "a certain Father", especially in connection with "colourable colours", or specious pretexts covering a treasonable intent, such as were commonly attributed to Persons by his Protestant, and even his Catholic, enemies. In these years hardly a book of Catholic controversy with some political slant was published but was seen to issue from the prolific pen of Persons in Rome, however much it might be disguised by anonymity or pseudonymity. This might be interpreted as indicating that even if Shakespeare was a Catholic, he might still be willing to satirize Persons for his political activities, as did not a few of that father's opponents among the secular clergy. Yet on Persons' behalf, one might plead that the implicit reference to him, rather than to *Pierce Penniless*, was intended by the dramatist as (in contemporary terms) "a sop to Cerberus", a means of raising a cheap laugh from among Protestant members of his audience while disguising his own Catholic sympathies. He might also have added the mention of "a certain Father" with his "colourable colours" for the amusement of the queen, when he came to refurbish his play for presentation at court in the Christmas season of 1597, before it was printed in the 1598 quarto with the description "newly corrected and augmented". In that case, it would have come conveniently after the publication of the *Conference concerning the Next Succession* in 1595. Though this work was commonly ascribed to Persons, he himself rejected the ascription, but it was regarded by contemporary readers, and not least by the queen herself, as charged with the "colourable colours" of treason.

Within the wider dramatic context, however, and in view of the characters into whose mouths the offending words are put, their anti-Jesuit implications are greatly weakened. Sir Nathaniel is evidently a minister of the established Church, no doubt a chaplain at some university college, especially considering the probable identification of Holofernes with the Puritan opponent of Nashe, Gabriel Harvey of Cambridge. At the same time, there is another probable identification of him with the Earl of Southampton's Italian tutor, John Florio. Not only had he changed his religious allegiance from Catholic to Protestant on coming to England, but he may have been planted in Southampton's household as a spy for Lord Burghley, in view of the Catholic sympathies of that young man, whose father had been one of the leading Catholic nobles early on in Elizabeth's reign. One may recall Macbeth's words to Lady Macbeth on such nobles and his spies: "There's not a one of them but in his house/ I keep a servant fee'd" (III iv.133). As for the words of Holofernes, their effect coming from such a man, whether identified with Harvey or Florio or both together, would surely have seemed deeply ironical to those who could have perceived the hidden irony. It becomes all the deeper when we go on to consider how cruelly Holofernes is treated by the nobles at court, even as "Monsieur Judas" the traitor, with a deliberate pun on the name of Judas Maccabaeus, whose part Holofernes is playing in the pageant of the Nine Worthies (V ii.596ff). Sir Nathaniel, too, is subjected to similar treatment in his role as Alexander.

Moreover, an interesting theory assigns the first performance of the play to the date of 1593 and to the house of Southampton himself, whether at Holborn in London or at Titchfield in Hampshire. This seems to be indicated by the sonnets, composed by the lords in honour of the visiting ladies, which imply a date of composition close not only to the early sonnets but also to the two long poems, *Venus and Adonis* and *The Rape of Lucrece*, which were dedicated to the young earl in the years 1593 and 1594, respectively. Further, considering that Southampton was still adhering to the "old faith" in which he had been brought up, though he may have slackened in his profession of it under James I, we may justly incline to a Catholic rather than a Protestant interpretation of the play, in which Holofernes is seen (in part) as a caricature of Southampton's irksome tutor. On the other hand, we have to see Southampton sharing the honours of the play with another young Catholic noble, Ferdinando Stanley, Lord Strange, who was soon to become the short-lived Earl of Derby, besides being patron of Shakespeare's company of players. This is sufficiently implied, considering the rarity of "Ferdinando" as an English name, as well as the royal title invested in the Earls of Derby as kings of Man, in the name Shakespeare gives the King of Navarre as the central figure of his play. But then in

1594, this patron was, as we have noticed, mysteriously poisoned on his return from the queen's court to his Lancashire home, and a new company of players was formed under the patronage of the queen's cousin, Henry Carey, Lord Hunsdon. Thus the play with all its attendant circumstances could have been interpreted by Southampton as a warning for him to proceed, like Hamlet, very carefully in dealing with his mighty opposite, Lord Burghley.

Lastly, we may reflect on the various penances imposed by the ladies on their lovers for having been forsworn. The king is first consigned by the princess to spend a year in some "forlorn and naked hermitage,/ remote from all the pleasures of the world" (V ii.803), as though to taste a real monastic life in contrast to the snobbish luxury of the academy he had been envisaging at court. Berowne is similarly consigned by his mistress Rosaline to a life spent visiting "the speechless sick" and conversing with "groaning wretches" (V ii.859), apparently in some hospital run by a Catholic religious order, such as that recently founded by St. Camillus de Lellis in 1591. Such institutions had for the most part been closed in England with the suppression of the monasteries under Henry VIII, and so it looks as if Shakespeare, in his unconventional conclusion to *Love's Labour's Lost,* is looking away from the romance of courtly love to the practical works of love as practiced either on the European continent or in mediaeval England.

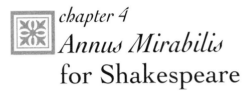

chapter 4
Annus Mirabilis for Shakespeare

Romeo and Juliet

THE YEAR 1595—or thereabouts, since it is so difficult to be certain as to the precise dating of Shakespeare's plays—seems to have been a veritable *annus mirabilis*, a year of marvels, for the budding dramatist. It marks a turning point between his early or apprentice plays and those of his masterful maturity. For it is about this time that scholars date three plays which have in common a notably lyrical quality. Moreover, between them the plays cover all three traditional divisions made by Shakespeare's fellow actors, Hemings and Condell, in their editing of the First Folio of 1623, namely, the tragedy of *Romeo and Juliet*, the comedy of *A Midsummer Night's Dream*, and the history play of *Richard II*. These plays stand out as a kind of literary or dramatic watershed between those that have gone before and those that come after. Yet few scholars seem to have stood back from them to ask the question, Why? All too often the plays of Shakespeare are taken for granted as simply there, like the Himalayas—as it were beyond our questioning owing to the privilege of genius. Yet they challenge our question. What, we may ask, took place in the year 1595 to bring the genius of Shakespeare to the level of such lyrical expression as we find in these plays? Was it, as some conjecture, the outcome of the poet's romantic or homosexual love for the young Earl of Southampton—assuming him to have been the Young Man of the Sonnets, as he was undeniably the dedicatee of the two long poems? After all, isn't it out of the period of the early sonnets and these long poems, composed as they evidently were in 1593–94, that the three plays take their rise—beginning with *Romeo and Juliet*, which is unique among Shakespeare's plays with two sonnets for prologues to the first two acts? It is as if after the March winds of *Venus and Adonis* and the April showers of *The Rape of Lucrece* come the May flowers of *Romeo and Juliet*.

Yet another conjecture may be advanced in accordance not just with the biographical but rather with the religious background of the dramatist. What, we may ask, of special interest to Catholics took place in the year 1595 such as might have an important bearing on the dramatist and his lyrical genius? What, I answer, but the trial and execution, or "martyrdom", of the Jesuit poet Robert Southwell on February 20–21 (still in the old year of the Julian calendar)? The relevance of Southwell's poems, especially his *Saint Peters Complaint*, to Shakespeare's plays and poems, especially *The Rape of Lucrece*, has been cogently presented by the poet's biographer, Christopher Devlin. What is more, not only did Southwell die a martyr's (or a traitor's) death at Tyburn on that date, but hardly had he died and his limbs been "lopped" by the executioner than his poems were published with the presumed approval of the Archbishop of Canterbury, John Whitgift, as being the person responsible for the censorship of printed books. How, we may ask, did these poems of a Jesuit "traitor" elude his censorious eye? Was he perhaps overswayed by some "great command" (*Hamlet* V i.250), maybe that of the Earl of Southampton?

Not that Shakespeare had to wait for the publication of these poems to inspire him to dramatic composition, for he may well have seen them and familiarized himself with them while they were still in manuscript. He may even, as Devlin suggests, be the "Master W. S." to whom the poems are dedicated, with an appeal for some "finer piece, wherein it may be seen how well verse and virtue suit together"—a piece that Devlin identifies with *The Rape of Lucrece.*

Turning now to the first and most lyrical of the plays under consideration, once we ask of *Romeo and Juliet* what significance it might have had for a Catholic spectator, we are all but overwhelmed by an abundance of evidence, in contrast to the relative dearth of it in the preceding plays. From the outset we have the same setting of civil strife that we noted in the history plays on the Wars of the Roses and the revenge play of *Titus Andronicus,* and of strife between neighbouring cities that we noted in *The Comedy of Errors* (between Ephesus and Syracuse), *The Two Gentlemen of Verona* (implicitly between Verona and Milan), and *The Taming of the Shrew* (supposedly between Mantua and Padua). Here, however, it is between two families or houses, those of Montague and Capulet, within the one city of Verona. These family names were taken by the dramatist from his sources, since the story was already well known in Italy, France, and England long before he came to write his play. For English readers and spectators in particular it had been retold not only in Shakespeare's main source, Brooke's Protestant version of *Romeus and Juliet* (1562), as well as Painter's *Palace of Pleasure* (1566), but also in a dramatized form mentioned by Brooke that has not come down to us. All the same, in view of his Catholic background, Shakespeare could hardly have used the name of Montague without thinking of the title of the great

Catholic nobleman in West Sussex, Anthony Browne, Viscount Montague, grandfather to his patron, the Earl of Southampton. As for Capulet, while this name is also derived from the old story, it may be noted that in his play Shakespeare twice (in Act V) speaks not of Capulet's but of Capel's monument, and Capel is the name not only of an English family but also of a village in Surrey just across the border from West Sussex.

When we pass from the story as retold in poetic form by Arthur Brooke to its dramatized form by Shakespeare, we may well have a feeling akin to that which we have noticed in *King John*, that here we have a dramatist taking a Protestant source and refashioning it as a Catholic play, if without making the contrast too obvious. (The same phenomenon we will also have occasion to notice in dealing with *Henry IV*, both Parts, and *King Lear*.) In this contrast, we first notice the change in atmosphere. On the one hand, Brooke betrays the stern, moralistic attitude of the Puritan in condemning the irresponsibility of the lovers and their indulgence in "dishonest desire" and, even more, the way the Catholic friar panders to them in letting them use his cell as "little better than a house of assignation". On the other hand, what Shakespeare presents is an ideal love, not without realism, particularly in his depiction of Juliet's character, in a sympathetic Catholic setting. Then, too, after the wearisome Petrarchan love convention, with Romeo shown from the outset in hopeless love for Rosaline, he shows how the hero is transformed on his unexpected meeting with Juliet into a Catholic pilgrim. She, too, responds to his transformation with a continuation of the same imagery. If he speaks of his lady as "this holy shrine" and his lips as "two blushing pilgrims", she responds by reminding him that "saints have hands that pilgrims' hands do touch,/ and palm to palm is holy palmers' kiss" (I v.98ff). What is more, however remote and heavenly Rosaline may have appeared to Romeo in his Petrarchan mood, he never uses the word "grace" of her, but in reporting his new love to his "ghostly father", Friar Laurence, he insists that "she whom I love now/ doth grace for grace and love for love allow" (II iii.85). In his words we may notice what to Puritan ears may have sounded blasphemous, with their evocation of two passages from the Bible. One is the angel's greeting of the Virgin Mary as "full of grace" (Luke i.28), and the other is John's proclamation of the incarnate Word, "And of his fullness have all we received, and grace for grace" (John i.16). The same divinity is again implied in Juliet's declaration, "My bounty is as boundless as the sea,/ my love as deep. The more I give to thee,/ the more I have, for both are infinite" (II ii.133). Hers is the divine love of giving, or *agape*, while his is the human love of desiring, or *eros*, which comes all too close to that "rude will" against which the friar has to warn him (II iii.28).

When the dramatist goes on to dramatize the friar, in contrast to Brooke's depiction of him as a sanctimonious pander, he goes out of his way to multiply testimonials to the honesty and sanctity of Friar Laurence. Thus, for example, Capulet respects him as a "reverent holy friar" (IV ii.32); Juliet reassures herself, before taking the drug he has given her, that "he hath still been tried a holy man" (IV iii.29); and the Prince of Verona, even in the face of the friar's admission of guilt, allows for his good intentions, with an echo of Juliet's words, "We still have known thee for a holy man" (V iii.270). When he is first introduced to the audience, before Romeo's coming to his cell, he is not infrequently portrayed by producers as a doddering old fool, mouthing irrelevant, sententious, rhyming couplets that are hardly religious or Christian but merely moralistic. But when we take a closer look at his commonplaces, we find in them a deep Christian wisdom that is aptly related both to his religious profession, as a "holy Franciscan friar" (V ii.1), and to the dramatic function he is to fulfil. As a friar he finds, like the exiled duke in *As You Like It*, "good in everything" (II i.17), and he quotes the contemporary Christian classic *The Imitation of Christ*—contemporary in the sense that it achieved the peak of its popularity in the Elizabethan age, when it was twice translated even under Protestant auspices and went into numerous editions. Thus, for example, his observation that "nought so vile that on the earth doth live,/ but to the earth some special good doth give" (II iii.17) seems to echo the words of à Kempis, "There is no creature so small and vile, but shows forth the goodness of God" (II iv). A little further on in his speech, in his mention of the "opposed foes" that "encamp them still/ in man as well as herbs, grace and rude will" (II iii.27), not only does he anticipate his contrast between the grace of Juliet and the rude will of Romeo, but Shakespeare in him may be recalling the meditation in the *Spiritual Exercises* on "The Two Standards" of Christ and Satan from the time he may have made them in Lancashire under the direction of Edmund Campion.

Yet another echo of those Exercises, from the other meditation on "The Kingdom of Christ", is where the exercitant is imagined as a knight responding to the call of Christ and is expected to offer himself wholeheartedly, not just in outward show but in his inmost thoughts and affections. Such, we may say, is the response of Juliet to Romeo, once she has reassured herself of his sincerity in promising to marry her, when she vows to lay her fortunes at his feet and to follow him as her lord "throughout the world" (II ii.147). The same sentiment, we may note, is twice repeated in *As*

You Like It, first, where Celia says of the clown Touchstone, "He'll go along o'er the wide world with me" (I ii.135), and secondly, where Adam promises his master Orlando, "Master, go on and I will follow thee/ to the last gasp with truth and loyalty" (II iii.69).

To return to the friar, we may further note how accurately he speaks of "this osier cage of ours" (II iii.7). He says not "mine" but "ours", with reference to his religious vow of poverty, according to which he can have nothing of his own. This is a point of religious observance which Shakespeare would have known as a Catholic, but which few Protestants in his audience would have even noticed. Later, when Juliet wants him to tell her the appropriate time for her to come to his cell, she accurately asks, "Shall I come to you at evening Mass?" Even in those days Mass was not celebrated in the evening, but Verona was a privileged exception, and Shakespeare knew it.

So far we have been dwelling on the Catholic ideal and what may be called, in the meaning of Dante's *Divina Commedia*, the comic part of the play. But once we turn to the tragic part, we pass from the Catholic ideal to a harsh, recusant reality. Impressive in this respect is the prince's doom on Romeo for his slaying of Tybalt—not the heavy punishment of execution but the seemingly lighter one of banishment. Yet in Romeo's ears the word "banishment", associated as it is with the long-drawn-out sufferings of the poor Catholic exiles on the continent, is intolerable. He compares it to "purgatory, torture, hell itself" (III iii.18), where he refers not only to hell, with its extreme "pain of loss", but also to the Catholic doctrine of purgatory (rejected by Protestants, as typical of popery), and the torture of the rack. On Juliet's side, while she stays at home, without having to eat what Bolingbroke in *Richard II* calls "the bitter bread of banishment" (III i.21), she is expected by her tyrannical father to marry Count Paris. And when she refuses, he threatens that, if she will not go with Paris to Saint Peter's church, he will drag her "on a hurdle thither" (III v.156), implying a comparison between such a forced wedding and the manner of execution for Catholic martyrs on their way from prison to Tyburn.

As for the Nurse, she may be a minor character in the play, with all her vivid characterization as a chatterbox, but in one point at least she stands for the remnants of the "old faith" and the pieties of pre-Reformation England. As mentioned above, one of the main changes brought about in the lives of ordinary Englishmen by Protestant teaching was due to its rejection of the Catholic doctrine of purgatory and the consequent practice of praying for the dead. For if between heaven and hell there is no purgatory, but the souls of the dead are either blessed in heaven or damned in hell, there can be no point in praying for them. Yet the chatter of the Nurse recalling her memories of the deceased is interspersed with such instinctive prayers as "God rest all Christian souls!" and "God be with his soul!" (I iii.18, 39). In her it is as if Shakespeare is looking back to the good old days of Queen Mary, in much the same way as he speaks through the mouths of old Gobbo in *The Merchant of Venice* (II ii) and of the mad Ophelia in *Hamlet* (IV v).

On the part of Mercutio, however, who somehow balances the Capulet Nurse as the comic friend of Romeo, there is little enough to record of either a Catholic or a Protestant flavour. What he says is, as Romeo observes of him, a deal of "nothing" (I iv.97). Yet it is he who, as noted above, pronounces "a plague o' both your houses" (III i.105), with reference in the dramatic context to the houses of Montague and Capulet, but also perhaps in a wider, contemporary context to the conflicts and controversies between Catholics and

Protestants. In these words he no doubt expresses the deep feeling of the dramatist concerning the religious strife surrounding him in England, which the secular government only makes worse with their cruel repression and persecution of English Catholics, whose only desire is to remain true to their "old faith". This, however, need not be taken to mean that Shakespeare was indifferent to the religious issues of his time, as one of the so-called *adiaphoroi*, who were commonly seen as little better than atheists. Such were above all the Machiavellian politicians for whom religion was a mere matter of expediency and with whom, as the Stranger in *Timon of Athens* laments, "Policy sits above conscience" (III ii.95).

A Midsummer Night's Dream

Though the precise dating and chronological order of Shakespeare's plays often remains unclear, it certainly looks as if *A Midsummer Night's Dream* comes very soon after *Romeo and Juliet*. For one thing, it is appropriate for the comedy to follow the tragedy, as it were in the spirit of Milton's "Lycidas": "Return, Alpheus, the dread voice is past." For another, the play-within-the-play of "Pyramus and Thisby", presented by the Athenian tradesmen before Theseus and Hippolyta in the final act, looks very like a parody of *Romeo and Juliet*. It is even suggested that the original Italian story was developed out of the classical tale of Pyramus and Thisby as narrated by Ovid in his *Metamorphoses* and translated into English by Arthur Golding in 1567. So we may conjecture that, in spite of the lyrical genius manifested in his romantic tragedy, the dramatist was somehow dissatisfied with what he had written. He may have regretted having treated the romantic love of Romeo and Juliet so seriously and sentimentally, even to the extent of permitting the lamentable death of Mercutio owing to Romeo's rashness and Juliet's indignant rejection of her Nurse as "ancient damnation" (III v.235)—the two comic characters who might have brought the play to a happy ending. In this he may also have been following, if indirectly, the lead of his great predecessor Sir Thomas More, to judge from the cartoons of the story of Pyramus and Thisby printed by Tottel on the title-page of his *Dialogue of Comfort against Tribulation* (one of the Tower writings, composed in 1534–35, printed in 1553). Then by entrusting this "most lamentable comedy" (I ii.11) to the clumsy hands of the "rude mechanicals of Athens" (III ii.9), Shakespeare skillfully transforms it into "very tragical mirth" for the entertainment of the noble couples, who turn out to be much better behaved than their counterparts in *Love's Labour's Lost.*

As a romantic comedy, however, *A Midsummer Night's Dream* has its own plot of romantic love, in line with *The Comedy of Errors* and *The Two Gentlemen of Verona.* Here, while Lysander and Hermia are happily with love with each other from the outset of the play, Demetrius has his heart set on Hermia, with her father's approval, after having turned from his former love Helena, who still has her heart set on him. Thus Shakespeare provides us with another love triangle, in which he seems to take no less pleasure than his mischievous fairy Puck. But since the play is a comedy, for the celebration of some aristocratic wedding, we may be sure that its problems will all be happily solved by the end. Then, as Puck sings, "Jack shall have Jill,/ nought shall go ill"—as if echoing the words of the fourteenth-century anchoress Juliana of Norwich, "All shall be well." Nevertheless, over this typical situation of romantic love there hangs a shadow of tragedy, not unlike that which hangs over the whole plot of *The Comedy of Errors,* that of the death penalty for infringement of a severe law. Here we are introduced to Hermia's father, whose name of Egeus oddly echoes that of Aegeon in *The Comedy of*

Errors, though the one threatens to enforce, whereas the other is threatened with the enforcement of, the harshness of the law. It may be doubted whether there was ever such a law at Athens, no less than at Ephesus, but there was certainly (as we have seen in dealing with the former comedy) such a law in England. And in England, too, it may be added, divisions of religion not infrequently appeared within the same family, as Gloucester laments in *King Lear* (I ii.118). In fact, however, Theseus here tempers the harshness of Athenian law by offering Hermia the option, similar to that Friar Laurence offers to Juliet in consideration of Romeo's death, to put on "the livery of a nun" and "for aye to be in shady cloister mew'd" (I i.70). Instead, she and Lysander take a third option, by escaping into the forest outside Athens and living as exiles, like the exiles in the other Forest of Arden in *As You Like It*. After all, so long as they are together, like Lear and Cordelia in prison, they need not eat the "bitter bread of banishment" like Bolingbroke in *Richard II* (III i.21).

Subsequently, however, during their temporary exile in the forest, where everything is subject to the fickle rule of the fairies, Lysander comes to reject his former love on the odd analogy, "As the heresies that men do leave/ are hated most of those they did deceive." (II ii.139) In recusant terms, this might be taken to mean that as exiles in the forest the two have taken refuge on the Catholic continent, but that for some reason Lysander has come to see his old Catholic allegiance as a heresy he now hates. Then for another reason he returns to Hermia and his former allegiance. In the same way, when Helena is bewildered at the strife between Lysander and Demetrius over her, she sees it as an instance of a time "when truth kills truth" and she exclaims at it as a "devilish-holy fray" (III ii.129). Thus in her Shakespeare seems to interpret the lovers' strife, in maintaining what they severally view as "truth" or "fidelity", in terms of the religious strife of the age—not that he rejects religion itself, but that he rejects strife in the cause of religion.

In this main plot of the Athenian lovers, moreover, we may note that, unlike the two lovers in *Romeo and Juliet*, none of the four stand out as individual characters. They are little more than four names, two men and two women. So when they go into the forest, Lysander with Hermia, Demetrius pursuing Hermia, and Helena pursuing Demetrius, their identities are hardly distinguishable in the darkness. This confusion is only accentuated by the magic juice, now of Cupid's flower, now of Dian's bud, as used by Puck under the remote control of Oberon. Eventually, with the former juice remaining on the eyes of Demetrius and the latter applied to the eyes of Lysander, the harmony of the lovers is restored and "Jack has Jill". This all seems to be trivial and irrelevant to Shakespeare's religious background—apart from the two possible exceptions noted above. Only, once the lovers come to themselves on waking up the following morning, they feel as if they are reborn and can see the world with new eyes—as in a dream, yet a waking dream. It may even be compared to the religious experience of being reborn. Yet it is presented, like so much else of a religious nature in Shakespeare's plays, in a secular manner—save insofar as they now make their way to the "temple", corresponding to the "church" in *Romeo and Juliet* and the "chantry" in *Twelfth Night*, for the celebration of their weddings.

Now we may turn to the background not of Shakespeare himself but of the play, namely the forest outside Athens. In the city during the daytime, as in the city of Ephesus in *The Comedy of Errors* or the court of Duke Frederick in *As You Like It*, all is under the harsh rule of the law or the harsh will of the tyrant. But in the forest at night all is under the benign, if fickle, rule of the fairies. And it is the fairies, rather than the lovers, who control the atmosphere, if not the action, of the play. Then, it may be asked, do these fairies—considering that among them, too, there is a strife between their king, Oberon, and their queen, Titania—have any symbolic connection with the religious strife between the Catholics and the Protestants? Don't they rather stand for a reversion to the pagan ages of England before the coming of Christianity, and long before the controversies engendered by the Reformation? On the contrary, it may be urged that it was the Protestant reformers who banished the fairies from England with their insistence on keeping the Christian Gospel pure of all contamination with paganism. In the Catholic Middle Ages, from the first preaching of St. Augustine in the kingdom of Kent it had been the wise policy of the Pope at Rome, St. Gregory the Great, to retain all that was harmless from the old paganism and to baptize it with a new Christian meaning—as in the names of "Yuletide" for Christmas-time, "Lent" for the period of fasting leading up to Holy Week, and "Easter" for the feast of the Pasch or the Resurrection of Christ.

For this reason, we find an interesting poem of the early seventeenth century by the Anglican Bishop of Norwich, Richard Corbet, entitled "A Lament for the Fairies", in which the passing of the fairies is associated with the spoliation of the "old abbeys", when "their songs were Ave-Maries, their dances were processions". Shakespeare, too, by introducing these fairies of old English folklore into this play, and thus keeping their memory alive for unborn generations, is effectively conveying his nostalgia for the old religion—as he goes on to do in even more unmistakable terms in *As You Like It.* This nostalgia may further be seen as coming to a climax in the final night scene of the play, when the fairies come in to bless the house "with fairy grace" and to sprinkle it "with this field-dew consecrate" (V i.29, 45)—as if recalling the old liturgical *benedictio thalami*, or blessing of the marriage bed, prescribed for the end of the wedding ceremony in the Old Sarum Use of the Catholic missal.

Finally, in Act V we may point to two speeches with a deep, though not demonstrably Catholic, meaning put into the mouths of the ducal pair, Theseus and Hippolyta, in whose honour all is being prepared. First, in his speech summing up his impressions of the strange "story of the night" as he has heard it from the mouths of the lovers, Theseus comments on "the lunatic, the lover, and the poet" as being "of imagination all compact" (V i.7). On the face of it, there seems to be nothing particularly Catholic in his words, till we compare them with similar words used by the Jesuit martyr Robert Southwell in the dedication of his recently published poems to "Master W. S." There the author complains of poets who "by abusing their talents . . . have so discredited this faculty that a poet, a lunatic and a liar are by many reckoned but three words of one signification". Secondly, Hippolyta's response to Theseus may well be interpreted as Shakespeare's reply to Southwell, when she points out how "the story of the night", however extraordinary it may seem, "more witnesseth than fancy's images/ and grows to something of great constancy" (V i.23). We may, incidentally, be reminded of Hamlet's response to Horatio, another of Shakespeare's rationalists, on the recent appearance of the ghost: "There are more things in heaven and earth, Horatio,/ than are dreamt of in your philosophy" (I v.166).

(What is more, these words of Hippolyta and Hamlet I may in turn make my own in urging the Catholicism of Shakespeare's plays against the old Shakespearian "orthodoxy". The items I offer one by one in support of my thesis may well, I recognize, be called in question. They are but sparks of light gleaming here and there in the plays. But when taken together, according to the argument proposed by Newman in his *Grammar of Assent* from a convergence of probabilities), they may be seen as growing "to something of great constancy".

Richard II

Even more than the plays considered till now, that of *Richard II* must have elicited resonant echoes in the hearts of all Catholic members in Shakespeare's audience. While it deals with the themes of enforced banishment (as in *Romeo and Juliet*) and self-imposed exile (in as *A Midsummer Night's Dream*), and thus attains a kind of climax among these three plays of lyrical genius, this play may also be seen as looking forward to two others which deal with the related themes of disinheritance and dispossession, *As You Like It* and *King Lear*. These three plays I would go so far as to identify as those in which the heart of the Catholic dramatist is most clearly revealed, and for which he must have stood in most danger from some suborned informer in his audience—as he did in fact come close to standing when the first of the three was revived at the request of Essex's followers on the eve of his rebellion in 1601.

Why then, it may be asked, did the dramatist expose himself to such danger in these plays, particularly in that which we are now considering? And what steps, if any, did he take to minimize the danger? First, one may point to the way he distributes the sympathies of his audience, now for Bolingbroke as he is sent into banishment for no fault of his own, now for Richard as he is deposed and sent to prison, not without his own fault. In the first half of the play the sympathies of the dramatist seem to be on the side of Bolingbroke, son and heir to John of Gaunt, Duke of Lancaster, when he is sent by the arrogant young king into banishment. But in the second half, on Bolingbroke's return to England and Richard's subsequent deposition, the dramatist seems to shift his sympathies to Richard, giving the impression that in either case his feeling is for the underdog.

Secondly, one may point to the strong patriotic emphasis in the play, as though carrying on from the concluding speech of the Bastard in *King John*, and culminating in the famous speech of old John of Gaunt on "This England" in Act II. No Catholic at that time, it is often assumed, would have been so outspokenly patriotic, seeing that patriotism was then coming to be regarded as the characteristic of the Protestant supporters of Queen Elizabeth, now (since 1584) leagued together to defend their queen from the continual Catholic conspiracies against her. There is also an undercurrent throughout the play of seeming support for the typically Anglican doctrine of the divine right of kings, championed as well by Richard himself as by his critics.

Thirdly, one may also paradoxically point to the inclusion of the deposition scene in Act IV, though at the time it was seen as charged with "colourable colours" (to borrow the phrase of Holofernes in *Love's Labour's Lost* IV ii.158), and so it had to be omitted from the first quarto of the play in 1597. Subsequently, the old play was specially commissioned by the followers of Essex, with the inclusion of this scene, of the eve of their rebellion in February 1601. Then the queen herself was said, by the antiquarian courtier William Lambarde, to have made the comment, not without indignation, "I am Richard II, know ye not that!" That must have been Shakespeare's moment of greatest danger, when not only was Essex himself beheaded in the Tower, but his second-in-command Southampton was also sentenced to death—only, the sentence was in his case commuted to one of life imprisonment in the Tower, thanks (it was said) to the personal intercession of the powerful minister Sir Robert Cecil. Shakespeare's company were also interrogated in connection with the trial, but they escaped being arraigned by a plea of ignorance, and partly no doubt because the queen was reluctant to lose her favourite players and her favourite playwright. In such ways the attention of prospective informers may have been deflected from the more subversive, as more Catholic, parts of the play before and after the deposition scene.

To go back now to the beginning of the play, what most prominently stands out in the first and third scenes is the theme of banishment, where it is emphasized even more strongly than in Act III of *Romeo and Juliet*. Oddly enough, whereas the sentence passed on Mowbray, Richard's loyal henchman in his murder of the king's uncle Thomas of Woodstock, Duke of Gloucester, is banishment for life, the one who most vehemently complains is Bolingbroke, who is sentenced to only ten years—and that sentence is almost immediately reduced to six years in view of his father Gaunt's sad face. This word "banishment" is used exclusively either by or about Bolingbroke, as when Richard sentences him to "tread the stranger paths of banishment" (I iii.143) and when Bolingbroke speaks of death as the outcome of his combat with Mowbray, either for one or the other, when "one of our souls had wander'd in the air,/ banish'd this frail sepulchre of our flesh" (I iii.195). Again, on his return to England, Bolingbroke recalls the time when "I sigh'd my English breath in foreign clouds,/ eating the bitter bread of banishment" (III i.20). How clearly this all relates to the fate of English Catholics in exile, whether by free choice of exile or by sentence of banishment, must have been keenly felt by Catholic members in Shakespeare's audiences. Then, as if to underline this emphasis, we come in the same early scene of Act I upon the added image of "pilgrimage", which is also used in *Romeo and Juliet*—only there it is used not of Romeo's banishment but of his approach to Juliet in Capulet's house. Here it is used by Bolingbroke before the tournament, when he compares himself and Mowbray to "two men that vow a long and weary pilgrimage" (I iii.49). He also goes on to describe his banishment as "an inforced pilgrimage" (I iii.264), while his aged father, Gaunt, refers to his own long life as a "pilgrimage" (I iii.320).

Then in Act II what most stands out is the impressive speech of John of Gaunt, which he makes just before his death, as "a prophet new inspir'd" (II i.31)—both on behalf of England and against the king of England for his reckless policies and his undue reliance on flatterers. Most impressive to the ears of most English audiences both then and now, not least to the twentieth-century novelist Graham Greene (for all his maverick tendencies), is the first half of the speech. This almost entirely consists of one long subject, beginning with the words, "This royal throne of kings", and going on for nineteen lines, with seventeen repetitions of "this" preceding a series of nouns ranged in apposition to each other (II i.40–58). In all English literature it may be doubted if there is a more ringing affirmation of patriotism. But all that Gaunt utters in the first half of his speech in favour of patriotism, or even jingoism, he takes back in the triple verb that follows in the second half, "is now leas'd out . . . is now bound in with shame . . . hath made a shameful conquest of itself"—with a significant change from "this England" to "that England" (II i.59–66). It all shows that, despite his real love of England, the dramatist did not regard patriotism as involving an uncritical allegiance to the rulers of England, whether Richard II or Elizabeth I. Rather, in this as in other matters, he seems to have made his own the self-description he puts into the mouth of his villain Iago, "I am nothing if not critical" (*Othello* II i.119).

From this moment onwards, as Gaunt dies and Richard seizes his lands to finance his ill-fated expedition to Ireland, and Bolingbroke returns to claim his rightful inheritance, Richard begins to affirm what Gaunt has long since affirmed, the Tudor doctrine of "the divine right of kings". This doctrine goes back not, as many imagine, to the Middle Ages but to the time Henry VIII claimed this right in the teeth of papal claims, yet paradoxically in virtue of the title *"Fidei Defensor"*, which he had received from the Pope in reward for his *Assertio Septem Sacramentorum* against Luther in 1521. There is an interesting book, published as late as 1689 by one Abednego Seller, and entitled *The History of Passive Obedience*, showing how universally this doctrine had been accepted by Anglican authors from the time of William Tyndale (following Martin Luther), except for the one theologian, Richard Hooker, in Book I of his monumental *Laws of Ecclesiastical Polity* (1594). It was also, incidentally, criticized about the same time by the Jesuit Robert Persons, if he is indeed the author of the notorious *Conference concerning the Next Succession* (1595). In this play of *Richard II* it is affirmed by John of Gaunt in the second scene. Then he urges the widowed Duchess of Gloucester to put her quarrel against the king "to the will of heaven", since it is the king who has caused her husband's death, and so "God's is the quarrel, for God's substitute,/ his deputy anointed in his sight,/ hath caus'd his death", and as a subject, he "may never lift/ an angry arm against his minister" (I ii.6, 56). Subsequently, it is reaffirmed by Richard himself, in his claim that "the breath of worldly men cannot depose/ the deputy elected by the Lord" (III ii.56). In such utterances it is pointed out by proponents of "the Elizabethan world-picture" that the dramatist was duly echoing the orthodox Anglican doctrine as stated in the two homilies "On Order and Obedience" (Volume I, 1547) and "Against Disobedience and Rebellion" (Volume II, 1571). It is also assumed that the words put so impressively into the mouths of Gaunt and Richard, anticipating similar words put into the mouth of Ulysses in *Troilus and Cressida* (I iii.85ff), express the dramatist's own Anglican orthodoxy against the subversive ideas of such Jesuits as Robert Persons. But to assess the real opinions of Shakespeare, it is (as always) necessary to take his words not only in themselves but also in their dramatic context. As for their context in this play, the theory enunciated in such a rhetorical, and such an unrealistic, manner by Richard is soon disproved by the course of events. No angels appear in support of Richard against Bolingbroke's rebellion. And Bolingbroke not only invades the country but also succeeds in supplanting the king, with the consent of Parliament and of the king himself.

Once, however, Bolingbroke comes to power as Henry IV and Richard is legally deposed, according to the theory not of divine right (as proposed by Luther and Tyndale) but of a contract between the ruler and his subjects (as proposed by Hooker and Persons), then he is displaced by Richard in the sympathy of both the dramatist and his audience. It is interesting to note how Richard, in prison at Pomfret Castle, still imagines himself as king, though now reduced by Bolingbroke to nothing. Yet now he rules over the hearts of the people, at least in the audience, as represented by the anonymous individual who comes and plays music, if discordantly, outside his cell as "a sign of love" (V v.65). It is even more interesting when, on his previous way to prison, not yet in Pomfret but in the Tower, Richard encounters his weeping queen, Isabella, and then he advises her, "Hie thee to

France,/ and cloister thee in some religious house," adding, "Our holy lives must win a new world's crown" (V i.22).

Here we may pause to reflect on the implications of these words. At this point in the play, Richard is being led to prison in the Tower, as if in memory of a similar occasion when Sir Thomas More was also being led back from his trial in Westminster Hall to his prison in the Tower, to await his execution on Tower Hill. Then his favourite daughter, Margaret, broke through the crowd and embraced her father. We are not told what he then said to her, but we do know that soon after his execution in 1535 she retrieved her father's head from London Bridge (where it had been set up as a warning against noncompliance with the king's wishes) and retired with her husband, William Roper, to his home in Canterbury. It may be added that not a few of More's female descendants followed Richard's advice to Isabella, going to France or the Low Countries and there entering religious houses. Many of his male descendants, too, became priests and/ or religious and returned to work on the English mission. Moreover, in Richard's advice to Isabella to seek refuge in "some religious house", we may notice an interesting echo of similar advice given on similar occasions in the other two plays considered in this chapter. In *Romeo and Juliet* Friar Laurence urges Juliet to hasten from the tomb of death, and he will dispose of her "among a holy sisterhood of nuns" (V iii.137); in *A Midsummer Night's Dream* Theseus informs Hermia of the alternative of accepting "the livery of a nun" and living as "a barren sister" (I i.70). Later on, in *Much Ado About Nothing*, which is a kind of sister play to *Romeo and Juliet*, Friar Francis proposes his plan for poor Hero, while anticipating the possibility of failure, and then—like Friar Laurence—he can conceal her "in some reclusive and religious life" (IV i.244). Yet another echo may be recognized in *Hamlet*, where the prince roughly tells poor Ophelia, "Get thee to a nunnery!" (III i.124).

Further, with reference to the other poor Catholics remaining in England and facing possible charges of treason along with other, lesser charges, we may note three passages in *Richard II* that echo the insistent Catholic reply to such charges—as stated by William Allen in his dignified *Defence of English Catholics* (1584) against the accusations of Lord Burghley in *The Execution of Justice in England* (1583). First, early in the play we have Mowbray's protest against Bolingbroke's accusation, "If ever I were a traitor,/ my name be blotted from the book of life!" (I iii.201). Secondly, in Act III we see Bolingbroke on his premature return from banishment accused by his uncle York of the crime of "gross rebellion and detested treason" (II iii.109), but he indignantly rejects the accusation, saying that he has come to defend his "rights and royalties", in lawfully succeeding to the duchy of Lancaster (II iii.120). Thirdly, on York's discovery of his son Aumerle's plot against King Henry, it is York who now accuses his own son, blaming him for thus bringing his life with dishonour to the grave, and so he protests against the king's pardon, "The traitor lives, the true man's put to death" (V iii.72). Similarly in *King Lear*, Albany is reported to have said much the same thing to Oswald, criticizing him for having "turn'd the wrong side out" (IV ii.9).

Then, by way of postscript, I may add two sets of general remarks that seem to echo the dramatist's own feelings of frustration at his inability to give more open expression to his grievances. First, there is the complaint of Ross under the oppressive rule of Richard, "My heart is great, but it must break with silence" (II i.229), and later on, the similar complaint of Richard himself, now that the tables have been turned on him, "My grief lies all within" (IV i.295)—both anticipating the similar words of Hamlet at the end of his first soliloquy, "But break, my heart, for I must hold my tongue!" (I ii.159). Then, there is the cry of the poor queen Isabella on overhearing the allegorical talk of the gardeners, "O, I am press'd to death through want of speaking!" (III iv.72)—which is also matched by the cry of the Lady Constance in *King John*, "O, that my tongue were in the thunder's mouth!" (III iv.38). The cry of Isabella, in particular, may be seen as pointing (as noted above) to the physical manner of Margaret Clitherow's death at York in 1586 for her refusal to plead on a charge of giving shelter to priests.

All this, however, fails to exhaust the Catholic implications in *Richard II*. For example, we may note the pious language of Richard (like that of Romeo on approaching Juliet) when making up his mind to abdicate in favour of his cousin Henry: "I'll give up my jewels for a set of beads,/ my gorgeous palace for a hermitage . . ./ my sceptre for a palmer's walking-staff,/ my subjects for a pair of carved saints" (III iii.147ff). He thus seems to be anticipating the known piety of his successor Henry VI. Nor is there, in such an utterance, we may add, any trace of Protestant revulsion in the dramatist's voice. Again, when Richard's reputedly "Machiavellian" cousin comes to the throne as Henry IV, he shows another form of piety in his repentance at having sent Exton to Pomfret for Richard's murder, in vowing "a voyage to the Holy Land,/ to wash the blood off from my guilty hand" (V vi.49). Thus, with all the several sins of murder committed by the two antagonists, Richard and Henry, it may be said that *Richard II* remains throughout a deeply Catholic play about a deeply Catholic England.

chapter 5 Master of Catholic Comedy

The Merchant of Venice

THERE CAN BE no doubt about the lyrical genius and the dramatic versatility shown by Shakespeare in *A Midsummer Night's Dream*, with its appeal to audiences of all ages and nations. It has such a light, fantastic touch with its airs of fairyland. Yet with all its deserved popularity, there is some lack of that maturity for which a master touch is needed. Such is the maturity we unquestionably find in the dramatist's next comedy, *The Merchant of Venice*, in which the fantasy of both main plots is transcended by the realism and humanity of its characterization. This realism even threatens to bring out the tragedy implicit in the fantasy, and it has to be kept firmly under control. All the same, not a few readers, critics, and producers nowadays interpret the play as more tragedy than comedy, with Shylock rather than Antonio as the real hero and perhaps even as the merchant mentioned in the title. But this is going to an opposite extreme, in the interests of modern social "relevance", without making due allowance for the uniqueness of a comedy that gives full rein to its tragic potential, in what the French call "la comédie humaine", while remaining a genuine comedy.

To begin with the tragic element, which is strangely akin to that in *The Comedy of Errors* and *A Midsummer Night's Dream*, we find it introduced in the first three scenes of the play. First, we have the mysterious sadness of Antonio, which persists throughout the play, secondly, the parallel world-weariness of the lady Portia, and thirdly, the loan of money from Shylock, with the condition of a pound of flesh as the bond. Now we may dwell on each of these scenes in turn, considering the relevance they may contain to the situation of English Catholics, in whom the fantasy of the two main plots is seen as transformed into harsh reality.

First, we have the opening words of Antonio, "In sooth, I know not why I am so sad" (I i.1). His different friends offer different explanations for his sadness, but he waves them all away. It is not what they imagine, and yet he himself hardly knows the reason either. Only when Bassanio enters and asks Antonio for a loan of money, to enable him to go to Belmont and woo the lady Portia, are we given some inkling of the true reason. As Salanio later remarks of Antonio's friendship with Bassanio, "I think he only loves the world for him" (II viii.50). Now his friend is about to leave him for a far country, and he is about to subsidize that friend's journey even at the risk of his own life; according to the words of Jesus, "Greater love than this has no man, than to lay down his life for his friends" (John xv.13). We need not seek a homosexual implication in Antonio's love for Bassanio, as modern psychoanalytic critics like to do, remaining as they do on the mere surface of the plot. Rather, when we look deeper into Shakespeare's meaning, as his plays compel us to do, we find unmistakably recusant implications, akin to those already noticed in *The Two Gentlemen of Verona* and *The Taming of the Shrew*. For, as we have seen, in the theme of going abroad for education in the world, which soon turns into a love affair, there is a hidden reference to those recusants who followed the guidance of the priests in sending their sons, as though on a secret pilgrimage, for religious and seminary formation on the Catholic continent. Already in the first scene we may notice this imagery of "pilgrimage" emphasized by Bassanio, as by Romeo on his first meeting with Juliet, once he is left alone with Antonio and can tell his friend about his inmost desire. It is Antonio who begins the conversation by inquiring, "What lady is the same/ to whom you swore a secret pilgrimage?" Then Bassanio declares, "In Belmont is a lady richly left,/ and she is fair and . . ./ of wondrous virtues" (I i.162). Here the very residence of the lady in Belmont, though (like the name of Montague in *Romeo and Juliet*) derived from the Italian sources, would have been associated in the dramatist's mind with another Belmont in Hampshire, the home of Southampton's recusant cousin, Thomas Pounde. From the time of Edmund Campion onwards he had been a notable helper of the Jesuits and had spent much of his adult life in prison for his faith, till in his last years he had the happiness of being admitted into the Society of Jesus.

To return to Antonio, the way he goes on to engage Shylock in a quasi-scholastic disputation on the morality of usury indicates a mind trained in the casuistry of the Jesuit schools. Later, he is described by Bassanio as "one in whom/ the ancient Roman honour more appears/ than any that draws breath in Italy" (III ii.295)—where "Roman" has the implication rather of Christian than classical Rome.

In the second scene we are carried across the seas to the residence of the lady Portia, though where exactly it is located we are given no idea. The way we are introduced to her belies the romantic ideal of her entertained by her lover

Bassanio. So far from shining in "wondrous virtues", she appears as excessively sharp with her tongue at the expense of all her suitors—till mention is finally made of a young Venetian scholar and soldier, one Bassanio. No wonder, as she declares at the beginning of the scene, she is "aweary of this great world" (I ii.2), in which she is allowed no choice of a husband but has to wait on the fortune of a right choice among three caskets. She realizes that "it is a sin to be a mocker" (I ii.60), but she cannot resist the temptation to mock at all her suitors, with the one exception of Bassanio. No wonder she is among the few ideal heroines in Shakespeare's plays to whom is granted every attribute human and divine but that of "grace". The most that is said in praise of her, after the opening words of Bassanio, is when Jessica says of him that in having her "he finds the joys of heaven here on earth" (III v.82) and of her that "the poor rude world hath not her fellow" (III v.88). All the same, her Catholic dimension appears, as a worthy object of Bassanio's pilgrimage, in the reasons she gives for absenting herself from Belmont, when it is her true intent to go to Venice in lawyer's disguise to save Antonio. Before she goes, she pleads "a secret vow/ to live in prayer and contemplation" at a nearby monastery (III iv.27), and before she returns, she is described by her servant Stephano as straying about "by holy crosses, where she kneels and prays/ for happy wedlock hours", accompanied only by "a holy hermit and her maid" (V i.31). She is indeed a pious Catholic, one whose mind is, by contemporary Puritan standards, entirely given over to superstition.

In the third scene we are introduced to Shylock, according to Shakespeare's usual order in his plays—first, the young hero Bassanio, after his merchant friend Antonio, then, the heroine Portia, and lastly, the villain who turns out to be the central character in the play, Shylock the Jew. More than in other sources of the play, where the Jew is portrayed as, in Stephen Gosson's words from his *School of Abuse* (1579), "representing the greediness of worldly choosers, and the bloody minds of usurers", Shakespeare gives him a more human, realistic, even sympathetic characterization. Not that he makes Shylock the hero rather than the villain, but he vividly depicts his human motives for revenge, as in the speech, "Hath not a Jew eyes . . .?" (III i.63). This characterization is largely due to the abundant use of biblical echoes and allusions which Shakespeare puts into Shylock's mouth—where it is interesting to note how many of these echoes and allusions come more from the New than the Old Testament. It may even be said of him that he evidently knows the New Testament better than any of the Christians in the play, apart from Antonio and Portia. Yet this familiarity of his with the Bible suggests that beneath the surface of the story, which Shakespeare has taken from his Italian sources, just as Antonio may be seen as a Catholic priest, if not a Jesuit in disguise, so Shylock may be seen not as a Jew but a Puritan, like so many of the city merchants in London, who were among the leading enemies of the theatre.

What a strange thing, one may wonder, to suggest that Shylock may be seen not as a Jew but a Puritan! And how contrary to both his commonly assumed character and his traditional place in the story! Needless to say, on the level of the story, as borrowed by Shakespeare from his Italian sources, Shylock is a Jew, no less or more genuinely so than Marlowe's Barabas in *The Jew of Malta*—which may have been the occasion for Shakespeare's company to request another topical play on a Jew, following on the execution of the queen's Jewish physician, Roderigo Lopez, in 1594. But what we are now considering is the deeper, recusant level of the play, at which the Puritanism of Shylock becomes more obvious in contrast to Antonio as Catholic priest. Take, for instance, Shylock's declaration to Bassanio just before the arrival of Antonio, "I will buy with you, sell with you, walk with you, and so following, but I will not eat with you, drink with you, nor pray with you" (I iii.36). Or take his defence of usury with reference to the biblical story of Jacob and Laban, against the more scholastic arguments of Antonio (I iii.78ff). Or take his insistence on the virtues of sobriety and thrift in speaking to Jessica, before (somewhat inconsistently) going to supper with the Christians (II v.13). Though he is a Jew of Venice who says all these things, he might just as well have been, as he was no doubt in the dramatist's mind, one of the Puritan merchants in London. In fact, each of these characteristics is ascribed to the Puritans by celebrated Anglican authors of the time—by John Whitgift, later Archbishop of Canterbury, writing against the Puritan leader Thomas Cartwright; by Richard Bancroft, later Bishop of London and subsequently Archbishop of Canterbury, against the anonymous Puritan authors of the Marprelate tracts; and by Matthew Sutcliffe, Dean of Exeter, when returning to the attack on Cartwright and openly accusing him of engaging in detested usury. Moreover, this superimposition by Shakespeare of a Puritan character on a Jewish villain—which seems so paradoxical to traditionally minded Shakespeare scholars—is the more understandable when we reflect how little he would have had to do with Jews in his dramatic career, and how much with Puritans.

Not that I am the first to propose such an identification. The usury of Shylock has already been related to that of the London merchants by two American scholars, Elmer Stoll and Paul Siegel. Only, they limit their attention to his usury, without realizing how his whole characterization is indebted to contemporary ideas about the Puritans, as outlined above. Still less does it occur to their minds to draw the contrast with the characterization of Antonio as implicitly a Catholic priest in Elizabethan London.

Yet even on the surface level of the play we come upon two transparent allusions to the Puritans. From the outset, while listening to the seeming "nothings" pouring from the mouth of Gratiano, we admire his vivid description of "a sort of men whose visages/ do cream and mantle like a standing pond", with their assumption of "wisdom, gravity, profound conceit,/ as who should say, 'I am Sir Oracle' " (I i.88ff). Here he is evidently speaking (to use Maria's words) of "a kind of Puritan", such as Malvolio in *Twelfth Night* (II iii.153)—as is further apparent in his mention of "this melancholy bait" (I i.101). Then the same type of character may be recognized in Bassanio's speech on "outward shows", where he criticizes "some sober brow" (in a religious context) that will bless a "damned error" and "approve it with a text", in the manner for which the Puritans of those days were notorious.

Turning now from the main characters of the play as introduced to us in the first three scenes of Act I, we may follow the development of the parallel plots of the Three Caskets and the Pound of Flesh to their respective climaxes in Acts III and IV. In them both we find the recusant dimension steadily deepening. Even in the happy outcome of the plot of the Three Caskets, the success of Bassanio in making his choice of lead is preceded by a serious, if not tragic, conversation between him and Portia, as hero and heroine. To not a few readers and spectators, who are interested only in getting on with the plot, this extended conversation may seem to be a waste of dramatic time. And not a few producers are tempted to cut the whole thing. After all, they reason, what is it for? We know that Bassanio himself wants to get on with it and make his choice. "Let me choose," he urges Portia, "for as I am, I live upon the rack" (III ii.24). But this is too much for the recusant in Portia, or rather in Shakespeare. So she cannot help taking him up on "the rack" and demanding, "Upon the rack, Bassanio! Then confess/ what treason there is mingled with your love" (III ii.26). This is not the first time in the play that Bassanio is somehow associated with the rack. Even before he departed from Venice, when he was approaching Antonio for a loan, he was told by his friend who lacked the ready money, "Try what my credit can in Venice do./ That shall be rack'd even to the uttermost" (I 1.181). This image is now further racked by Portia, when she responds to her lover's protest of innocence, "Ay, but I fear you speak upon the rack,/ where men enforced do speak anything" (III ii.32). The whole of this riddling conversation takes up the best part of twenty lines, while many of the audience are no doubt fidgeting in their seats and perhaps yawning—whereas more fortunate readers can skip it if they wish. At last they must feel relieved when Portia ends her speech and maybe sings the song, while Bassanio prepares to make his choice. But first he has to make his soliloquy, in the course of which he refers not only to the above-mentioned Puritan preacher but also to the propaganda of the time put out by crafty men like Lord Burghley, or "the seeming truth which cunning times put on/ to entrap the wisest" (III ii.100). From a recusant point of view, their enemies employed two methods to win them over. One was the cruder method of brute force, such as the torture of the rack, said by the victims to be worse than death. The other was the seeming truth of official propaganda, such as

Burghley's defence of the use of torture against "traitors" in his *Execution of Justice in England* (1583).

Then in the moment of joyful success, when Bassanio has Portia in his arms, comes the turning point, when he is informed of the bad news that Antonio has been unable to repay the loan within the stated time and is now in the hands of Shylock, who insists on his bond. Now everything in the play moves from Belmont to Venice, from the happy outcome of the one plot, or fantasy of the Three Caskets, to what threatens to become the tragic outcome of the other plot, or fantasy of the Pound of Flesh. This brings us to the trial scene in Act IV, with Bassanio and Gratiano there to provide poor Antonio with little more than moral support, while shouting pointless abuse at Shylock. The Jew is bent on what might have been termed (in an earlier play) the "lopping" of a pound of Antonio's flesh, though he stands to gain nothing from it but the satisfaction of his revenge. So now he rejects even twice the amount of the loan offered by Bassanio. Meanwhile, Portia has made her way to Venice in lawyer's disguise, taking the place of the renowned Bellario for the defence of Antonio. At first, her line of defence is no more than an appeal to the Jew for mercy, with the famous speech beginning, "The quality of mercy is not strain'd" (IV i.184). In this she seems to be summing up the many Catholic appeals to Queen Elizabeth, such as Robert Southwell's *Humble Supplication to Her Majesty*, which was ready for the printer by the time of his death in 1595, but not actually published till 1600. Needless to say, her appeal, like that of the duke before her, falls on deaf ears, as Shylock insists on his just revenge, according to his bond. So Portia has to fall back on what unfriendly critics call a trick, though it includes a law that has been overlooked till that moment. She presents it in three stages: first, by insisting on a precise pound of flesh, neither more nor less, with scales to check the weight, next, by forbidding the shedding of a single drop of Antonio's blood, and thirdly, by pointing out a provision in the law to protect the lives of citizens from all attempts, direct or indirect, upon their lives. To Shylock and his modern sympathizers this is all merely legal quibbling. But to Portia, as it was also no doubt the dramatist's intention, it is a dramatic way of turning the tables on him, by giving him the justice he demands, but in a way not of his demanding. She is, in effect, telling him, "If what you want is justice, then justice you will have." Indeed, she has already warned him in her appeal for mercy, "Though justice be thy plea, consider this,/ that in the course of justice none of us/ should see salvation" (IV i.198). This is also the meaning of Shakespeare in the biblical title he goes on to give to the related play of *Measure for Measure*, where the place of Portia before Shylock is taken by Isabella before Angelo. It is also perhaps what Shakespeare, no less than Southwell, is implicitly saying to his sovereign lady, Queen Elizabeth.

Such is the happy outcome of the trial scene and the plot of the Pound of Flesh. But now, we may ask, if the two main plots have their respective outcomes in Acts III and IV, what more can the dramatist have to provide for our entertainment in Act V? Here we see him as it were unwilling to end his comedy in the city, whether of Venice or of London. Rather, it seems to be his wish to bring his good characters back with him to Portia's country home in Belmont—with all its Catholic associations. In the same way we may think of the Gospel accounts of the resurrection, where Jesus, both in his own words and in the message of the angels, looks forward to a reunion with his disciples not in the city of Jerusalem, with all its tragic memories, but in the countryside by the lake of Galilee. Accordingly, from the beginning of Act V we find ourselves back at Belmont, waiting for the night to give place to daytime and for the good characters to reappear in their appropriate setting. This night is no longer the tragic night of the trial, with the prospect of death hanging over the head of Antonio, like the sword of Damocles. It is rather as it were a continuation of Romeo's "blessed, blessed night" (II ii.139), with the other lovers Lorenzo and Jessica singing a duet whose stanzas are introduced by the refrain, "In such a night", repeated seven times (V i.1ff). To Catholic ears, moreover, this refrain enshrines a liturgical memory of Christ's Resurrection, when prominent in the celebration of the Easter Vigil in Catholic countries is the solemn chant of *"Exultet iam angelica turba caelorum"*—Let now the angelic host in the heavens—with its repetition of *"Haec nox est"* and *"O vere beata nox!"*—This is the night, and O truly blessed night! It also looks forward to the similar expression of joy which Shakespeare puts into the mouth of the "holy Gonzalo" in the last scene of *The Tempest* (V i.206), including other echoes of the same hymn of joy. It has even been taken as evidence that, before setting out on his dramatic career in the Catholic household of Alexander Houghton, Shakespeare had some experience of seminary life at Rheims or Rome, where he could have enjoyed the full celebration of the Catholic liturgy in Holy Week without fear of the proceedings being disrupted by government agents, who were ever on the watch for such "seditious" activities.

Much Ado About Nothing

Shakespeare is, it may be said, nothing if not paradoxical, no less than critical. Once he achieved mastery and maturity in the craft of comedy with *The Merchant of Venice*, we find him going on to produce three more comedies, each a work of comic art in itself, yet all with such trivial sounding titles: *Much Ado About Nothing, As You Like It,* and *Twelfth Night*, or *What You Will.* How far these titles are trivial, and how far their seeming triviality is reflected in the plays, remains to be considered in each of the plays one by one. So for the time being it may be sufficient for us to focus our attention on the "nothing" in *Much Ado About Nothing.* To what extent, we may ask, is this "nothing" substantival, and not merely negative, in the play? And to what extent does it look forward, as well in the title as in the content of the play, to the great tragedies from *Hamlet* to *King Lear*, and even to the romance of *The Winter's Tale*, in all of which "nothing" takes on a substantival meaning? At the same time, considering the recurring theme of this book, in what way, we may ask, does this "nothing" have a bearing on what I presume to be the Catholicism of Shakespeare in the circumstances of Elizabethan England? May not Shakespeare have perhaps said of himself, like Edgar in *King Lear*, "Shakespeare I nothing am" (II iii.21)?

Certainly, this is one theme that is consistently explored within the play, according to the implication in its title. Insofar as the word is used in anything but its merely negative sense, its substantival potentiality points unmistakably to the character of Benedick, who is chiefly brought to life as hero with Beatrice as heroine in the main plot of *Much Ado About Nothing*—while in the subplot we are kept amused with the "humours" of Dogberry and his companions. In contrast to those two principal characters, who are always sparring with each other in their wit combats, the other characters of Claudio and Hero, for all their seeming centrality to the main plot, are but pale and two-dimensional. As for Don Pedro and his brother Don John, for all their royal blood, they are mere nonentities. True, Benedick is not explicitly described in terms of "nothing", but he comes very close to it, as third in a line of comic characters who are more openly described in this manner. Thus we have Mercutio in *Romeo and Juliet*, who is criticized by Romeo for his unceasing chatter on "nothing", in connection with his long speech on Queen Mab and her fairies (I iv.97). This speech is thought to have suggested the fantasy of *A Midsummer Night's Dream* to the fantastic mind of the dramatist in his *annus mirabilis*. More explicitly, Gratiano is criticized by his friend Bassanio for his readiness to speak an "infinite deal of nothing", in contrast to those Puritan time-pleasers who "only are reputed wise for saying nothing" (I iii.113, 96). In Benedick's case, however, nothing of this kind is explicitly said against him, but Beatrice's snide remarks at his expense all tend in that direction, from her first words to him in the first scene, "I wonder that you will still be talking, Signior Benedick. Nobody marks you!" (I i.121), to the more positive climax of their witty exchanges in Act IV. Then, in response to Benedick's indirect profession of love for her, "I do love nothing in the world so well as you," Beatrice answers, "It were as possible for me to say I loved nothing so well as you, but believe me not, and yet I lie not. I confess nothing, nor I deny nothing" (IV i.217ff).

Here is indeed "much ado about nothing"! But how exactly are all these nothings, proceeding from a line of comic characters, which the dramatist has in turn produced out of nothing in his sources, to be applied to the Catholic recusants of the Elizabethan age? That remains to be seen more clearly, and more substantively, in the tragedies mentioned above. As for the earlier plays, we may note that *Much Ado About Nothing* shares with *Romeo and Juliet* a common source in Matteo Bandello's *Novelle* (completed in 1572), possibly by way of Belleforest's *Histoires Tragiques* (completed in 1582), though in neither of their respective stories do the characters of Mercutio or Benedick appear. We may conjecture that the emergence of Benedick in *Much Ado* is due to the dramatist's remorse at having so outrageously killed off Mercutio, after having allowed him an outrageous pun in his dying moments—comparable to the three jests uttered by Sir Thomas More on the very scaffold of his execution on Tower Hill. After all, it is an unwritten law of drama, unmentioned by Aristotle in his *Poetics*, that "comic characters are not to be killed".

Turning from the comedies to the tragedies, we may note how the ghost of Hamlet's father, visible to Hamlet in the closet scene with his mother, remains invisible to her and is therefore described by her as "nothing" (III iv.129ff). We may further reflect how, as ghost of the past, he may be taken as representing the old order of Catholic England. More clearly, on coming to *King Lear*, we find both champions of the old order, Cordelia and Edgar, characterized in terms of "nothing" from the very outset. First, Cordelia can only answer "Nothing" to her father's impossible question. So she finds, as her father is also soon to find, the truth of Aristotle's axiom, "Nothing will come of nothing" (I i.89ff). Secondly, when Edgar is forced to flee from his own home and to assume a beggar's disguise, like the hunted priests in the Elizabethan persecution, he declares of himself, "Edgar I nothing am" (II iii.21). The original of Edgar's "nothing" we may find portrayed by Robert Southwell in his *Humble Supplication* (1600), speaking for himself and his fellow priests, "We are the common theme of every railing declaimer, abused without hope or means of remedy, by every wretch with most infamous names, no tongue so forsworn but it is of credit against us, none so true but it is thought false in our defence." In other words, they are mere nothings.

Nor is that all there is to be said about the meaning of "nothing" in *Much Ado About Nothing*, in view of Shakespeare's notorious propensity for punning. For there is another meaning in "nothing" on which emphasis is laid at a certain point in the play. This is when the singer Balthazar is invited to sing, but he coyly hesitates, saying, "Note this before my notes. There's not a note of mine that's worth the noting." Such word-play is an open invitation to further punning, and Don Pedro readily takes him up, "Why, these are very crotchets that he speaks, notes, notes, forsooth, and nothing!" (II iii.57ff). In this context it is often remarked that "noting" was an occasional pronunciation of "nothing" in Shakespeare's day, and in a recusant connection it may be further noted that many of the leading composers in that golden age of English music, such as William Byrd, were recusants, or at least Catholic in sympathy. This fact may seem less surprising when we recall the genealogy of that music from the monastic choirs after they were disbanded and/or secularized with the dissolution of the monasteries.

This trivial meaning of "nothing" leads us to the third and more tragic meaning of noting or noticing, observing, and more precisely spying. Not only the meaning but also the reality of this word is everywhere present in this play, more than in any other of Shakespeare's plays except *Hamlet*. We may find it not just in a few incidents of the play, but pervading it as a kind of atmosphere. This appears notably in what has been termed "the recurrent device of overhearing" as characteristic of *Much Ado*. It was also the atmosphere in which Catholic recusants, who stayed at home instead of going into exile, had to lead their lives. This is what Campion wrote of his experiences in England to his superior in Rome already in 1580: "The enemy have so many spies, so many tongues, so many scouts and crafts." In *Much Ado*, however, most of the spying is innocent and well-intentioned, since it is a comedy—unlike *Hamlet*, where the mutual spying is between "mighty opposites" (V ii.62). Only at the heart of the Claudio-Hero plot do we find the evil spying of Don John, whose spirits are said to "toil in frame of villainies" (IV i.191). From a recusant viewpoint, we might say that Don John stands for the great spymasters of the Elizabethan persecution, notably Sir Francis Walsingham (who had died in 1590), Lord Burghley (who was soon to die in 1598), and his crook-back son, Sir Robert Cecil, who was like his father a skilled manipulator in the murky underworld of espionage.

While still remaining on the trivial level implied in the "nothing" of the play's title and developed in the witty word-combat of most of the characters in the main plot, we may further note two particular exchanges concerning which we might say, with Sebastian in *The Tempest*, "There's meaning in their snores" (II i.226). In the opening scene, where the aristocrats are exchanging their opinions about love, Benedick affirms his scepticism about love, as "an opinion that fire cannot melt out of me. I will die in it at the stake." In the same vein, Don Pedro responds, "Thou wast ever an obstinate heretic in the despite of beauty" (I i.242ff). Here the topical reference is either to the burning of Protestant heretics at Smithfield in the reign of the Catholic Mary Tudor or to the autos-da-fé of other heretics in Catholic Spain. This apparently anti-Catholic imagery may, however, be balanced in Act III by another such exchange with its more topical reference to the frequent sights of the execution of Catholics as "traitors" in Elizabethan London. Then it is that, on Benedick's complaint, "I have the tooth-ache", Don Pedro advises him, "Draw it!", only to bring down on himself the exclamation, "Hang it!", followed up by the crowning pun of Claudio,

"You must hang it first and draw it afterwards" (III ii.21ff). We may think it extraordinary for Shakespeare to use such gruesome imagery from the religious persecution going on all round him, whether Catholic or Protestant, in a merely comic context. Hasn't he, we may demand, any sense of propriety? In his defence one might plead that the impropriety is not so much in the dramatist as in his aristocratic characters, who no doubt reflect the kind of exchanges commonly made at Elizabeth's court. Or one might add that this is what he had become inured to, with his audiences, from his experiences in London. Or else one might note that, whereas the reference to the burning of heretics at the stake is unique in Shakespeare's plays, the other image of hanging and drawing, followed by quartering (or lopping), recurs in several of those plays, notably in *King John*, where it is used in a sarcastic context by the Bastard (II i.504ff).

So we may come to the tragic climax of Don John's plot in Act IV, where Claudio, having been misled by him into imagining that Hero has played him false on the eve of their wedding, rejects his bride at the beginning of the ceremony with a blunt "No!" in reply to the priest's question. This naturally creates confusion in the church, such is the power of "No!" and "Nothing!" in the real world. Then the poor bride swoons. This reaction of Hero's, however, convinces the priest, Friar Francis, of her innocence, as he says, "by noting of the lady" (IV i.160). Hero herself has protested her innocence. If not, she adds, "refuse me, hate me, torture me to death" (IV i.186)—with reference to the torture of the rack, on which not a few Catholic prisoners in the Tower were done to death. So the friar proposes his plan, based on the general observation, which was all too familiar to English Catholics who had lived through the successive reigns of Mary and Elizabeth, "For what we have we prize not to the worth/ while we enjoy it, but being lack'd and lost,/ why, then we rack the value" (IV i.220ff). This was the frequent experience of a priest such as Campion, in the course of his visits to Catholic houses in Warwickshire, Derbyshire, Yorkshire, and Lancashire, ending up at Lyford Grange in Berkshire. How eager, he found, were the Catholics in each county to attend his celebration of Mass, to listen to his sermons, and to confess their sins, in contrast to the previous reign of Mary, when they had no need to take precautions against spies or pursuivants. What is more, this observation made by the friar occurs not just once in this play, but recurs in many of Shakespeare's plays (as remains to be noted on each occasion), indicating how deeply he had himself noted the reality.

Next, the friar goes on to offer a practical suggestion, to give out that Hero's swoon (like that of Hermione in *The Winter's Tale* III ii.202) has resulted in her death, since this may lead, as he foresees, to "a greater birth". He therefore exhorts Hero, "Come, lady, die to live!" (IV i.215, 255). Friar Francis's suggestion, while reminiscent of that proposed by Friar Laurence to Juliet, though without the need of resorting to a dangerous drug, further echoes—in view of the recusant background of the play—the exhortations of the Jesuit poet Robert Southwell in both prose and verse. (We may also note how frequently in the controversial literature of the time Jesuits were abused as "friars", though the term was accurate enough for the Society of Jesus as a mendicant order, and the literal meaning of "friar" is brother.) In his recently published poems (1595) Southwell often plays, in the contemporary manner of a "conceit", on the contrast between life and death, as in his poem "I die alive": "I live, but such a life as ever dies./ I die, but such a death as never ends . . ./ Thus still I die, yet still I do revive." Such is also the tone of his prose *Epistle of Comfort* (published in 1588), which he dedicated "to the reverend priests . . . and other of the lay sort restrained in durance for the Catholic faith".

Friar Francis's plan, unlike Friar Laurence's, turns out to be successful, partly for its reliance on human psychology rather than on the chances of fortune. Or more basically, we may attribute its success to the fact that the play, unlike *Romeo and Juliet*, is to be a comedy with a happy ending, not a tragedy. We may also conjecture, as noted above, that the dramatist was suffering from remorse both for having killed off Mercutio and for having allowed Friar's Laurence's ingenious scheme to fail owing to a mere accident, though we have to admit that his hands were tied by the existing story and the need for a tragedy to have a sad ending. The success of the plan is foreshadowed in the poem which Claudio has to read at Hero's tomb by way of penance: "So the life that died with shame/ lives in death with glorious fame" (V iii.7). Then the living Hero is restored to the overjoyed Claudio—just as the living Hermione is restored to her overjoyed husband Leontes in the climax of *The Winter's Tale* (V iii.104). In either case, it appears as it were a resurrection from the dead. Here, too, we may recall how, just as Friar Laurence fell back on the alternative idea of placing Juliet "among a sisterhood of holy nuns" (V iii.157), so Friar Francis allows for the possible failure of his plan, in which case he will likewise place Hero "in some reclusive and religious life" (IV i.244). All in all, we may conclude, this is indeed a play in which recusancy is as all-pervasive as "nothing", or "noting".

As You Like It

The path of Shakespearian comedy leads straight from *Much Ado About Nothing* to *As You Like It*. Here, too, we are prompted by the title to ask such questions as "Who likes what?" and "Why should we like it?" It sounds as if the dramatist nonchalantly handed his manuscript to the manager of his company without a title, and on being asked for a title he offhandedly replied, "As you like it"—implying that any title would do. Yet on comparing this play with its predecessor, we notice so many similarities between them that it looks as if the dramatist took what had proved successful in the former play and reworked it into his source-story adapted from Thomas Lodge's pastoral romance of *Rosalynde* (1590). It also looks as if he was perhaps unconsciously following the principle enunciated by Falstaff in Part II of *Henry IV*: "It was always yet the trick of our English nation, if they have a good thing, to make it too common" (I iv.44). Thus, on the one hand, in *Much Ado About Nothing* Shakespeare took Mercutio and Friar Laurence from *Romeo and Juliet*, bringing the one back to life and giving better success to the other's plan, so as to replace the sad ending of the tragedy with the happy ending suited to the comedy. Then, on the other, in *As You Like It* he takes the merry Beatrice from *Much Ado* and refashions her as the inimitable Rosalind. What we like above all in *As You Like It* is surely the character of Rosalind, who is in turn an improvement on the Rosalynde of Thomas Lodge. And what the dramatist also seems to like, in common with most members of his audiences, especially if they are Catholic, is the pastoral and crypto-Catholic setting of the play in the Forest of Arden.

So to begin with this forest, the first question may arise as to its precise locality. Lodge vaguely locates it not to the northeast of France, bordering on the Low Countries, in the forest and mountain area of the Ardennes, but to the southwest of France, somewhere between Bordeaux and Lyons. In his play, however, Shakespeare seems to have in mind rather the Forest of Arden in his native Warwickshire, the home of his ancestors on both sides, while his mother bore the name of Arden. This forest is introduced to us from the beginning of the play as a place of refuge for exiles, outlaws, and other fugitives. It is also implicitly compared, with its reference to "the old Robin Hood of England" (I i.124), to the other Forest of Sherwood in the North Midlands. It is shown, in particular, as the refuge of the old duke, whose ducal dignity has been usurped, as in the other case of Prospero in *The Tempest*, by his younger brother. There are, moreover, "three or four loving lords" who "have put themselves into voluntary exile with him", as well as "many young gentlemen" who "flock to him every day" (I i.107, 125). If we may look for a recusant parallel in Elizabethan England, we need not look far to discover the very same situation in the English college or seminary at Douai, founded by William Allen in 1568, moved to Rheims in 1578, brought back to Douai in 1593, and since Allen's death in 1594 presided over by Richard Barret. Besides the president, the original staff were mostly Oxford fellows in exile, and the students were the sons of English gentlemen sent there "every day" for their Catholic education and further priestly studies.

As the dramatist moves into the development of his plot, we find him thinking, as always, of his native England and specifically his native Warwickshire, with the Forest of Arden in its western division. This is perhaps why, unlike *The Merchant of Venice*, where Venice is so clearly identifiable as London, there is no comparable city in *As You Like It*, but only a vaguely defined ducal court swayed by the usurping Duke Frederick. (We may note that he alone is given a name. His elder brother, being an exile like Edgar in *King Lear*, has no name.) With the dramatist, we may see the usurping duke as corresponding to the upstart Earl of Leicester, whose grandfather had been a mere lawyer under Henry VII, and one of the most hated men in England as tax-gatherer for the royal treasury under the system known as "Morton's Fork". From his castle at Kenilworth to the east of Stratford, and through his agent, the "Puritan" magistrate Sir Thomas Lucy of Charlecote, he had projected his envy upon the Arden family at the time of the Somerville Plot in 1583, not least because of their noble ancestry and their Catholic faith.

Within the forest of the play we come upon such "old religious men" as Rosalind's uncle, who has taught her how to cure the disease of love (III ii.366), and the hermit (perhaps the same man as the uncle), who meets the usurping duke on the outskirts of the forest and miraculously converts him to a religious life after a single conversation (V iv.167). Such an old priest is historically to be found in the vicar of the village church at Temple Grafton, who may have performed the wedding for the young William and his older bride Anne Hathaway in 1582. We even know his name, Sir John Frith, from a Puritan *Survey of the Ministry* in Warwickshire (1593). We also know the residence of the bride at that time, from the diocesan register for wedding licences at Worcester, as Temple Grafton, near Shottery. The name of this place is also hinted at in the punning words of Touchstone the jester, "Here we have no temple but the wood" (III iii.52). The priest is further contrasted in the play with the Puritan "vicar of the next village", Sir Oliver Martext (III iii.45). His identity as a Puritan may be gauged partly by the evident derivation of his name from the Marprelate tracts of 1588–89 (ascribed by many scholars to the Puritan MP for Warwickshire, Job Throckmorton), partly from the "sober brow" mentioned by Bassanio in *The Merchant of Venice* (III ii.78) as one who will bless and approve any "damned error" with a text from the Bible.

Yet another recusant association we may discern in the reason Duke Frederick gives Rosalind for banishing her from the court. When she indignantly protests her innocence, he replies, in much the same spirit as Lord Burghley in dismissing the pleas of the Catholic exiles in *The Execution of Justice in England* (1583), "Thus do all traitors./ If their purgation did consist in words,/ they are as innocent as grace itself" (I iii.35). Thus he rejects the plea as well of Rosalind in the play as of William Allen in his responding *Defence of English Catholics* (1584). Further, when Rosalind insists, like Allen and other recusant authors, "Yet your mistrust cannot make me a traitor," the duke replies, "Thou art thy father's daughter, there's enough." Again she pleads, "Treason is not inherited, my lord," adding, "My father was no traitor." Her cousin Celia, the duke's daughter, also intervenes on her behalf: "If she be a traitor, why, so am I" (I iii.59ff). But all is to no avail. Here precisely is the main issue at stake in the Elizabethan persecution of English Catholics, which was justified by the Protestants as a just punishment for treason, if only because they were following the directives of their "holy father" in Rome, who had excommunicated the queen—and that made them "Papists". The Catholics, however, maintained that they were being punished not for any treason proved against them but only for their religion, and so if they were put to death for this reason, they died as martyrs. The same word "traitors" is again significantly used by the old servant, Adam, when commiserating with his young master, Orlando, "Your virtues . . . are sanctified and holy traitors", adding, "O what a world is this, when what is comely/ envenoms him that bears it" (II iii.12).

In contrast to such reflections on the iniquities of the present age, which form a chorus of disapprobation and lamentation arising from almost all the poems and plays of

Shakespeare, we find a converse expression of nostalgia, which may be seen as coming to a climax in this play. Thus, in response to the generous loyalty of his servant Adam, Orlando exclaims, "O good old man, how well in thee appears/ the constant service of the antique world!" adding, "Thou art not for the fashion of these times" (II iii.56). Similarly, when Orlando comes upon the exiles at their feast in the forest, he appeals to them to help him and his servant, in words charged with religious nostalgia: "If ever you have look'd on better days,/ if ever been where bells have knoll'd to church." And the duke replies in the same vein, "True is it that we have seen better days,/ and have with holy bell been knoll'd to church" (IV vii.113ff).

Yet another theme, not of nostalgia but of loyalty, attends the departure of both groups of characters for the forest—that of Rosalind and Celia with Touchstone, and that of Orlando with Adam. Celia says of the clown to her cousin, "He'll go along o'er the wide world with me" (I iii.135). In much the same vein Adam declares to Orlando, "Master, go on and I will follow thee/ to the last gasp with truth and loyalty" (II iii.69). Such is, as noted above, the ideal response of the loyal knight to his king that St. Ignatius envisaged in his meditation on "The Kingdom of Christ" in the *Spiritual Exercises*, a meditation that had evidently impressed the mind of the young Shakespeare when making those Exercises in Lancashire under (we may assume) the direction of Edmund Campion.

Now that the refugees from the court have reached the safety of the forest and satisfied their hunger on venison—the very meat for which (according to the legend) the young Shakespeare was caught poaching in the park of Sir Thomas Lucy and forced to leave Stratford—the thoughts of Orlando and Rosalind turn to the softer theme of love. First, we may note how Orlando in the excess of his love for her goes round hanging poems in her honour on every tree. Here it is that, as in so many of the preceding comedies, the lover inevitably uses the word "grace" of her: "Therefore Heaven Nature charg'd/ that one body should be fill'd/ with all graces wide enlarg'd" (III ii.150). This heavenly grace is not limited to just the person of Rosalind alone, as representing in this play the person of the Virgin Mary. Somehow it extends to the whole forest, from the moment it is introduced to us in the old duke's opening speech in Act II. Then he contrasts the good he finds everywhere in the forest, even in winter, with the evil, the painted pomp and the peril of envy, at the court. He goes on to descant, in the very words of à Kempis's *Imitation of Christ* (I xii. *"De utilitate adversitatis"*), on how "sweet are the uses of adversity"—as it were following in the footsteps of Friar Laurence from his opening speech in *Romeo and Juliet* (II iii)—culminating in his recognition of "good in everything" (II i.1ff). In such a context, his mention of "sermons in stones" prompts the suspicion that he is also a duke in friar's clothing, like Duke Vincentio as Friar Lodowick in *Measure for Measure.* This may be a further confirmation of my earlier suggestion that he stands for William Allen of Douai, which is in fact situated on the outskirts of the French Ardennes. The same mention in the other context of the Warwickshire Arden may have implied for the dramatist the familiar stones of Wroxhall Abbey, where two nuns bearing the name of Shakespeare, Isabella and Joan, had lived in pre-Reformation times. These stones may have seemed to him to be crying out, like those other stones over which Macbeth had to make his way for the murder of Duncan (II i.58). No wonder if in such a forest, with such holy ruins, those in authority may be seen as represented by Corin's new master, who is described as a man "of churlish disposition", who little recks "to find the way to heaven/ by doing deeds of hospitality" (II iv.81). Still, this master remains in the shadows of the forest, nor can he dispel the prevailing atmosphere of heavenly grace.

At the end of the play, a problem arises concerning the ceremony for the blessing of the various couples who have been brought together in the forest. This ceremony is conducted not by a good priest such as Jaques recommends to Touchstone and Audrey, "that can tell you what marriage is" (III iii.91), still less by "the vicar of the next village", Sir Oliver Martext, but by the pagan god Hymen, or one of the lords wearing a mask to impersonate this "god of every town" (V iv.153). What, we may ask, is the point of such a ceremony, coming as it does at the climax of such a Christian, even Catholic, play—especially when there seem to be so many religious men lurking in the forest? Does it perhaps show the dramatist's revulsion from denominational differences and his preference for a secular, even pagan, wedding? Or isn't it rather to be interpreted as an engagement ceremony, akin to that arranged by Prospero in *The Tempest* for Ferdinand and Miranda (IV i), before having their Catholic wedding celebrated back in Italy? At the same time, we may also note the dramatic principle of Shakespeare, never to present a full Christian ceremony on stage. (The wedding in *Much Ado About Nothing* was, we may remember, called off before it had properly begun.) We may also recall the parallel ending of *A Midsummer Night's Dream*, where the fairies come back to bless the marriage-bed of the newly married couples, whose weddings have been solemnized in the "temple" offstage. In both plays, moreover, the seemingly "pagan" element may stand for the "old faith", which, as noted above, made due allowance for such folk customs, in contrast to the Protestant insistence on the pure Gospel.

Twelfth Night

Yet another seemingly trivial title is attached to what is regarded as the maturest of Shakespeare's mature comedies and the happiest of his happy comedies, *Twelfth Night.* Yet again, in response to a manager's presumed request for a title to his bare manuscript, we may imagine the dramatist saying, or even shouting, "Call it what you will, anything you like, I don't mind!" Or again, he might have said, "Considering that the first performance is to be held on January 6, you may call it 'Twelfth Night'." Or if—according to the opinion of some scholars—the play was first performed, as recorded in the contemporary diary of John Manningham, on February 2, 1606, it might then have been entitled "Candlemas" for the occurring feast. As for the earlier date, January 6, 1601, it is based on the well-documented theory of Leslie Hotson, as set forth in his *The First Night of Twelfth Night* (1954), that the play was composed for performance before the queen herself at White-hall, partly in honour of a distinguished visitor from Italy, the Catholic, and even Papal Duke of Bracciano, Don Virginio Orsino, partly for the conclusion of the Christmas festivities at court, which came to an end on the feast of the Epiphany, the twelfth night after Christmas, commemorating the adoration of the infant Christ by the three wise men or magi (as told in Matt. ii).

In the play itself, however, we find no mention of either Christmas or the Epiphany. But considering that the day was also celebrated, like the earlier feast of the Holy Innocents on December 28, as a feast of fools, with the customary order of life turned topsy-turvy or upside-down, we may recognize the central importance in this play of the clown Feste as "lord of misrule". For it is he who in a sense presides over the events of the play on both sides of the stage, in the two houses of the Duke Orsino and the Countess Olivia. In himself he may be seen as illustrating the words of St. Paul to the Corinthians, "God has chosen the foolish things of the world to confound the wise" (I Cor. i.27). Because he knows himself to be a fool, Feste is, like Socrates before him, and like Socrates' Tudor counterpart Sir Thomas More, the wisest man among those around him, who all exhibit various forms of melancholy even to the extent of madness. Only one other character in the play, the heroine Viola, in the disguise of Orsino's page Cesario, appreciates him at his true worth, when she says of him, "This fellow's wise enough to play the fool" (III i.68). So if he is the "lord of misrule", she is his lady—though in the happy ending she becomes "fancy's queen" to the melancholy Duke Orsino, leaving the poor fool alone.

Turning now to two of the principal characters in the main plot, who may be seen as standing for the queen herself and her ducal visitor from Italy, Olivia and Orsino, we find in them an unusually ecumenical meeting—as at the little academy of the lords in *Love's Labour's Lost*—between Protestant and Catholic, namely the Protestant Queen Elizabeth and the Catholic Duke from the Papal States, Don Virginio. Further, unlike *The Merchant of Venice* with its contrast between a Protestant or Puritan Venice, swayed by the money-bags of Shylock the Jew, and the Catholic Belmont, and unlike *As You Like It* with its contrast between a Protestant court ruled by a usurping duke, such as the Earl of Leicester, and a Catholic Forest of Arden, whether in Shakespeare's Warwickshire or in the neighbourhood of Allen's Douai, in this play we have only the court of Whitehall with its contrasting "houses", one for the Countess Olivia, standing for the Virgin Queen in mourning for her deceased brother Edward VI, and the other for Duke Orsino, standing for the Duke of Bracciano. It may have been for this reason, out of respect for the feelings of the queen and in the spirit of the Christmas occasion, that Shakespeare seems to have deliberately toned down any Catholic bias on the side of the duke, while on the side of the countess he seems to have emphasized an anti-Puritan bias.

First, on the side of Orsino, there appears a typically Shakespearian "comedy of errors", when the duke uses the convenient arrival of Viola disguised as a young man named Cesario for his wooing of the lady Olivia—only to have Olivia fall in love with Viola-Cesario, who has herself already fallen in love with Orsino. All this is, moreover, typically presented for the main plot, in verse. Because of her disguise, however, Viola never becomes such an object of romantic love as to prompt a male lover to hail her, like the Virgin Mary, "full of grace". For Olivia, when falling in love with her, mistakenly supposes her to be a young man, and Orsino doesn't make her his "fancy's queen" till the end. The most, therefore, we find of a Catholic nature in the house of Orsino is his nostalgia for such relics of the past as "that old and antique song" which he has Feste sing for him, in contrast to "these most brisk and giddy-paced times" (II iv.3, 6). Much the same kind of nostalgia we also hear in Feste's own exclamation, "To see this age!" (III i.12). Nor is it absent from the mouth of Olivia herself, when she uses the common expression in Shakespeare's plays, not least in *Richard III*, " 'Twas never merry world" (III i.110). Such, too, was the nostalgia, as noted above, pervading *As You Like It*, recalling the good old days of the "old faith", before all the recent changes as well in religion as in social life and customs from the time of Henry VIII onwards.

On the other side, Olivia isn't entirely Protestant, though she stands for the Protestant queen. In the course of the play, thanks in part to the combined influence of Viola-Cesario with her twin brother Sebastian, she even shows in herself something of a Catholic tendency, as when, mistaking the one for the other, she leads Sebastian to a "chantry"—though the chantry chapels in England had all been suppressed under Elizabeth's brother, Edward VI—for a remarkably expeditious wedding. Then in the final scene, when she calls on the priest to tell the duke what has taken place, he turns out to be just the kind of priest recommended by Jaques to Touchstone, "a good priest that can tell you what marriage is" (*As You Like It*, III iii.91). Even before the priest enters, she calls him "the holy father", and on his entry she addresses him as "father" and charges him "by thy reverence" to explain "what thou dost know hath newly pass'd between this youth and me" (V i.146ff). Then the priest goes on to give a clear explanation of the wedding ceremony, to the full satisfaction of both Olivia and (presumably) Jaques (V i.160ff)—perhaps recalling the details of Shakespeare's own wedding to Anne Hathaway in the village church of Temple Grafton. This may remind us that, inasmuch as Olivia stands for Elizabeth, the queen was not so Protestant as to reject (with the Puritans) all the "rags and relics of Rome". She herself liked to retain certain Catholic ceremonies and ornaments, such as the crucifix, in her royal chapel. She insisted on the wearing of vestments at the altar, for the sake of decency. She disapproved of the clergy, especially the bishops, taking wives—though her own Archbishop of Canterbury, John Whitgift, was a married man. In these matters, however, as in most other matters, her motive was more political than religious—going along with the Puritans, so far as she considered it expedient to keep the Catholics down, while seeming to support the Catholics, or at least to relax the pressure of persecution, when it was in her interest to do so. She was, in fact, rather like Malvolio as seen through the eyes of Maria, "the devil a Puritan that he is, or anything constantly, but a time-pleaser" (II iii.161).

It is, moreover, on the side of Olivia that we turn from the main plot, involving the aristocratic characters, to the subplot of the lesser, more plebeian characters, though among the latter are two knights. Here, as befits plebeians, everything is in prose. But such is the topsy-turvydom of this play, as belonging to a feast of fools, that the subplot stands out over the main plot in the minds of most members of the audience, with Olivia's surly, Puritan steward Malvolio as the central character, if not quite the hero of the play. Here, too, it is that we find the anti-Puritanism of the play most in evidence, with the baiting of Malvolio by the others for his killjoy behaviour as "a kind of Puritan". First, he is shown up by Maria when he falls for the bait of a mysterious love letter written to him seemingly by Olivia but really by Maria. Secondly, he presents a ridiculous appearance before Olivia, and the audience, as he faithfully observes the precise instructions contained in the letter. Thirdly, and most laughably, he is baited in prison by the clown Feste, who masquerades as "Sir Topas the curate" or "Master parson" (IV ii.2, 13). In this scene it is interesting that the Puritanism of Malvolio is ironically taken over by the clown, who professes to be dissembling "in such a gown" (IV ii.7)—with reference to those Puritan ministers who refused to wear any vestments but their gowns at liturgical ceremonies, and so they were ejected from their livings in the 1560s by Archbishop Matthew Parker, and in the 1580s by Archbishop John Whitgift. At the same time, the clown is parodying the exorcisms undertaken by the Puritan John Darrell, whose activities against devils in the north of England had recently been satirized by the Bishop of London's chaplain, Samuel

Harsnet, in *A Discovery of the Fraudulent Practices of John Darrell* (1599), and subsequently recalled by Ben Jonson as "little Darrell's tricks" in his play *The Devil is an Ass* (1616). In detail, in his exhortation to Malvolio to "leave thy vain bibble-babble" (IV ii.107), the clown echoes the very words of Darrell in his *True Narration* (1600), where he speaks of those exorcized as "calling the word preached bible-bable".

Thus paradoxically even those involved in the baiting of Malvolio are also involved in his Puritanism. If the clown puts on the appearance of a Puritan minister for the sake of his exorcism—recalling the case of Dr. Pinch in *The Comedy of Errors*—there is a more substantial Puritanism in (believe it or not) both Sir Toby Belch and Maria. For in them both we find a profession of the basic Protestant tenet of *fides sola* as the condition of salvation. Sir Toby in his drunkenness, not unlike his so-called "cousin" Sir John Falstaff, parodies this teaching in his description of the young Viola-Cesario as the devil Lechery, when he exclaims, "Let him be the devil an he will, I care not. Give me faith, say I!" (I v.135). In other words, so long as he has faith, he may freely follow the temptations suggested by Lechery or Gluttony or Drunkenness or Sloth—which is no doubt the very teaching Bassanio condemns in his words "What damned error but some sober brow/ will bless it and approve it with a text?" (*The Merchant of Venice*, III ii.78). Maria also shows this way of thinking when she remarks on Malvolio's ridiculous behaviour, "There is no Christian that means to be saved by believing rightly, can ever believe such impossible passages of grossness" (III ii.78).

In addition to such passages of anti-Puritanism, or rather anti-Puritan parody, there remains in Olivia's house a tone of official Protestantism, which is opposed no less to the Catholics than to the Puritans. We may recognize it in Viola's need to come to the house in disguise, though this is also the policy she has had to observe from the time of her shipwreck on the coast of Illyria. We may find it again in the clown's easy mention of punishment for treason—recalling the "colourable colours" of *Love's Labour's Lost* (IV ii.157)—"He that is well hanged in this world needs to fear no colours" (I v.5). We may also recognize it in the same clown's catechizing of Olivia concerning her dead brother, when he baits her with the statement "I think his soul is in hell, Madonna", and she rises to the bait with her reply, "I know his soul is in heaven, fool" (I v.73ff). Here we may note what is rarely noted by commentators, that no allowance is made, as it is by Romeo and Hamlet, for the possibility of his soul being in purgatory and thus in need of prayer. Perhaps that would have been too obviously Catholic for a performance in the presence of the Protestant queen.

In the end of our discussion, we may turn to a question that might well have been raised at the beginning, namely, Where is Illyria? Needless to say, it is the old romantic name for the Dalmatian coast on the opposite side of the Adriatic Sea to Italy. Yet in view of the identification of Orsino Duke of Illyria with the other Orsino Duke of Bracciano, it seems rather to be identified with Italy itself, particularly the Papal States, which include the ducal fief of Bracciano. It is also the court of Queen Elizabeth at Whitehall in Westminster, where she is entertaining Don Virginio Orsino on the twelfth night of the Christmas festivities in 1600–1601. All these places—Illyria, Italy, and England—the dramatist brings together by the power of his dramatic imagination, as described by Theseus in *A Midsummer Night's Dream* (V i.12ff). At the same time, on a deeper level of meaning, we may interpret all this as a hint at rapprochement between the opposing religions represented by the queen and her ducal visitor. Only, the outcome of this ecumenical endeavour for the feast of the Epiphany, celebrating both wise men and fools, might be phrased in the opening words of the sad Sonnet xxxvi, "Let me confess that we two must be twain."

Such is perhaps the sadness echoed in the concluding song of the clown, which comes as a shock to those who, with John Dover Wilson, regard this as the happiest of Shakespeare's "happy comedies". Rather, this is a play dealing with the theme not only of wisdom (in Feste and Viola) but also of melancholy (in almost everyone else). So this melancholy song is appropriately put into the mouth of the wisest character in the play, the clown. And if the play was indeed, according to Hotson's theory, presented at court on January 6, 1601, the sadness of the song may be seen as prophetic both of the Essex rebellion, which erupted on the streets of London within a month of its first performance, and of the subsequent composition of *Hamlet* (in which the hero has been seen as inspired by the moody disposition of Essex on the eve of his rebellion), followed by the death of Shakespeare's recusant father in the summer. Nor is it only the sad song of the paradoxically named Feste that brings the play to an end. We may also remember Malvolio's unrepented resolution of revenge, which is as it were carried over into Hamlet's revenge—considering Hamlet, too, as "a kind of Puritan".

chapter 6
The Falstaff Plays

The Two Parts of *Henry IV*

THE TRADITIONAL division of Shakespeare's plays into comedies, histories, and tragedies, foisted upon them by his fellow players Hemings and Condell in their edition of the First Folio, is an exceedingly unfortunate one, particularly with regard to the plays of English history. While all are named after the reigns in which the dramatic events took place and therefore arranged in the chronological order of those reigns, from *King John* to *Henry VIII*, two are accorded the title of "tragedy" on their original title page, namely *Richard II* and *Richard III*. But the presence of Sir John Falstaff, that might well call for the title of "comedy" for the two Parts of *Henry IV*, is sadly ignored. Yet it is he who imparts life and interest to those two plays, and in contrast to the scenes in which he appears, the political events dramatized in the other scenes take on a merely secondary significance as the remote setting for the matches of wit between Falstaff and Prince Hal. These plays are indeed hardly deserving of the title of *Henry IV* at all. They are rather to be called "the Falstaff plays". It was, moreover, thanks to the immense popularity of Falstaff that the name of Shakespeare was first printed on the title pages of his plays—from the first quarto of *Love's Labour's Lost* in

1598—implying that his name had now at last come to have a market value.

During the first scene of Part I, as we listen to the lament of King Henry over the "riot and dishonour" that "stain the brow of my young Harry", in contrast to the other Harry, Hotspur of Northumberland, who is "the theme of honour's tongue" (I i.81ff), we nod our heads in conventional acquiescence to this next play in line of succession from the preceding history plays. But at the beginning of the second scene, we are woken up with a start at the sight of a fat old man waking up and asking the young prince, "Now, Hal, what time of day is it, lad?"—to which the prince replies with another question, "What a devil hast thou to do with the time of the day?" (I ii.1ff). Here we find ourselves in a completely different world, a world not of history but of comedy, a world that is not in but above time, reflecting the genius of its creator who was described (by Ben Jonson) as "not of an age, but for all time". Now for the first time we are introduced to Shakespeare's great comic creation, greater than all his other fools, clowns, and buffoons who throng his other comedies. He, Sir John Falstaff, may be called the very spirit and essence of Shakespearian comedy, as he boasts of himself in Part II, "I am not only witty in myself, but the cause that wit is in other men" (I ii.10). So he has won fans for himself in all ages and nations, from his first royal fan, Queen Elizabeth, to his latest academic fan, Harold Bloom—fans who delight to find more than something of themselves in him.

Now, we may ask, how did Shakespeare come to conceive such a comic creation and to introduce him so unexpectedly in the second scene of Part I of *Henry IV*, after having briefly sketched the political crisis facing the king from the North? Various answers can, and have been, given to this question with varying degrees of probability, all of them converging on this one figure of fun, this self-proclaimed "plump Jack", who sees himself as equivalent to "all the world" (II iv.534). At first, we find him, if only in the anonymous plural, in the final act of *Richard II*, where mention is made of the "unrestrained loose companions" of the young Prince Hal at certain unnamed taverns in London (V iii.7). One of these companions is named in what is commonly regarded as the source of these two plays with *Henry V*, the anonymous bipartite play of *The Famous Victories of Henry V*, the man who later became the Lollard leader and rebel against his king, Sir John Oldcastle. This name of Oldcastle we find still preserved for us in the text of Part I, where Prince Hal calls Falstaff "my old lad of the castle" (I ii.47), and in a stage direction of Part II. Evidently, it had to be changed at the last moment at the instance of the new Lord Chamberlain, who now came into power over Shakespeare's company, Lord Cobham. At this point the chronology is somewhat confusing, as the former Lord Chamberlain, Sir Henry Carey, Lord Hunsdon, died in July 1596 and was succeeded in his title as Lord Hunsdon, but not immediately in his office as Lord Chamberlain, by his son George Carey. The office was taken over at his death by William Brooke, seventh Lord Cobham, who soon died in March 1597, when the office passed to George Carey. Thus for a few months, from July 1596 till March 1597, the Chamberlain's Men were known as Lord Hunsdon's Men. Now Lord Cobham, who became Chamberlain during these months, was a direct descendant of Sir John Oldcastle, the first Lord Cobham, and he may well have objected to his ancestor being treated as a figure of fun, especially as that ancestor was now being hailed by John Foxe in his *Book of Martyrs* (1563) as morning-star of the Reformation. Consequently, the dramatist had to come up with a new name, which he found in Part I of *Henry VI*, in the cowardly knight Sir John Fastolfe (III ii.105)—though critics complain that neither the old nor the new Sir John was the cowardly ruffian he is made out to have been. Anyhow, from the name of Fastolfe it is an easy transition by metathesis to Falstaff, with a possible implication of "false" added to "staff", on analogy with "shake" and "spear", or "shake" and "shafte", or "shake" and "scene".

Still, we may further ask, how is it that from such small beginnings—like the simple sources mentioned by Helena in *All's Well That Ends Well* from which "great floods have flown" (II i.142)—Sir John Falstaff was developed by Shakespeare's genius from a mere name into so great a comic character? On the one hand, we may consider how, once Prince Hal is depicted as the prodigal son of King Henry, with biblical overtones from the parable of Jesus in Luke xv.11–32, his boon companion Sir John lends himself to characterization as the Vice or Devil of Prodigality. And so he can draw upon the rich dramatic and homiletic tradition from the Middle Ages—and Shakespeare, we know, is never averse to drawing upon such tradition. Then, this Vice, also known as Riot, from the "riotous living" on which the young man "wasted his substance", is obviously related to the other Vices of Gluttony and Drunkenness, Lechery and Sloth, who had long since lent themselves to vivid representation in sermons and plays. Shakespeare himself speaks of the devil Lechery in *Twelfth Night* (I v.132) and of the devil Drunkenness in *Othello* (II iii.300). Also in Part I of *Henry IV* he makes Prince Hal abuse Falstaff as "that reverend Vice, that grey Iniquity" (II i.505). No wonder Falstaff, with his addiction to eating and drinking, sleeping and whoring, is a very personification of the Vice, even or especially while speaking of himself as "plump Jack" who represents "all the world", namely the old Adam "in the days of villainy" (III iii.186).

On the other hand, as many critics observe, Shakespeare's character is far more than a moral Vice in the abstract. Rather, he is individualized on the basis of the Lollard knight, Sir John Oldcastle, portrayed in Foxe's *Book of Martyrs.* In this connection, a main point of Luther's teaching was, as noted above, the doctrine of *fides sola,* or justification by faith alone, apart from any merit claimed from good works, on which so much emphasis had been laid in the Middle Ages. This was understandably criticized by Catholic controversialists, such as Thomas Harding in his "great controversy" with John Jewel, as a "belly Gospel", for allowing free rein to such vices as Falstaff and Sir Toby Belch indulge in. But it is also what chiefly fascinates us in Falstaff, namely his freedom from any moral inhibitions. It is his appeal to the old Adam in us, from the old days of Queen Elizabeth to the postmodern age of Harold Bloom. Or rather, it is his appeal to one side in us, while on the other side we laugh at him and despise him as a figure of fun, if not evocative of moral indignation. Incidentally, it is at this figure of fun that the Jesuit Robert Persons was pointing his mocking finger in the course of his detailed critique of Foxe's *Book of Martyrs* in *A Treatise of Three Conversions* (1603–04). There he speaks of Sir John Oldcastle as "a ruffian, as all England knoweth, and commonly brought in by comedians on their stages"—notably by Shakespeare in his two Parts of *Henry IV.* Several years later, we find both Persons and Shakespeare incurring combined criticism as "this papist and his poet" by the Protestant historian John Speed in his *History of Great Britain* (1611). Here the "papist" is Robert Persons, who is taken to task for his particular depiction of Oldcastle as "a ruffian, a robber and a rebel, and his authority taken from the stage-players". In these words, it may be noted, Shakespeare is, for the first time and at the end of his dramatic career, explicitly associated not just with recusancy in general but with the arch-Papist Persons in particular.

Then how precisely, we may again ask, is Sir John Falstaff characterized in the two Parts of *Henry IV* not only as a figure of fun, a merry old man somewhat akin to our image of Santa Claus, but also as a Puritan, if in the old Lutheran mould? First, there is his adherence to the Lutheran doctrine of *fides sola*, which we may find implied in his remark on one of his companions, Poins, "O, if men were to be saved by merit, what hole in hell were hot enough for him?" (I ii.119). Here the implication is that, since men are to be saved not by the merit of good works but by faith alone, Poins is fortunate to be spared the pains of hell. Secondly, we find the old man appealing to the Bible, to St. Paul's teaching in Eph. iv.1–28, on the need of labouring in one's calling, in order to justify his pursuit of thieving. Thus he protests to Hal, " 'Tis no sin for a man to labour in his vocation" (I ii.116), overlooking the fact that in this very text St. Paul is drawing a contrast between an honest calling and thieving. This may remind us of the Puritan mentioned by Bassanio in *The Merchant of Venice*, who with his "sober brow" will bless a "damned error" with a text from the Bible (III ii.78). Thirdly, it is a noteworthy characteristic of Falstaff in both Parts of *Henry IV*, though not in *The Merry Wives of Windsor*, that he frequently uses biblical language—like Shylock. Yet he declares that he has "forgotten what the inside of a church is made of" (III iii.8), as if he is one of those Puritan recusants who refused to attend church with so many unregenerate people—in much the same way as

Shylock refuses to "pray with" Christians like Bassanio (I iii.39). Fourthly, there is yet another Puritan aspect of his to which his fans, from Queen Elizabeth to Harold Bloom, turn a blind eye, namely his indulgence in occasional moods of remorse, for which Poins nicknames him "Monsieur Remorse" (I ii.125). In such a mood he laments, "I would I were a weaver, I could sing psalms or anything" (II iv.148). He even vows to repent, though without any real intention of doing so (III iii.5).

Also in Part II, we find traces of Falstaff's Puritanism in his relationship with Justice Shallow in the wilds of Gloucestershire—insofar as that individual may be identified (according to an old tradition going back to the Anglican clergyman Richard Davies in the late seventeenth century) with Sir Thomas Lucy of Charlecote. This Lucy is the "Puritan" magistrate, formerly a pupil of John Foxe, who is said to have hounded the young William from Stratford in the 1580s and who led the prosecution of the Arden family after the Somerville Plot of 1583. Or if, as Leslie Hotson conjectures in his *Shakespeare Versus Shallow* (1931), Lucy has to be replaced by William Gardiner of Southwark as the real object of Shakespeare's satire, this other justice was notorious for his usury and malice, fraud and perjury, as well as for the vigour and animosity with which he prosecuted Catholic recusants. Yet, in neither Part of *Henry IV* do we come upon any anti-Catholic sentiments, so characteristic of the Puritans, in the words whether of Falstaff himself or of Justice Shallow. Only when we come to *Henry V*, in Mistress Quickly's description of Falstaff's dying moments, do we hear of his ravings about "the whore of Babylon" (II iii.41)—as the Puritans commonly spoke of the Church of Rome, not least in their numerous commentaries on the Book of Revelation.

Now, we may go on to ask, after all this discussion of Falstaff and his Puritanism, where in these two Parts of *Henry IV* may we find any positive mention of Catholic recusancy? May we not find it, for example, in the characterization of Prince Hal, as opposed to Falstaff? In Prince Hal, I fear, we look in vain for any clear sign of his presumed Catholic faith, at least not till he emerges as King Henry V in the play that bears his name. True, he is no less ready than Falstaff to bandy biblical language with him in their exchanges of wit. But he stands out rather as a Machiavellian before his time, even more than his father Henry IV—for all the latter's supposed usurpation of the English throne, but more like his Yorkist successor Richard III. From the very first scene in which he accosts Falstaff, the prince betrays his Machiavellian cast of mind in his closing soliloquy, "I know you all, and will a while uphold/ the unyok'd humour of your idleness" (I ii.217). For all the human vices of Falstaff as the old Adam, Prince Hal is much less acceptable with his cold-blooded calculating character, which comes to a climax both in his rejection of Falstaff at the end of Part II and when Falstaff is reported in *Henry V* to be dying of a broken heart. Poor Falstaff!

All the same the Catholic recusants of the age are not altogether unrepresented in the two Parts of *Henry IV*. For when we turn from Falstaff and his friends to the political background, we may notice that what characterizes both Parts is the common threat of rebellion from the North. In Part I it is the rebellion led by Henry Hotspur, but without the needed support of his father, the Earl of Northumberland. So the play concludes with the battle of Shrewsbury, when King Henry is victorious and Hotspur is slain by Prince Hal. In Part II it is the subsequent rebellion of the Archbishop of York, Richard Scroop, which ends with the capitulation of the rebels owing to a trick played on them by Hal's younger brother, Prince John of Lancaster. In either case (as Lily Campbell has shown in her study of *Shakespeare's Histories*, 1947), the dramatist is evidently thinking of similar movements in the North of opposition to the religious changes inaugurated by the Tudor rulers. First, there was the Pilgrimage of Grace in 1536, protesting against the dissolution of the monasteries. Then, there was the rising of the Northern earls in 1569, in support of the imprisoned Mary Queen of Scots. The analogy may not be drawn so explicitly in these two plays, but it hardly needed to be pointed out to Elizabethan audiences, it is so clearly implied. At least, the cause of religion, which hardly surfaces in Hotspur's rebellion, comes to the fore in that of the archbishop.

In particular, in the opening act of Part II we may notice the similarity between the archbishop's feelings in his complaints "What trust is in these times?" and "Past and to come seem best, things present worst" (I iii.108) and those of Elizabethan recusants—not to mention those of Shakespeare himself in Sonnet lxvii, where he looks back with nostalgia to "days long since, before these last so bad". Later in Act IV the archbishop is flattered by the Machiavellian Prince John—in whom we may see a pallid replica of Prince Hal, lacking as he does the presence of Falstaff—as "the imagin'd voice of God himself,/ the very opener and intelligencer/ between the grace, the sanctities of heaven,/ and our dull workings" (IV ii.19). Then, once his men have been taken in by John's deception and laid down their arms, he is arrested by Westmoreland on a charge of "capital treason" (IV ii.108). Incidentally, this Westmoreland is Ralph Neville, the first of that title and ancestor of the sixth, Charles Neville, who was one of the leaders of the rising of the Northern earls with Thomas Percy, the seventh

Earl of Northumberland, whose ancestor, the first earl, had been behind both the rebellions against Henry IV. Moreover, just as the first Earl of Northumberland was planning to take refuge in Scotland in the event of Scroop's likely failure (II iii.67), this is in fact what his descendant, the seventh earl, did in 1569, only to be handed back by the Scots to the English and beheaded as a traitor in 1572—and so to be honoured among the English martyrs as Blessed Thomas Percy.

Finally, it remains for us to consider the Epilogue to Part II. It was, no doubt, on the insistence of Lord Cobham that Shakespeare was obliged to issue a formal disavowal of any intent to identify Sir John Falstaff with Sir John Oldcastle. So we have the statement in the Epilogue, "Oldcastle died a martyr, and this is not the man" (34). How, we may wonder, could Shakespeare have really meant what he says? Clearly, he did not. What he really meant is clear enough from the context, in which the whole country, as Persons attests, was ringing with laughter at the discomfiture of Lord Cobham, particularly the eighth lord, Henry Brooke, who succeeded to his father's title in March 1597 and who was already being identified with Sir John Falstaff—no less than his ancestor Sir John Oldcastle. This we may see in two letters of the time, one from the Earl of Essex in 1598 and the other from the Countess of Southampton in 1599, neither of whom had any reason to be fond of him. Accordingly, what Shakespeare wrote in his Epilogue, if it was indeed he who wrote it, has to be interpreted as written with tongue in cheek, and as overswayed by "great command" (*Hamlet* V i.250).

Henry V

A unique characteristic of *Henry V* is its novel insertion of a series of patriotic, and presumably Protestant, utterances by a Chorus before and between the five acts of the play. They all lead up to the triumph of the young king over a seemingly superior French army at the battle of Agincourt—as it were in anticipation, from the year 1415, of the similar triumph of the English navy over the seemingly superior fleet of the Spanish Armada in 1588. The probable dating of the play in 1599, moreover, seems to indicate that the dramatist was striving his utmost to produce a play worthy of being presented for the inauguration of the Globe Theatre, "within this wooden O" (Prol.13), that year. Yet dramatically speaking, apart from the choruses, the play as a whole comes as something of an anti-climax after the two Falstaff plays which share the title of *Henry IV*, failing as it does to fulfil the promise made in the Epilogue of Part II to "continue the story, with Sir John in it" (30), and only describing his death offstage. Part II had ended with the famous scene of Falstaff's rejection by the newly crowned king, which was subsequently so deeply deplored by the great Victorian critic A. C. Bradley. Now in this new play of *Henry V* we have not long to wait before hearing of Falstaff's death in the touching words of Mistress Quickly (II iii.9ff). At least, we may say that he is exempted from the martyr's or traitor's death which had been the fate of his historical predecessor at the hands of King Henry, his erstwhile boon companion, while being allowed to make a Protestant rejection of "the whore of Babylon" in his dying words (II iii.41). Now, without the living presence of Falstaff, we hardly recognize the old Prince Hal in the newly reformed character of King Henry, apart from that Machiavellianism which is his constant trait and which, as noted above, he shares with his brother Prince John. Now we are back to the political history of England, from which not all the humours of a Pistol, a Nym, or a Bardolph, can distract our attention for long. What we are left with is no longer a comedy, still less a tragedy, but a shallow patriotic play about political success which is dramatic failure—as we may see from the long gap in recorded performances of *Henry V* from 1605 to 1735.

Not that the new king is left without any profession of Catholic piety, such as we fail to find in the former prince. Now he is shown as hardly less pious than his son and heir Henry VI, whose excess in this regard (as "the pious king") proved to be the cause of his undoing. In Henry's opening address to the Archbishop of Canterbury, we find the name of God recurring as it were "trippingly on the tongue" (*Hamlet*, III ii.2), as when he repeatedly declares, "God forbid . . . God doth know . . . We charge you in the name of God . . .", and when he goes on to exhort the archbishop to be sure "that what you speak is in your conscience wash'd/ as pure as sin with baptism" (I ii.13, 18, 23, 31). (Here we may note the Catholic implication in his words, that in baptism all sin, both original and actual, is washed away, whereas for the Lutheran it remains but is not imputed.) Also in his concluding speech in the same scene, the king makes appeal to "God's grace", to "the will of God", "to God", and "God before" (I ii.262, 289, 307). No wonder the two bishops in the opening scene are so ready to admire the young king's unexpected "reformation" (I i.33), though we know he has been deliberately planning it from the outset of Part I of *Henry IV*—for political rather than religious reasons. This also serves him as a convenient cover-up for his bare-faced aggression against the peaceful land of France. This is, moreover, an aggression that seems all the more bare-faced in view of his plan by this means to comply with his father's dying advice to "busy the giddy minds" of the English nobles with "foreign quarrels" (Part II, IV ii.212). Subsequently, on the eve of Agincourt we are shown King Henry in solitary prayer, admitting "the fault/ my father made in compassing the crown" and appeasing his conscience with the thought that he has atoned for the death of Richard II by building two chantries, "where the sad and solemn priests/ sing still for Richard's soul" (IV i.313, 320)—chantries that were subsequently pulled down in the reign of Edward VI under the ironical pretext of "reformation". Even so, as the king rightly realizes, like Claudius at prayer in *Hamlet* III iii, all he can do is worth nothing, "since that my penitence comes after all" (IV i.324). That is to say, he wants to repent, while keeping his ill-gotten crown. Then, once the battle is crowned with victory, he reverts to his pious language, declaring, "O God, thy arm was here,/ and not to us, but to thy arm alone,/ ascribe we all" (IV viii.112).

We may well appear to be ungracious in not admitting such abundant signs in King Henry of religious conversion, or "reformation". But the signs are too suspiciously abundant, and in their abundance they ring hollow—as Gertrude says of the Player Queen in *Hamlet*, he "doth protest too much" (III ii.242)—especially when we contrast the pious words of the king with his impious deeds, and with the doubtful validity of his position no less in England than in France. Like Claudius in *Hamlet*, he wants to have his cake and eat it. That is, he wants to retain his crown and yet repent, while making compensation on his own and his father's behalf for the way they have achieved it. He wants to invade France, while still unsure of his title as well in France as in England. Like Claudius, too, he is a notable example of what St. Ignatius in an exercise for the second week of the *Spiritual Exercises* calls "the second class of men"—that is to say, the class of those who would like to remove a disorderly affection, while retaining the thing they have gained by following that affection, and so, instead of doing God's will whatever it may be, they aim at bringing God round to their own way of thinking and willing. This is a spiritual issue that is not merely raised by the dramatist in this one soliloquy, but is central to the play. It is also raised in a pointed manner by the common English soldiers on the eve of battle, when the king comes round their tents in disguise. From them he hears many home truths about himself and his enterprise, which none of his professional advisers, least of all the bishops, have dared to tell him. Such is the truth put to him most forcefully by the young soldier Michael Williams:

> But if the cause be not good, the king himself hath a heavy reckoning to make, when all those legs and arms and heads, chopped off in a battle, shall join together at the latter day and cry all, "We died at such a place"—some swearing, some crying for a surgeon, some upon their wives left poor behind them, some upon the debts they owe, some upon their children rawly left. I am afeard there are few die well that die in a battle. (IV i.141ff)

Here again we may recognize an echo of the *Spiritual Exercises* of St. Ignatius, also from the second week, in which there occurs the contemplation on the Incarnation. Here the three persons of the Holy Trinity are imagined looking down from heaven to earth and observing men in all their diversity of appearance, clothing, and gestures, "some white and others black, some in peace and others in war, some weeping and others laughing, some in health and others in sickness, some being born and others dying", and then "how they swear and blaspheme . . . how they strike and kill one another, and so they go to hell."

Such a view, so strongly implied in this central scene of *Henry V*—not at the battle itself but on the eve—is a kind of judgment passed on the king not directly by God but by his own soldiers and by the continuing echo of the words he has spoken in soliloquy as it were out of his own conscience. It is the more strongly implied in the contrast between his outward victory over the French, as emphasized on the title page of the first quarto, "with his battle fought at Agincourt in France", and his inner mind. It is the contrast between his public utterances, which sound so brash from the time of his arrival in France, comparable to the words of some overweening public schoolboy leading his scrum in a game of rugby, and his private self, as when he reassures the English soldiers that "the king is but a man as I am" (IV i.105). It is also the contrast between the patriotic utterances of the Chorus, glorifying him in pagan terms as having "the port of Mars" (I Prol.6) and the mien of "young Phoebus" (III Prol.6), and the content of each act in which the legal weakness of the king's position in both England and France is emphasized. These utterances seem to be making their appeal to the patriotic spirit of Protestant Englishmen under the rule of their "gracious empress", as the queen is flatteringly described by the Chorus (V Prol.30), in view of the continuing danger from Spain, while her noble general, the Earl of Essex, is on his way to Ireland to bring back "rebellion broached on his sword" (Prol.32). But they ring no less hollow than the public speeches of Henry himself, which we may see reflected no less in the outcome of his brief reign on the accession of the infant Henry VI than in Essex's own ill-fated expedition to Ireland, which ended not only in his failure there but also in his equally ill-fated rebellion back in London.

Here, if we are looking for some contemporary reference in the play, we may find it in this combination of Elizabeth and Essex in the situation of Henry V and this comparison between Essex's expedition to Ireland and Henry's to France—except that in Ireland Essex encountered no Agincourt. That victory, moreover, comes almost at the end of *Henry V*, while it also suggests a comparison or contrast with the beginning. For who, we may ask, are the two prelates assigned to the sees of Canterbury and Ely in the opening scene? Do they really belong to the reign of Henry V, or not rather to the later reign of Elizabeth I? In the former case, they may look like the corrupt prelates of the mediaeval Church, as envisaged by the Protestant readers of Foxe's *Book of Martyrs*—such prelates as we may find depicted in Cardinal Beaufort in Parts I and II of *Henry VI*, Cardinal Pandulph in King John, and Cardinal Wolsey in *Henry VIII*. In the latter case, there seems to be something typically Anglican in Canterbury's statement that "miracles are ceas'd" (I i.67), which was the official attitude adopted by the Anglican Church to the Catholic claims of miracles as proofs of the true Church. Such was the controversy that broke out from 1604 onwards between Anglicans and Catholics concerning certain miracles alleged to have been worked at a shrine of Our Lady in Brabant, a controversy that is evidently reflected in *All's Well That Ends Well* on the miraculous cure of the French king worked by Helena. Then Lord Lafeu remarks how shocking this must be to "our philosophical persons" who "say miracles are past"(II iii.1–2). And this in turn echoes Hamlet's famous remark, "There are more things in heaven and earth, Horatio,/ than are dreamt of in your philosophy" (I v.166).

Then, too, it is the same Archbishop of Canterbury who insists on the remarkable "reformation" of the erstwhile prodigal, and who goes on in the next scene to encourage him to undertake the expedition to France on what seems to be, judging from his round-about speech, the flimsiest of reasons. In this he conveniently overlooks the warning of Christ, "All that take the sword shall perish by the sword" (Matt. xxvi.52). Not that King Henry perishes by the sword, as he no doubt deserves. Rather, the play is given a happy ending in a happy marriage between King Henry and Princess Katharine, which is blessed by Queen Isabella of France in the name of God as "the best maker of all marriages" (V ii.387). This conclusion, however, has to be balanced by the brief Epilogue, in which the Chorus in an altered tone of voice foretells the tragic future under the reign of the infant Henry VI, whose many advisers "lost France and made England bleed", as "oft our stage hath shown" (V ii.414). Consequently, the audience leave the theatre with little of that triumphant feeling which the same Chorus has striven, not without dramatic irony, to elicit in them. No wonder this play, popular though it may have been with Elizabethan audiences in the aftermath of the Armada, and appealing as it may have been to their Protestant patriotism, fell out of favour from the Jacobean age onwards—only to be revived in wartime Britain owing to the patriotic fervour of Sir Laurence Olivier.

The Merry Wives of Windsor

If there is a feeling of anti-climax on passing from the two Falstaff plays of *Henry IV* to the absence and subsequently reported death of Falstaff in *Henry V*, much stronger is this feeling on passing from these three "history" plays to the "comedy" of *The Merry Wives of Windsor*. This purports to show "Falstaff in love", at the special request, it is said (by John Dennis and Nicholas Rowe), of the queen herself, who had been so delighted with the figure of Falstaff in the plays of *Henry IV*. Not only is she said to have been "very well pleased" with the performance, but it has proved to be just as popular with audiences ever since, though it is more farce than comedy, with a record proportion of prose over verse. Among scholars, however, it is not so favourably received, as Falstaff hardly seems to be the same character when deprived of the company of Prince Hal and the opportunity provided by him for witty banter. Here in his crude attempts to make love to the "merry wives", Mistress Ford and Mistress Page, he is but a shadow of his former self. Before, in every contest of wit he invariably came out on top, like a doll that is all paunch below, which, however much pushed from one or other side, always returns to the upright position. Now, however, he is all too easy a victim for the wiles of the merry wives. Yet in spite of the successive reverses he suffers at their hands, he retains his demeanour of solemn dignity to the end. True, in his use of language he reverts to his familiar phrases from *Henry IV*—in his reflections on "what a man is" with all "his frailty" (III v.51), in his complaint about "the villainous inconstancy of man's disposition" (IV v.113), in his occasional biblical references as to the Book of Job (V i.25, V v.168), and in his futile resolution to "repent" (IV v.107). Such words may recall the Puritan aspect of his character noted above in *Henry IV*, but they still fail to convince us that this is the same old Falstaff. In *Henry IV* he is the quintessential Vice of Prodigality to Prince Hal as the Prodigal Son. But in *The Merry Wives of Windsor*, with no Prince Hal at his side, he is little more than a mere Vice of Lechery, in relation no longer to whores such as Doll Tearsheet but to honest wives whose fidelity to their husbands he seeks in vain to undermine. Only when we forget his memory from the two Parts of *Henry IV*, or preferably when we have no such memory, can we really enjoy the episodes concerning him in this comedy—not so much for his character, which is here reduced to mere nonentity, as for his victimization, in being made a butt for the laughter of others. What a change is here from his boast in Part II of *Henry IV* (where he is already on the decline), "I am not only witty in myself, but the cause that wit is in other men" (I ii.10). Here he is another man masquerading as "Sir John Falstaff", the name without the reality.

In this play, moreover, Falstaff is not so clearly Puritan but that he betrays certain Papist associations. The slapstick jest played on him by the merry wives, and on the jealous husband of Mistress Ford, in enabling him to escape from the other's jealous wrath by bundling him into a smelly laundry basket and dumping him into the foul water of the Thames, is oddly reminiscent of the way hunted priests in Elizabethan times sometimes eluded capture by pursuivants. Thus, when Mistress Page warns Mistress Ford, "Your husband's coming . . . with all the officers of Windsor" (III iii.113), and when Falstaff recalls his predicament to Master Brook on the arrival of Ford with "a rabble of his companions" (III v.79), we may be reminded not only of Judas coming with soldiers for his betrayal of Jesus in the garden, but also of a sheriff coming with his search party to apprehend a hunted priest in some recusant house. Campion himself, for example, once eluded capture thanks to the presence of mind of a housemaid, who laughingly pushed him into a stagnant pond. Persons, too, managed to get out of a similar situation by diving into a haystack.

The plot of Falstaff's baiting by the merry wives is, however, by no means the only or even the main centre of attention in this play. Shakespeare in his comedies is nothing if not complicated as well as comic, and this comedy is no exception. If there is a plot on "Falstaff in love" to meet the queen's express wishes, there is another plot that might be called "main" to which the Falstaff plot is subordinated. After all, even in the two Parts of *Henry IV*, Sir John is essentially a subplot character, however large he may loom in the minds of the audience—and in the intention of the dramatist. He belongs to low life, with his inseparable companions, Pistol, Nym, and Bardolph, and he invariably speaks in prose, though Pistol may affect a Marlovian, melodramatic verse. While in the course of the subplot we are entertained by three successive ruses of the merry wives on their easy victim, in the main plot we are introduced to three successive suitors for Mistress Page's pretty daughter, Anne. First comes Abraham Slender, a witless cousin to Justice Shallow, then Doctor Caius, the irascible adversary to the Welsh parson Sir Hugh Evans, and lastly Master Fenton, one of the few characters in the play who consistently speaks in verse and who wins Anne's heart.

Of these three suitors, from a religious viewpoint, first Slender may be regarded as "a kind of Puritan"—as Maria might have described him (*Twelfth Night* II iii.161). This appears partly in his name of Abraham, considering that the Puritans of the time were notorious for affecting names from the Old Testament, in preference to "popish" names of saints. Partly, too, in his almost pathetic dependence on the advice of his cousin Shallow, who is, as noted above, identified by old tradition with the "Puritan" magistrate of Charlecote, Sir Thomas Lucy. Again, partly in his surly demeanour, recalling the "willful stillness" attributed to such people by Gratiano in *The Merchant of Venice* (I i.90), and producing remarks that are hardly calculated to ingratiate him with Anne. Thus in his boorish manner he declares his puritanical preference for "godly company", even to the extent of involving himself in the absurd contradiction, "If I be drunk, I'll be drunk with those that have the fear of God, and not with drunken knaves" (I i.189). Secondly, as for the fiery Doctor Caius, there is nothing particularly religious in his words, and he shows no qualms of conscience in challenging the parson to a duel for love of Anne, even with the intent to kill this "scurvy Jack-dog priest" (II iii.65). Still, in view of his French nationality he might seem to be a Catholic, if more Gallican than Papist, while in view of his name he might be seen as a parody of the famous Papist doctor of Cambridge, Dr. John Caius, who was physician to both Edward VI and Mary Tudor before his dismissal from court by Elizabeth for his papistry. Thirdly, Master Fenton, as the successful suitor to Anne, may be compared with such other lovers as Romeo and Bassanio and Orlando, in that he is the character with least colour in this colourful play, even to the extent of an uncertain religious allegiance.

On the other hand, the most colourful of all the characters in this play, more colourful than Falstaff himself or his companions or the merry wives themselves, and more colourful than any of Anne's suitors, is the one with the most obvious religious allegiance, the parson Sir Hugh Evans. He not only declares himself from the outset as "of the Church" (I i.32), but he frequently intersperses his words with pious remarks and echoes from the Bible, as when in the opening scene he declares (in his Welsh accent), "There is no fear of Got in a riot" (I i.37), and exclaims, "Got deliver to a joyful resurrections!" (I i.53). When it comes to deeds, however, he is less than pious and shows himself no less ready for a fight than the irate French doctor. And that, one may add, is what chiefly contributes to his colour. In this respect, however, he is hardly the mirror of "a curer of souls" or "a wise and patient churchman" such as Justice Shallow would hope to find in him (II iii.40, 57), but he is a student of both "the sword and the word", much to the scandal of that same justice (III i.44).

Here a question may be raised about Sir Hugh Evans—though recognized as Master Parson by the other characters in the play, in view of his profession—how he would have been regarded by the dramatist himself and his Elizabethan audiences. Would they have taken him as a Catholic priest of the early fifteenth century, under the reign of Henry V? Or wouldn't they rather have seen in him a typical Protestant parson of the late sixteenth century, under the reign of Elizabeth I? At first sight, there seems to be little in his words or deeds to show him as either Catholic or Protestant. He seems to be altogether nondenominational. But the contrast between the way he unhesitatingly peppers his speech with religious language and the absence of any religious propriety in his actions would point to the typical behaviour of not a few Anglican ministers of the age, as reported by their own contemporaries. Thus the Puritan Thomas Cartwright, in responding to his Anglican adversary John Whitgift, complains of such as give "one leap out of the shop into the church" and are suddenly changed "out of a serving man's coat into a minister's cloak", thereby bringing about what William Harrison calls, in his *Description of England* (1577), "the general contempt of the ministry". It is in virtue of this Anglican identity that Shakespeare might well have based his characterization of Sir Hugh on personal observation, and that might be the reason for his having such a colourful character. It has even been suggested that Sir Hugh, as a fiery Welshman and tutor to the little William Page, could be a parody of one of Shakespeare's schoolmasters at Stratford, Thomas Jenkins.

His name betrays his Welsh origin, though he is said to have come from London, via Oxford, where he had been a colleague of Campion's at St. John's College, and from Stratford he went on to become an Anglican minister.

Yet another plot remains to be mentioned as contributing to the variety and humour of the play, namely the jealousy of Ford on learning that Falstaff is making love to his merry wife. The two wives conspire to show up the folly not only of Falstaff in his lechery but also of Ford in his jealousy, and in both undertakings they are eminently successful. In the contemporary background to their exposure of Ford's folly, there is an interesting connection between the pseudonym Brook chosen by Ford in his dealings with Falstaff and the real name of the new Lord Chamberlain, William Brooke, Lord Cobham, who took over the office on the death of Henry Carey, Lord Hunsdon, in 1596. Lord Cobham, with his claim to descent from the Lollard martyr Sir John Oldcastle, may well have been, as noted above, responsible for the change of name from Oldcastle to Falstaff in the plays of *Henry IV*, and for his puritanical attitude Shakespeare may have wished to take a dramatic revenge on him—as Sir Toby and Maria do on Malvolio—by parodying him as Master Brook, alias Master Ford, while the chamberlain could do nothing against him while he enjoyed the queen's favour. In the play Ford is by no means unreligious even in his jealousy. He even exclaims in premature triumph, "God be praised for my jealousy!" (II ii.327). He also goes on to declare with a strange combination of glee and anger, "Our revolted wives share damnation together" (III ii.41). On the other hand, in his exposure as a would-be cuckold, he comes close to being treated by the others as a case for exorcism, recalling the plight both of Antipholus of Ephesus in *The Comedy of Errors* and of Malvolio in *Twelfth Night*. So

Page warns him, "Master Ford, you are not to go loose any longer, you must be pinioned." And Sir Hugh adds, "Why, this is lunatics! This is mad as a mad dog!" (IV ii.132). Later on, in his discovery of one whom he takes to be the old woman of Brainford (but who is really Falstaff in disguise), he shouts at her, "A witch, a quean, an old cozening quean!" and accuses her of working "by charms, by spells, by the figure" (IV ii.184ff), as if for him Windsor is a kind of Ephesus in need of exorcists like Dr. Pinch. This may look back by implication to the Jesuit exorcisms held at Catholic houses to the north of London in the mid-1580s, and even perhaps to the Puritan exorcisms practised by John Darrell in the north of England in the late 1590s. At least, we may find an interesting verbal similarity between the "pribbles and prabbles" of Sir Hugh Evans (I i.56, V v.172) and the "prittle prattle" and "bible bable" mentioned by John Darrell in his *True Narration* (1600) as having occurred in the scurrilous speeches of the possessed children he was attempting to exorcize by means of the word of God.

If only, we may regretfully reflect, Falstaff had been called by some other name in this pleasant comedy, we might have been able to sit back and enjoy it without any odious comparison to his greater namesake in the plays of *Henry IV*. But then, we may ruefully recall, it had been the wish of the queen herself to be shown "Falstaff in love", and the poor dramatist had to do his best at short notice, and so to come out with this farce in prose. Juliet may have asked, "What's in a name?" But there is so much implied in the name of Falstaff that we can hardly help applying to his namesake in *The Merry Wives of Windsor* those other words of Juliet, "O be some other name!" (*Romeo and Juliet*, II ii.42).

chapter 7
Religion in the Roman Plays I

Julius Caesar

THREE PLAYS seem to have been specially composed by Shakespeare for the opening of the new Globe Theatre in 1599, plays that between them cut across the traditional division of comedies, histories, and tragedies—as though repeating the similar achievement in the *annus mirabilis* of 1595. In the comedy of *As You Like It* occurs the speech of Jaques, whose first line, "All the world's a stage", corresponds to the Latin motto of the Globe from Petronius, "*Totus mundus agit histrionem*"—All the world plays the player. In the history play of *Henry V*, the last of the series on mediaeval English history, the new stage is introduced to us by the Chorus as "this wooden O" (Prol.13). Now, as it were a sequel to *Henry V*, while moving from mediaeval England to classical Rome, we have the tragedy of *Julius Caesar*. In it the dramatist takes up the central event of mediaeval English history, the assassination of Richard II, and looks back to the central event of ancient Roman history, the assassination of Julius Caesar. Also in that tragedy we may note the theatrical reference in the words of Cassius, "How many ages hence/ shall this our lofty scene be acted o'er/ in states unborn and accents yet unknown!" (III i.111). Moreover, if *Julius Caesar* comes at the end of these three productions for the opening of the Globe, as well as at the end of the series of plays on mediaeval English history, it also comes at the beginning of a new series of three Roman plays. Thus we have three series coming together at an important turning point in Shakespeare's dramatic career, both between his comic and tragic periods and at the turn of the century. For the time being, however, this first Roman play stands alone, as the dramatist turns his mind to new, unsuspected problems. And only when the tragic period is over does he return to the subject of Rome, in two more plays which are ranged with the tragedies, though there is in them (in Miltonic phrase) "nothing for tears".

At the same time, while we are thinking in terms of series, we may note yet another series of three plays, from *Richard II* by way of *Julius Caesar* to *Hamlet*. What is common to the plays in this series is that they all deal with the sensational and topical theme of regicide. For Julius Caesar was king in all but name, and the main reason for his assassination was that he was on the verge of being formally offered the crown by the Roman senate. In this way we may see Shakespeare moving as it were from the centre of English to the centre of Roman history. Further, we may consider that with the play of *Henry V* Shakespeare had come to the end of his material from Holinshed's *Chronicles* for the history of mediaeval England (though for him, of course, it was not yet "mediaeval") and that, instead of entering upon the more recent, and dangerous, events of the Tudor period, he now preferred to transfer his attention to classical Rome. There, in the clash between republican and imperial Rome, as represented by the followers of Pompey and Caesar, he may have seen an ambivalence similar to that between the popular Bolingbroke and the imperious Richard. Moreover, the very name of Rome would have set up the other ambivalence between classical and Christian Rome noted above in *The Merchant of Venice*, where the merchant Antonio is described by his friend Bassanio as "one in whom/ the ancient Roman honour more appears/ than any that draws breath in Italy" (III ii.296).

In theory, therefore, we might expect to find a layer of recusant meaning in *Julius Caesar*, in spite of the unusual degree of fidelity shown by the dramatist in drawing on his main sources, the lives of Caesar, Brutus, and Antony in Plutarch's *Lives*, which had been translated into English by Sir Thomas North in 1579. We even get the impression, from a recusant viewpoint, that here more than ever before Shakespeare has sought to cover up all traces of recusancy by using his source material in such a way as to offer no ground for any suborned informer to accuse him, in contrast to the ample ground he had offered in *As You Like It*. After all, in the religious situation of the *fin de siècle* at that time, the very mention of Rome in a play might have excited suspicion on both sides, for and against Rome in a contemporary sense. Yet "thought is free" (*The Tempest*, III ii.134), and Shakespeare may have taken a perverse delight in playing on the differing sympathies of Protestant, Papist, and Puritan in his audience, those three religions which were distinguished by Robert Persons in his contemporary tract, *Elizabethae, Angliae Reginae* (1592).

From the Puritan viewpoint, the imperial Rome of the Caesars, founded by Julius and established by Augustus, would readily have been seen in terms of Papal Rome—considering that even one of the contemporary popes, Sixtus V (pope from 1585 to 1590), is said to have referred to himself as "Caesar" at the time of his election. It is Caesar's enemies, the republican tribunes Flavius and Marullus, who from the outset seek to "disrobe the images" and to disrupt the ceremonies in honour of Caesar (I i.68) and who are consequently, in Casca's words, "put to silence" (I ii.291). They may be seen as corresponding to the Puritan iconoclasts and opponents of ceremony. On the other hand, Caesar himself is characterized as superstitious and over-fond of ceremony (I ii.6). In the climax of the play, just before he is stabbed by the conspirators on the steps to the Senate-house, his proud assertion, "I am as constant as the Northern star" (III i.60), may be heard as an echo of the papal claim to infallibility. As for Cassius and Brutus, there seems to be something Puritan in them both. They are both republicans, followers of the great Pompey, who has been defeated by Caesar and brought to his death before the play begins. As such they may both be seen as anticipating the achievement of a republic in England with the triumph of Oliver Cromwell and the downfall of Charles I in 1649. The Stoic idealism of Brutus is not unlike the moral idealism of the Puritans. Then, the "lean and hungry look" noted by Caesar in Cassius, together with his dislike of plays and music and his seldom smiling (I ii.193, 202), all smack of Elizabethan Puritanism as caricatured by Gratiano in the opening scene of *The Merchant of Venice* (I i.88ff). Even the cry "Liberty! Freedom!" (III i.77, 81), uttered by the conspirators in the moment of their assassination of Caesar—repeated in less savoury circumstances by Caliban in *The Tempest* (II ii.199)—has an unmistakably Puritan ring. So if the sympathies of the dramatist are seen as siding with the republicans and their "necessary" killing of Caesar—as when Brutus says, "It must be by his death" (II i.10)—may he not also be seen as siding with the Puritans, at least within this play and in a political connection?

All the same, we may well ask, are the dramatist's sympathies entirely on the side of the republicans? They are, to some extent. Certainly, he enters more fully into the mind of Brutus than into the mind of any other character, including Caesar. For the real hero of the play is Brutus, though the title might seem to point to Julius Caesar. Compared with Brutus, Caesar is merely a nonentity. Well may we wonder, with Cassius, how such a puny man with such a feeble temper could have got "the start of the majestic world" so as to "bear the palm alone" (I ii.130). Yet if Caesar himself is weak, his cause, represented by his ghost, is strong. This is what Brutus recognizes, on encountering the corpse of Cassius on the battlefield of Philippi: "O Julius Caesar, thou art mighty yet!" (V iii.94).

Not that this seeming vindication of Caesar, and implicitly of Papal Rome, necessarily indicates a recusant sympathy on Shakespeare's part. It might still indicate an Anglican sympathy, directed as much against the Papists as against the Puritans. After all, from the Anglican viewpoint, both Papists and Puritans were conspirators, or potential conspirators, against the English establishment. In the long run, it was the Puritans under Oliver Cromwell who succeeded in their conspiracy against the monarch with his bishops and their vestments and ceremonies. But by the end of Elizabeth's reign there had already been a long line of conspiracies attributed to the Papists, if the work of agents provocateurs on behalf of the government—including the ridiculous Squire Plot against the queen, which had been brought to light only the year before. So when Brutus speaks of the conspirators who come to his house by night as "the faction", and when he inconsistently—in view of his resolve to join them—goes on to exclaim, "O conspiracy,/ sham'st thou to show thy dangerous face by night,/ when evils are most free?" (II i.77), he might well have been seen by an Elizabethan audience as more Papist than Puritan.

Further, the mention of their conspiracy as an "enterprise" both by Cassius (I iii.123) and by Brutus (II i.133)—while anticipating the similar use of this word by Hamlet in his soliloquy, "To be, or not to be" (III i.86)—may remind us that this was an all but technical term on the recusant side for forcible attempts, whether by the Duke of Guise or the King of Spain, to relieve the persecuted Catholics during the 1580s. The very scene, too, in which Brutus exclaims on "conspiracy" is all but prophetic of the preparations for the Gunpowder Plot of 1605.

Yet another line of reasoning may indicate that the republican cause upheld by Brutus and Cassius against Caesar is more Papist than Puritan. For whereas Caesar is regarded by the republicans as an upstart with his regal ambitions, it is Brutus and Cassius who represent the traditional values of Rome. In this respect they are more Papist than Puritan, like the old duke in *As You Like It.* On the other hand, in this respect Caesar himself is more Anglican than Papist or Puritan, being comparable to Henry VIII, who was the first in English history to claim the novel title of Supreme Head of the English Church, on the basis of the equally novel doctrine of the divine right of kings, proposed by Luther's English follower William Tyndale in his *Obedience of a Christian Man* (1528). This book, when introduced to the king by Thomas Cromwell, was warmly welcomed by Henry—though he pursued its author to his death for heresy in 1536. Further, whereas the doctrine of divine right was consistently taught by Anglican theologians and preachers from Tyndale onwards—with the notable exception of Richard Hooker, who relied in his writing of *The Laws of Ecclesiastical Polity* (1595) rather on such mediaeval scholastics as Aquinas and Scotus than on the Protestant reformers—the opposite doctrine of the right of the people (or the social contract) was upheld not only by the Puritans but also by the Papists in their *Conference about the Next Succession* (1595), attributed to Robert Persons (though he denied the attribution). It is significant that this latter book was twice reprinted in the following century, first by the Puritans on the eve of the Civil War in 1642, and secondly by the Whigs at the outset of their Revolution in 1689. Thus Brutus and Cassius might be regarded as Papists and even Jesuits before their time!

What then may we conclude from this bewildering ambivalence concerning the sympathies of the dramatist in *Julius Caesar*? Many will, no doubt, see his true mind in the words of Cicero, commenting on the interpretation of the many portents in the night sky on the eve of Caesar's assassination, "Men may construe things after their fashion/ clean from the purpose of the things themselves" (I iii.34). Cicero himself, it may be remembered, was regarded by Cassius as a friend of the republican cause, and as such he was subsequently pricked down by Octavius and Antony among the seventy senators "that died by their proscriptions" (IV iii.176). In that case, the words of Cicero may in turn be construed not in favour of their seeming scepticism, but on the side of that tradition which had preceded the religious changes introduced into England under Henry VIII with his Machiavellian minister Thomas Cromwell.

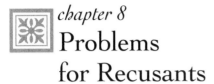

chapter 8
Problems for Recusants

Hamlet

FROM A ROMAN viewpoint there is an obvious connection between *Julius Caesar* and *Hamlet.* At the climax of Caesar's assassination in the former play the people are said, somewhat anachronistically, to "stare, cry out and run/ as it were doomsday" (III i.97). Then the same theme of doomsday is taken up, with reference to the same event, at the beginning of *Hamlet,* when Horatio is reminded of the portents at the time of Caesar's death, with the moon becoming "sick almost to doomsday with eclipse" (I i.120). It is as if the dramatist has deliberately inserted this reference into the latter play in order to imply the same Roman meaning, with all the ambivalence we have noted, in the one play as in the other. In *Hamlet* the reference to Julius Caesar is particularly applied to the strange appearance of the ghost, bearing as it does "the majesty of buried Denmark" (I i.48). In this way our attention is directed back to a past age that is recalled as ideal in contrast to the harsh reality of the present. For the young Hamlet that age was bound up with the memory of his living father, as he describes him to Horatio: "He was a man, take him for all in all./ I shall not look upon his like again" (I ii.187). For Shakespeare, in his composition of this drama, there may also have been a combined memory of his revered father, John, the declared recusant, who died in the very year of this play, 1601, and of his dear son Hamnet, named after his recusant godfather Hamnet Sadler. Also in 1601 Shakespeare had celebrated the feast of the wise men, the Epiphany, or the "twelfth night" after Christmas, with a play involving a contrast between the wise fool Feste and the foolish wise man Malvolio, in whom there is something of Hamlet in his concluding resolve to be revenged on the whole pack of his shallow enemies.

From the beginning of the play there is a mystery about this young Hamlet, with his "inky cloak" and dark, brooding demeanour, which serve to disguise "that within which passeth show" (I ii.77, 85). In contrast to the bright, colourful world of Claudius and his court, the presence of Hamlet is a cheerless, melancholy, threatening shadow. If they exist in and for the world, he is but a nonentity uttering gloomy, foreboding comments that come to nothing. But once we see him as the central figure in the play to which he gives his name, we find that—"handy-dandy", as the mad Lear says (IV vi.158)—they are all but shadows of himself, shadows of which he would dearly like to be rid, only he can't see a way to get rid of them without putting an end to himself. From this viewpoint, it is no accident that the place of his education at Wittenberg, Luther's university, is mentioned no less than four times in the second scene—once each by Claudius and Gertrude in speaking to Hamlet, and twice by Hamlet himself in speaking to his fellow student Horatio (I ii.113, 119, 164, 168). Why, we may wonder, does the dramatist make such insistent repetition of the name of Wittenberg, whose university was only founded in 1502, with Martin Luther as one of its first teachers from 1508, almost five centuries after the events of the play as narrated in the Danish chronicle of Saxo Grammaticus? Here already we may note the strange juxtaposition in the play between old and new, not only between Hamlet father and son, but also between the remote origins of the English and Danish people and the present world of Renaissance and Reformation in Elizabethan England. In presenting such a play, as the first quarto announces on the title page "in the city of London and the two universities of Oxford and Cambridge", the Chamberlain's Men were indeed making themselves what Hamlet calls "the abstracts and brief chronicles of the time" (II ii.555), both in early eleventh-century Denmark and in sixteenth-century England.

Now, we may argue, if Claudius, Gertrude, and their Danish court stand for the colourful, if not garish, world of the Elizabethan Renaissance, what do Hamlet and Horatio, both fresh from Wittenberg, represent but the Lutheran Reformation—as it was brought to England in successive waves, at first secretly under Henry VIII, then openly under Edward VI, and at last imposingly (in both meanings of the word) under Elizabeth I? This Lutheran aspect of Hamlet's character may be recognized in his brooding sense of sin, no less in himself than in all men and all women. First, in flat contradiction to the Renaissance ideal of man—which also came down from the Bible and found notable expression in Robert Persons's best-selling *Book of Resolution* from 1582 onwards—"What a piece of work is a man! How noble in reason!", Hamlet adds with all the pessimism of a Luther, "Man delights not me. No, nor woman neither!" (II ii.323). Secondly, he rounds on Polonius with a sudden, unexpected outburst concerning the entertainment of the players: "Use every man after his desert, and who should 'scape whipping?" (II ii.561). Thirdly, in the nunnery scene with Ophelia, he no less angrily rounds on Polonius's daughter, while directing his criticism even more strongly against himself, "We are arrant knaves all, believe none of us!" (III i.125). Thus he urges her—as it were in line with similar proposals made by Friar Laurence and Friar Francis, King Richard and Duke Theseus—to go to a nunnery as the only way to avoid becoming a "breeder of sinners" (III i.125).

Yet if Hamlet were no more than a Lutheran pessimist or a Puritan killjoy—as we might also conclude from his moral disapproval of the king's carousals and the jests of the clowns at their grave-digging—the play would have been exceedingly dull and monochrome, in conformity with the mourning cloak of the prince. What makes him such an interesting character, and what makes his interest transcend the restrictions of his age and nation, is the strange juxtaposition in his character between Lutheran and Catholic, or in more contemporary terms, between Puritan and Papist.

The Catholic aspect of Hamlet's character returns to him almost as soon as he returns to Denmark. Here his brooding on the original sin of man, echoed in his opening soliloquy comparing his father and mother to Adam and Eve in a garden that has now, alas, run to seed (I ii.135), is offset by his memory of those good old days when his father was alive and his very ideal of man (I ii.187). It is perhaps this memory of his father that now assumes visible form both to himself and to his friends on the castle battlements. And it is from his father's ghost, played according to an old tradition by the dramatist himself, that he learns not only about the original murder (whose truth he already suspects) but also about the ghost's actual location. This is neither heaven nor hell, the only alternatives allowed to the dead by Protestant theologians, but the "prison-house" of purgatory, where "the foul deeds done in my days of nature/ are burnt and purg'd away" (I v.12). Then, when Horatio comes on the scene after the ghost's departure, Hamlet uses the unusual oath (unique in all Shakespeare's plays), "By Saint Patrick" (I v.136), with reference to St. Patrick's Purgatory in Ireland, about which the dramatist may have read in Holinshed's *Chronicle* of Ireland—in a passage originally composed by Edmund Campion. Thus, under the influence of his father's ghost and his own reviving memory of the good old days, we may see Hamlet moving away from his brief period of Lutheran indoctrination at Wittenberg back to his earlier Catholic formation. All the same, he still entertains doubts about the identity of the ghost, whether a Catholic ghost from purgatory or a Protestant devil masquerading as a ghost to abuse and damn him. Only in the outcome of the play-within-the-play is he at last satisfied that the ghost has told him the truth and is therefore to be accepted and obeyed as the spirit of his father from purgatory.

All the same, it seems that Hamlet has to be seen as more than just a Catholic converted from a temporary lapse into Lutheranism by the revival of memories from his Catholic past. He is also a Papist in the full sense of a recusant Papist—not just a "church Papist" or "crypto-Papist"—who is fundamentally opposed to the new order that he finds already established on his return to Denmark. That order is bound up with the persons of the new king and queen, his uncle, Claudius, and his mother, Gertrude, not without the help of the old councillor Polonius, to whom they evidently owe their position on the throne. Nor is Hamlet merely opposed to this new order in a passive manner, as shadow to light, or as inner light to surrounding darkness. He also feels the deep need to resist that order, especially once he has met his father's ghost and received the injunction of revenge. He himself has no wish to take revenge or to commit the crime of regicide. But he can't get it out of his mind that his is a mission to cleanse what is "rotten in the state of Denmark" (I iv.90) and to "set things right" (I v.189).

From now on Hamlet begins to put on his "antic disposition", as he forewarns his friends (I v.172), though we may suspect much of it is not just feigned but close to real madness. This comes to the dramatist from his remote sources, where it has a point in enabling the avenger to conceal his real intent. But in the play it has the opposite effect of eliciting concern about the cause of Hamlet's "distemper" or "transformation", and so two other fellow students of Hamlet are sent by the king to spy on him (II ii.5.55). Here we find a primitive kind of spy-system, devised by Claudius and Polonius and used against Hamlet—strangely parallel to the more elaborate spy-system devised by Lord Burghley (the probable model for Polonius, whose name sounds like a Welsh-Latin form of "Burghley") with the aid of Sir Francis Walsingham. The latter spy-system was used not least against the English Catholics, both at home and abroad, not only to find out what plots they might be hatching against the queen and her government, but also to promote such plots as agents provocateurs (such as Anthony Munday, who may have been the "suborned informer" mentioned in Sonnet cxxv) and to reveal them at the right time for the discrediting of Catholics. The outcome of their "lawful espials", as Polonius calls them (III i.32), is the nunnery scene Polonius stage-manages between Hamlet and Ophelia while he and Claudius are eavesdropping on them from behind the arras. Polonius expects that in this way they will reveal their secret love for each other, but Claudius is not so easily convinced. Rather, what he catches of their conversation confirms him in his opinion that Hamlet is dangerous both to himself and to the state of Denmark, and so he must be put to silence.

Not that Hamlet is content to remain a passive victim of their plots against him and his inner mind. He is also actively intent on catching "the conscience of the king" (II ii.642), in order to find out how far he can rely on the ghost's word before carrying out his revenge. So while they are spying on him, he is in turn spying on them. This is what we also find in Elizabethan England, with the Jesuit Robert Persons organizing his own form of counterespionage, or "intelligence", through fellow Jesuits at work in England, such as Anthony Rivers, and trusted laymen in the Low Countries, such as Richard Verstegan, probably the author of an exposé of Burghley entitled *A Declaration of the True Causes* (1592). Most of his spying Hamlet seems to do for himself, as when he evidently (according to the probable theory of J. D. Wilson) overhears the plot of Polonius with Claudius to "loose my daughter to him" (II ii.162). This may explain why Hamlet goes on to call the old man a "fishmonger", or whoremaster (II ii.174), and why he behaves so rudely to Ophelia in the nunnery scene, knowing that her father and Claudius are hiding behind the arras (III i.135). He speaks of yet another source of intelligence when, to the king's conditional "If thou knew'st our purposes", he makes the cryptic reply, "I see a cherub that sees them" (IV iii.51). As for the outcome of his plot against the king, it comes to a climax with his play-within-the-play. Then Hamlet is overjoyed at the terrified reaction of Claudius in hastening from the room and calling for "lights" (III ii.286). For him it is sure proof both of the king's guilt and of the ghost's words, not to mention the Catholic doctrine of purgatory. All the same, he isn't ready to take his revenge on Claudius when he comes upon his enemy at prayer. For then it seems as if Claudius is purging his soul and repenting of his sin—though ineffectually, as he realizes (according to the teaching of St. Ignatius, in his meditation on "The Three Classes of Men") that he cannot genuinely repent so long as he retains his attachment to the things for which he committed his sin, "my crown, mine own ambition, and my queen" (III iii.55). Rather, Hamlet prefers to go on and take revenge both in words on his poor mother, when she turns out to be more truly repentant than his uncle, and in deeds on the old councillor who, more than Claudius, "popp'd in between the election and my hopes" (V ii.65). He may say over the corpse of Polonius, "I took thee for thy better", but he must have known that it could be none other than Polonius (III iv.32).

Meanwhile, we may find a sure proof of Hamlet's recusancy in his central soliloquy, opening with the famous dilemma, "To be, or not to be" (III i.56). On first hearing, the speech seems to have nothing to do with the play, and it might easily be omitted by an impatient producer in order to get on with the main action. The content of Hamlet's words—for all their seeming anguish as a dramatic expression of what Shakespeare says in his own voice in Sonnet lxvi, "Tir'd with all these, for restful death I cry . . ."—bears little relation to anything we have so far witnessed or heard in the play, in contrast to his first soliloquy, which is full of such reference (I ii.129). Rather, we may find the anguish of Hamlet proceeding straight from the Book of Job, as if he has just been reading this book on entering the lobby. Or rather, it is perhaps because he derives his reflections from that book in order to deceive the "lawful espials" whom he knows to be hiding behind the arras. Thus he is spying on his spies. He is having "the enginer hoist with his own petar" (III iv.206). For all that, we may also recognize an inner layer of meaning in his soliloquy with reference not just to the limited context of the play in an imaginary

Denmark, but to its wider context in Elizabethan England. For who in Elizabethan England could utter the words "To be, or not to be" with more urgent meaning than the persecuted recusants, not least those desperate young men, many of them Shakespeare's own cousins on his mother's side, such as Robert Catesby, son of that Sir William at whose Warwickshire home Campion had found hospitality in the summer of 1580 and handed to John Shakespeare his copy of Borromeo's Spiritual Testament? For them above all "to be" meant "to suffer the slings and arrows of outrageous fortune", that is, to go on enduring the outrageous persecution inflicted on them by the queen and her cruel ministers, the two Cecils, father and son. For them it increasingly came to seem as if the only way out of their sufferings was "to take arms", namely to engage in plots against the queen and her government, which soon came to the notice of government spies, if not actively fostered by them, and so "not to be", to die in the process. Robert Catesby in particular was such a young man—though not so young, being in his late thirties—who from assisting Essex in his ill-fated rebellion of 1601 went on to become ringleader of the Gunpowder Plot of 1605. For Hamlet, however, less impulsive and more given to brooding than Catesby, there remained the insoluble dilemma between "enterprise" ("Do something!") and "conscience" ("Don't do anything!"), both of them keywords for the recusants of those days.

Now we may turn from Hamlet, with all his problems, to the tragedy of poor Ophelia. Now we are increasingly shown how that tragedy is being inflicted on her, first with her father's strict injunction to have no further dealings with Hamlet, then with Hamlet's strange and sudden appearance in her room, then with his inexcusably rude behaviour to her both in the nunnery scene and during the play-within-the-play, and finally with the impulsive revenge he takes on her father. It all culminates in Act IV, during Hamlet's absence from Denmark on his way to England, with her pitiful madness. This is, moreover, what prompts her brother, Laertes, newly come from Paris, to seek his revenge on Hamlet—in much the same spirit as Tybalt sought his revenge on Romeo. At this point, we may note a movement of mind in Ophelia strangely parallel with that in Hamlet. In Hamlet we noted a change from his adolescent indoctrination in the teachings of Luther at Wittenberg to a new appreciation of his Catholic past in a revived memory of the good old days associated with his deceased father, and even an aggressive, recusant attitude of opposition to the new regime in Denmark-England. In the same way, we may note a similar change in Ophelia from the distinctively Puritan family portrayed in the third scene—in which they all, brother to sister and sister to brother, then father to both son and daughter, address words of moral advice and exhortation to one another—to a reversion in the girl's mind to memories of a Catholic girlhood. That was a time when it was still customary for people to go on pilgrimage to such shrines as Our Lady of Walsingham and St. James of Compostela and to pray for the dead, or at least when those pious customs were still recent memories. This is what we may notice in the snatches of song chanted by the mad Ophelia, in which she asks, "How should I your true love know/ from another one?" and then answers, in words referring to pilgrims, "By his cockle hat and staff/ and his sandal shoon" (IV v.23ff). Then in her further ravings about her true love, in whom memories of her dead father and her absent lover are strangely intermingled, she prays, "God ha' mercy on his soul! And of all Christian souls, I pray God!" (IV v.198). Such prayers we also find on the lips of old Gobbo in *The Merchant of Venice* (II ii.78), of the Nurse in *Romeo and Juliet* (I iii.18, 39), and of the grave-diggers later in *Hamlet* (V i.146). What they all have in common is that they are disregarded for their age or folly or sex or occupation by those citizens of an enlightened country who have adapted themselves to the fashion of a new world—such as Lord Fitzwater in *Richard II*, who readily switches his allegiance from the former King Richard to the new King Henry, declaring his intention "to thrive in this new world" (IV i.78).

Now what, we may ask, is the effect of this change in Ophelia, bringing about her tragic death by drowning and her burial in the churchyard, on the mind of Hamlet, when he returns to Denmark and finds himself in the churchyard where her funeral is taking place? At first, it is for him just a funeral, prompting him to make general reflections on the vanity of human wishes—till he suddenly realizes whom it is all for. "What!" he exclaims, "the fair Ophelia?" (V i.264)—when we might have expected him to say, "the poor Ophelia". He might also have reflected, if he had any conscience, that this must be the result of his cruel treatment of her. For all his pride in himself and his imagined superiority over others, he has been nothing but a fool!—and that not least when he roughly told Ophelia, "I loved you not!" (III i.122). Then he was not only a liar but a villain as well, to use a poor lady so. Then, so far from belonging to the old age, when courtesy was prized as a virtue and respect was paid to all ladies, he came to learn both from his mother and his lover (as he thought) the frailty of woman—and of man as well. Then he was taken in by the heresy of Luther, which he had learnt at Wittenberg, and from which he now has to purify himself at the grave of Ophelia. In him we now recognize a new, reborn Hamlet, as a result both of his experiences at sea on his way to England, enabling him to return to Denmark, and of his further experience beside and even within the grave of Ophelia. And at last he is led to make his belated profession of love, "I lov'd Ophelia!" (V i.291).

Now in conversation with Horatio Hamlet professes a new belief in divine providence, not just in general over the whole world but in particular over each individual. So he speaks of "a divinity that shapes our ends,/ rough-hew them how we will" (V ii.10). He himself has shown how adept he is at rough-hewing, making a mess of everything he turns his hand to, and it seems as if only when he turns his mind away from himself and his particular aims is he able to achieve anything. Again, he speaks of "heaven" as being "ordinant" in arranging for him to have his father's signet ring in his purse at just the right moment for him to escape from his prison ship and to make his way back to Denmark. Lastly, and most impressively, he echoes the very words of Jesus in his remark, "There's a special providence in the fall of a sparrow" (V ii.232, Matt. x.29). Moreover, in the oddly repetitious words that follow, "If it be now, 'tis not to come . . ."—words that no commentator has satisfactorily explained—Hamlet half quotes a passage from St. Augustine's commentary on Psalm 95(96), "He will come, whether we like it or not. The fact that he has not come yet is no reason to think that he will not come. He will come, but when it will be you do not know. If he finds you ready, it is no disadvantage that you do not know." His famous conclusion is, therefore, "The readiness is all." (V ii.236). From then onwards, instead of seeking to control the course of events any more, he allows them to control him, in the belief that somehow behind them is the guiding hand of that "greater power than we can contradict" mentioned by the friar in *Romeo and Juliet* (V iii.153). And so

Hamlet dies, after having involved in his death almost everyone else on the stage, while uttering the uncharacteristic words, "The rest is silence" (V ii.372).

Still, we may ask, echoing Kent's question, "Is this the promised end?" (*King Lear* V iii.265). Is this the outcome imposed on Hamlet's conscience by a seemingly divine command? After all, what kind of being was the ghost? Was he a ghost from purgatory, according to Catholic teaching? Or was he a devil from hell, sent to abuse and damn Hamlet, according to Protestant teaching? Or was he perhaps a pagan ghost, rising out of the revenge plays of Seneca? We may never know. Perhaps the dramatist himself was not particularly interested in deciding the question, while yet contriving to suggest all these possibilities, as if playing cat and mouse with his critics. But we do have the silent end of the young prince, uttered in words that are somehow parallel to Christ's dying words on the cross, "Father, into your hands I commend my spirit" (Luke xxiii.46). This is what elicits from the mouth of the otherwise sceptical yet stoic Horatio the liturgical prayer, "Goodnight, sweet prince,/ and flights of angels sing thee to thy rest" (V ii.373). It is a transparent echo of the old Gregorian antiphon, to be sung while the coffin is borne to the grave, *"In paradisum deducant te angeli"*—May the angels escort you to paradise. Such was also, it may be added, the dying prayer of the Earl of Essex at his execution in 1601: "Send thy blessed angels which may receive my soul and convey it to thy joys in heaven."

Finally, before the silence of Hamlet descends upon the stage, there remains his last will and testament, which he has entrusted to his faithful friend Horatio as executor, saying, "Report me and my cause aright" (V ii.353). Why, we may ask, does Hamlet show such concern at the end, mystifying all those who, like T. S. Eliot, are always looking for an "objective correlative" within the limits of the play? Within the play the only satisfaction of this concern is to be found in the unsatisfactory generalities of Horatio's concluding words "to the yet unknowing world" (V ii.393). He doesn't really say anything that satisfies us, or that might have satisfied his departed friend. Only outside the play can this concern, like so much else in this baffling play, be satisfied in terms of that religious background which, more than in any other of Shakespeare's plays apart from *King Lear*, is so abundantly implied in it. As for Hamlet's particular concern about his "wounded name" (V ii.358), where is it more abundantly to be found if not in the recusant cause of the dying Elizabethan age—a cause that seems to have been dying with the age? Consider all that Sir William Cecil, Lord Burghley (or Polonius), had done from the moment he arranged for the smooth accession of Elizabeth I to the throne in 1558 till the time of his death in 1598—a full forty years—to ensure the triumph of the Protestant cause. Then consider all he had done with this end in view, first to suppress, then to persecute the Catholic faith of his own fathers, to torment and torture on the rack—supervised by himself in the Tower of London—those priests and laymen who had the misfortune to fall into his hands, to spread disinformation and lies not only in his own official documents and proclamations but also in the writings he persuaded willing Puritans to publish under their own names or to translate from the French, to spawn an unceasing succession of plots as planned by Catholics and especially Jesuits, when they were really the devices of his own spies and agents provocateurs. Considering all this, of which the dramatist was fully cognizant, no wonder the Catholic recusants, who had somehow managed to survive in their thousands and ten thousands, were concerned, like Hamlet in his dying moments, about their "wounded name"! But then, as if all this were not enough, hardly had the old Burghley died than his cunning, crook-backed son Sir Robert Cecil, like Don John and Iago combined, took over from where his father had left off, and he so arranged the accession of the Stuart King James VI of Scotland to the English throne that all the new monarch's assurances of toleration to the Catholics were thrown to the winds. Then a new master plot, well worthy of the father's ingenuity in such proceedings from the Ridolphi Plot onwards, came to be hatched by the son, with the collaboration of desperate fools such as Robert Catesby, who had already implicated themselves in the Essex rebellion and now lent themselves as convenient objects of blackmail. This new plot was now foisted as before upon the Catholics, as it were rubbing salt on their wounded name and leaving it to fester for subsequent time with the annual commemoration of Guy Fawkes Day on the fifth of November. The outcome today is that the Elizabethan myth is flourishing as never before, not only among the common people, who are easily entertained by movies celebrating the myth, but even in the academic world of Elizabethan historians such as A. L. Rowse and of Shakespeare scholars such as Harold Bloom, who ought to know better. And what is even worse, the very play of *Hamlet*, with its unfortunate playwright, is drawn into the myth, and his true genius is lost from sight.

Troilus and Cressida

What on earth, we may wonder, could have induced Shakespeare, so fresh from composing and producing his masterpiece of *Hamlet*, to prostitute his mature genius on the composition of so evidently inferior a play as *Troilus and Cressida*? Even in its own age we have no clear evidence of any performance of it on the stage, though some scholars conjecture it was written for performance at one of the inns of court for an audience of lawyers and legal students. On this point we have the strange contradiction in the quarto of 1609, with two title pages that seem to cancel out each other. Whereas one proclaims "The History of Troilus and Cressida, as it was acted by the King's Majesty's servants"—or the King's Men, as Shakespeare's former company of the Chamberlain's Men had come to be known since the accession of King James I in 1603; the other omits all mention of its having been acted, but adds a preface "To the reader", introducing it as "a new play never staled with the stage" (that is, never yet acted) and implying that it is rather to be read and enjoyed as a comedy, or what Ben Jonson would have termed a "comical satire". There is no doubt a bewildering variety of genre in the play, including the historical background of the Trojan War, with a strong comic element featuring the bitter fool Thersites and a tragic ending both for Troilus in his disillusionment with Cressida and for Hector when he is surprised and killed by the trickery of Achilles. But to justify all this variety there is, alas, no unity. There is no one viewpoint, whether religious or recusant, to draw the various themes or plots of the play together.

On the surface of the play, the main themes that stand out are those of love and war, which might perhaps be put together in terms of the Beatles' saying "Make love, not war." Everything is seen, at least on the Greek side, through the sarcastic, disillusioned eyes of the fool Thersites, who is yet something of a philosopher, enjoying much the same function in this play as Apemantus in *Timon of Athens*. As he sees things, all around him is nothing but "war and lechery" (II iii.82). Nor can we help agreeing with him. By his means Shakespeare seems to be setting out to rival his friend Ben Jonson's vaunted "comedy of humours", and it has been conjectured that this play is the dramatist's response to a challenge from his friend, who also happened to be an avowed recusant at the time. It is also commonly considered to be the "purge" Shakespeare is said, in the contemporary student play *The Return from Parnassus* (Part II, 1601–2), to have administered to Jonson.

The love between Troilus and Cressida is shown from the outset, unlike that of Romeo and Juliet, as distempered—on the side both of Troilus, infected as he is with a fever of lust or lechery, prompting him to desire a merely sexual union with Cressida, with no hint of marriage, and of Cressida, characterized as she is with a coquettishness that stimulates both Troilus, so long as she remains in Troy, and Diomede, as soon as she crosses over to the Greek camp. Seen through the disillusioned but perceptive eyes of Ulysses, she is but a sluttish "daughter of the game" (IV v.63). So her falsehood, as she has all unthinkingly predicted, passes into a proverb, rather than the truth asserted of himself by Troilus (III ii.198). And so, when Troilus on his visit to the Greek camp finds her dallying with Diomede, he is disillusioned in her and in all created order—even more profoundly than Hamlet in the men and women around him. Such is the satirical, if not tragic, climax of the play, when Troilus exclaims, "The bonds of heaven are slipp'd, dissolv'd and loos'd" (V ii.153). In such a context there can be no worthy mention of "grace", least of all concerning such a heroine as Cressida. Instead, the only use of the word is put into the mouth of an ignorant servant, in addressing the bawdy uncle Pandarus with this title, which he immediately disclaims as the preserve of princes. All he claims are the titles of "honour" and "lordship", though they are for him but names, not signifying any reality. It is indeed this absence of any real "grace" from the play that sets it apart from almost all other plays by Shakespeare—as a play he ought to be ashamed of having written.

It is also for this reason that, in the total impression made by the play, the romantic plot of these would-be lovers takes second place to the background of war and/or peace between the Trojans and the Greeks. In this background what the dramatist depicts is undermined by the absence of order on either side. On the Trojan side, there is neither order nor reason in the love between Troilus and Cressida, as she herself confesses: "To be wise and love/ exceeds man's might. That dwells with gods above."(III ii.163–164) So, too, in the council of war among the Trojan princes, Hector, who at first stands for the ideal of reason and natural law, soon yields to the unreasonable importunity of Troilus, who maintains that "reason and respect/ make livers pale and lustihood deject" (II ii.49). So he allows the futile war on behalf of the whore Helen to go on, and in so doing he effectively signs his own death warrant. On the Greek side, with the foul-mouthed Thersites standing for freedom of speech in a new, democratic society, there is no order or degree among the leaders, least of all between the general Agamemnon and the hero Achilles. It is only the wily politician Ulysses who in the Greek council of war upholds the ideal with his famous "degree" speech (I iii.83ff). Here he presents in a poetical or rhetorical manner ideas which Shakespeare had already presented in his unprinted, unperformed play of *Sir Thomas More* (or rather, in his generally recognized contribution of 147 lines to that play), in More's speech to the rioting apprentices of London. For the statement of this ideal the dramatist seems to have drawn on two major Anglican sources, the homily "On Order and Obedience" from the first book of Homilies (1547) and the first book of Richard Hooker's *Laws of Ecclesiastical Polity* (1594), which are rightly regarded as expressing the thought of the Anglican establishment in the Elizabethan age. For this reason, some are led to see this play as more Protestant (in the Anglican sense of the word) than Papist or Puritan. Yet it may be observed that Shakespeare subverts this thought by placing the words in the mouth of a politician such as Ulysses. At the same time, we may recall that he rarely uses such words as "policy" and "politician" in a favourable sense, but he more often than not attaches to them the epithet "vile". It is also in the mouth of Ulysses, we may note, that he places the ironical speech on the mystery "in the soul of state", which "hath an operation more divine/ than breath or pen can give expressure to" (III iii.202). Here we may suspect that the mystery in question is more diabolic than divine, especially in view of what Ulysses has just said about "the providence that's in a watchful state", which is almost diametrically opposite to that "divinity" and "providence" emphasized by Hamlet in his renewed frame of mind (V ii.10, 233). Here we may rather recognize an allusion to the elaborate spy-system set up by Burghley and Walsingham from the time of the Ridolphi Plot and chiefly used by them against what they gave out to be the threat from seminary priests and Jesuits to the security of the realm.

Here, from a recusant viewpoint, is perhaps the only significant reference in the play to the situation of English Catholics. Otherwise, we may point to another of Shakespeare's flippant allusions to the torture of the rack in the second scene. When Pandarus begins, "I must needs confess," he is jestingly interrupted by his niece, "Without the rack," and he goes on to cap her jest by adding, "And she takes upon her to *spy* a white hair upon his chin" (I ii.149ff). It is all very frivolous and inconsequential, with little bearing on the reality of recusant life, but it is all too typical of the generally satirical tone of the play. Hence, if *Troilus and Cressida* is to be counted as the second of Shakespeare's problem plays in succession to *Hamlet*, it is mainly because of this deep undercurrent of irony and satire as part of that mood of *fin de siècle* which prevailed no less among Anglicans than Catholics towards the end of the Elizabethan era. Only, whereas there is something more positive in *Hamlet*, what we find in *Troilus and Cressida* is almost entirely negative. It is noted in general that, if the Trojans with their mediaeval ideals of chivalry and honour look back to the Catholic past of England, the Greeks with their new-fangled ideas stand for the present Anglican establishment, which is more political (in a Machiavellian sense) than religious. Then we may further imagine the dramatist himself looking equally askance on both sides and exclaiming, in Mercutio's exasperated words, "A plague o' both your houses!" (*Romeo and Juliet*, III i.105). Only, in view of the inferior quality of the play, we may also imagine not a few of its first spectators (if there were any) leaving the theatre with the similar exclamation, "A plague on your play!" And Shakespeare would have deserved it!

chapter 9 The Religious Problem in the Problem Comedies

Measure for Measure

FOR ALL THE uniqueness of *Measure for Measure* among Shakespeare's plays, and its close association with the other problem comedy of *All's Well That Ends Well*, the play is also to be paired at a deeper, religious level with *The Merchant of Venice*, both for its moving appeal for "the quality of mercy" and for the implicit contrast between Papist and Puritan in the light of its religious background. To many this contrast as seen only in *The Merchant of Venice*, in the persons of Portia and Shylock, may have seemed unconvincing, seeing that Shylock is so obviously a Jew. But when we find the same contrast presented more openly in Isabella and Angelo as Papist and Puritan, the former interpretation may carry more conviction. In the former play, in the 1590s, the dramatist had to be more cautious in presenting his plea for mercy (on the persecuted Catholics), and then the Puritan persecutor might appear in the guise of a Jewish money-lender (like many of the Puritan city merchants), while Portia could be portrayed in Catholic terms as an aristocratic lady of the Italian Renaissance. But now, at the beginning of the new reign of James I, presumably in 1604, the dramatist may have felt free to dispense with disguise and to offer a comedy that has been described as the most Catholic of all his plays. Here in *Measure for Measure* his plea is still for mercy, and the arguments Isabella puts forward before Angelo are much the same as those Portia uses in dealing with Shylock. Only here Isabella, unlike her prototype in all the dramatic sources, is characterized as a "novice" (or postulant) intending to enter "the cloister" of "the sisterhood, the votarists of Saint Clare", the female branch of the Franciscan order (I ii.188, I iv.5). Her very name seems to have been chosen by the dramatist from that of a possible relative and former prioress of Wroxhall Abbey in the Forest of Arden, Isabella Shakespeare. As for Angelo, though the setting of the play is Catholic Vienna, he is described by the duke as "precise", which was in Elizabethan English all but a technical term for the Puritans, "the precise brethren" (I iii.50). Moreover, the unique use of "prenzie" by Claudio and Isabella with reference to Angelo in Act III may be a corruption (in a notably corrupt text) for "precise" (III i.92, 95). Then again, Angelo's excessively strict interpretation of the old law in Vienna is reminiscent of the Puritan Thomas Cartwright's insistence on the need of applying the Mosaic law on adultery to the contemporary Christian world, adding—in defiance to his Anglican adversary John Whitgift—"If this be bloody and extreme, I am content to be so counted with the Holy Ghost" (*Second Reply,* 1575).

Meanwhile, behind Lord Angelo, who has been granted ducal power in Vienna by the duke himself before his departure (like the king in Christ's parable, Luke xix.12), there is the shadowy figure of the same duke, who has secretly returned to Vienna in the disguise of a Franciscan friar named Lodowick. It is his aim, as he admits, to spy on the behaviour of his deputy so as to see, "if power change purpose, what our seemers be" (I iii.54). The duke, therefore, as if in the footsteps of Isabella, applies to a Franciscan convent for authorized acceptance, "as 'twere a brother of your order" in the appropriate "habit" for bearing himself "like a true friar" (I iii.44ff). This request of his is granted without difficulty. Subsequently, however, he tells an apparent lie when introducing himself as "a brother/ of gracious order, late come from the See,/ in special business from his Holiness" (III ii.237). He even claims, without having been ordained priest and received the necessary faculties, to have heard the confession of Mariana: "I have confessed her, and I know her virtue." (V i.29) Strictly speaking, what he says is either a lie or, if true, a sacrilege. Yet few scholars have noticed the lie—and perhaps the dramatist expected few of the spectators to notice it either. But it has troubled the American scholar R. M. Frye, who says in his *Shakespeare and Christian Doctrine* (1963) that this was no doubt the reason why the Jesuit William Sankey, of the English College at Valladolid, had the whole play deleted from his copy of the Second Folio of 1632, before letting his students in the mid-seventeenth century make use of it. Yet the lie alone might easily have been deleted, as it occupies no more than a line at the end of the play, nor does it serve any integral function in it. Rather, the Jesuit was probably considering the impact of the more obviously bawdy element in the play on the impressionable minds of young boys. Anyhow, apart from this minor item in the characterization of the duke-turned-friar, one may be sure that the Catholic spectators or readers would have had no difficulty in accepting his disguise with a willing "suspension of disbelief". After all, they may have considered how well the would-be friar goes about his charitable task of visiting "the afflicted spirits here in the prison" (II iii.4, cf. I Pet. iii.19).

There is one more point to be noted about Duke Vincentio in his disguise as Friar Lodowick. In the play he appears as a Franciscan friar—just as Shakespeare seems to have preferred his Catholic priests to appear as friars, perhaps to make their religious identity quite clear. On the other hand, considering that few, if any, of the Catholic priests in Elizabethan England were Franciscans, but the religious priests were almost all of them Jesuits, and considering that the Jesuits were frequently described by their enemies as "friars", in a pejorative sense, it is not unlikely that the dramatist was looking, beyond Friar Lodowick in Vienna, to Jesuit priests working in London, many of whom from Campion onwards may have been personally known to him. This seems all the more likely in view of Lucio's slanderous description of him as "the old fantastical duke of dark corners" (IV iii.167), which echoes Burghley's denunciation of the "secret lurkings" of the Jesuits and seminary priests in England in his *Execution of Justice in England* (1583). Then, if any individual Jesuit is to be named, it might well be Robert Persons, though he had left England at the time of Campion's arrest in 1581, never to return. Or again, it might be the elusive Jesuit missionary in England, John Gerard. Both of them soon realized that one of the best, even safest, methods of missionary work was that of visiting prisons, where they might meet not a few imprisoned Catholics and even offer Mass for them inside the prison—even with the connivance of the jailer. So the white lies told by the duke as friar, such as that of his having heard Mariana's confession, may be explained by the probability that in his characterization of Vincentio the dramatist is thinking of a Jesuit priest.

As for the couple of lovers for whose welfare the duke-friar is principally concerned, Claudio and Juliet, there are two points of recusant interest worthy of mention. One is that Claudio is the first victim of Lord Angelo under the old law (= the Old Law of Moses) now being rigidly enforced by the new (= Puritan) judge. He has been caught *in flagrante delictu*, in the very act of fornication with his lover Juliet. Only, it turns out that his is no ordinary sin of fornication but the consummation of what he calls "a true contract" (I ii.155), or what is also called "a pre-contract" (IV i.73), by which Juliet is, he affirms, "fast my wife,/ save that we do the denunciation lack/ of outward order" (I ii.157). His situation is all the more interesting as it seems to echo that of the young William Shakespeare with his wife Anne. As noted above, it is likely that months before his application at the diocesan registry of Worcester for exemption from the customary marriage banns in view of the impending season of Advent 1582, when the name of Anne is given in the register as Whateley (for Hathaway) and assigned to the parish of Temple Grafton, Shakespeare had secretly married her at the village church in a Catholic ceremony performed by the old Marian priest Sir John Frith without ecclesiastical approval. So the dramatist could well sympathize with Claudio's predicament, while seeing in Juliet a type of Anne.

The other point is the strange procession of three couples joined in holy matrimony by three friars in three different plays. First, in *Romeo and Juliet* the lovers' hands are joined by Friar Laurence in a secret ceremony (II vi.35). Secondly, in *Much Ado About Nothing* Claudio and Hero are happily united by Friar Francis, in spite of the previous disruption of their wedding (IV i). Thirdly, in this play the pre-contract of Claudio and Juliet, coming as though in the conclusion of a syllogism of names—Romeo-Juliet, Claudio-Hero, and

Claudio-Juliet—is not indeed performed but rescued by Friar Lodowick. Here, too, the friar repeats the insistence of his fraternal predecessors on the need to "be absolute for death" (III i.5), as the way to "a better life, past fearing death" (V i.398), and Claudio for a time readily accepts his advice, by "seeking death" to "find life" (III i.43). In this advice, moreover, the dramatist echoes, as noted above, the similar paradoxical teaching of the Jesuit poet-martyr Robert Southwell.

To return now to Isabella, who is all too often described by critics as a "nun", though she hasn't yet taken the veil, it has to be emphasized that she is rather a postulant for the convent, or (in Lucio's words) "a novice of this place", and she first makes her appearance (in Claudio's words) on the day she "should the cloister enter" (I ii.188). That leaves her free to go with Lucio and do her best to save her brother. Unlike Ophelia in *Hamlet* or Cressida in *Troilus and Cressida*, she is regarded by Lucio, for all his depravity, as "a thing ensky'd and sainted" (I iv.34), and as possessed of "moving graces" (II ii.36), so as to sway the mind of Angelo from his intent to pass the death sentence on Claudio. Ironically, her "moving graces" have the effect of moving him in another sense, to sexual lust, as he himself admits on realizing the nature of his feelings for her, "O cunning enemy, that, to catch a saint," meaning his Puritan self, "with saints," such as the Catholic Isabella, "dost bait thy hook!" (II ii.181). To this temptation in himself Angelo freely yields, but Isabella refuses to accept his ensuing proposal or to gratify his lust, though in so doing she might save her brother's life. When she goes on to visit her brother in prison and informs him of the judge's offer, he pleads with her to accept it and save him. Then, what is for all too many critics the crux of the play, causing them to lose all sympathy for her and even to equate her with Angelo as partners in hypocrisy, she turns on him with the indignant exclamations: "O you beast! O faithless coward! O dishonest wretch!" (III i.134). Thus she follows her previously stated principle, "More than our brother is our chastity." (II iv.186) What her unfriendly critics fail to realize is that, from her point of view, which is presumably that of the Catholic dramatist, she is being asked by her brother for the exchange of her eternal life for his temporal life. For in yielding to Angelo's demand to commit the sexual sin of fornication with him she would, according to Catholic teaching—as repeated by St. Ignatius in his meditation on Hell in the first week of the *Spiritual Exercises*—be committing a mortal sin, and death in a state of unrepented mortal sin would consign the sinner to eternal punishment in hell. No wonder if Isabella, as an innocent girl on finding herself betrayed in such a matter by her own brother, loses her temper and abuses him with such vehement words. But to equate such a loss of temper with the cold, calculating solicitation of her by Angelo, who is shown to be all the more heartless by his intention not to keep his part of the bargain by sparing Claudio, reveals a strange lack of moral sense or sense of proportion.

Nor is that all. Once the unfriendly critics begin to shower their moral disapproval on the head of poor Isabella, they turn their evil eye to one after another of her supposed faults. They discern a contradiction between her appeal to Angelo for mercy on her brother and her subsequent insistence on "justice, justice, justice, justice" against Angelo (V i.25). What they fail to recognize is an important distinction between two kinds of justice. One is the legal justice on which Angelo, like Shylock before him, bases his position and which Isabella, like Portia before her, admits in her words, "O just but severe law!" (II ii.41). The other is the human justice for which Isabella, as victim with Mariana, pleads before the duke—the justice of which Christ himself speaks in the Sermon on the Mount (the very sermon from which the title of this play is taken), "Blessed are those who hunger and thirst for justice." (Matt. v.6, vii.2—only in Rheims among all Tudor versions). On the other hand, once the position of Angelo is reversed and his sin brought to light, Isabella also changes her plea for justice (while his sin remains hidden) to one for mercy (now he repents of his sin). This is surely the highlight of the play! Then, in spite of all that her critics say against her, Isabella stands out as an incarnation of mercy, personified as one of the four daughters of God, according to the mediaeval interpretation of Psalm 84(85), and dramatized in the fifteenth-century morality play *The Castle of Perseverance.*

Yet another character who calls for consideration in this play is Isabella's partner in distress, Mariana of the Moated Grange. She, too, like Juliet, has entered into a pre-contract of marriage. In her case it is with Angelo, but, though he should be her husband, he had reneged on his promise on account of a sudden loss of the money she needed for her dowry. It is because of this existing relationship that the duke-friar regards himself as lawfully entitled to arrange the bed-trick by which Isabella may consent to Angelo's unlawful offer, while Mariana may take her place in the darkness of the night. This plan is justified by the friar in the strange ditty he sings, as it were in between two parts of the play, "So disguise shall, by the disguis'd,/ pay with falsehood false exacting" (III ii.302). Here we may note another indication of his Jesuitry, in the way he seems to excuse his plan by the notorious Jesuit doctrine of equivocation. This doctrine had already become a topic of comment at the time of Robert

Southwell's trial in 1595, and it was shortly to be even more strongly emphasized at the trial of the Jesuit superior Henry Garnet in 1606, besides being subsequently defended in print by Robert Persons in his *Treatise Tending to Mitigation* in 1607. As for the Moated Grange, so oddly identified as the lonely dwelling of Mariana, it is precisely described, without any dramatic necessity, as having "a garden circummur'd with brick,/ whose western side is with a vineyard back'd,/ and to that vineyard is a planched gate" (IV i.30ff). The very place is not unlike the moated manor of Baddesley Clinton, a noted stronghold of Catholic recusants in the Forest of Arden not far from Wroxhall Abbey, and a common resort of Jesuits as mentioned in the autobiography of yet another noted Jesuit of the time, John Gerard.

Finally, we may return to the duke and his concluding offer of his hand in marriage to Isabella. To unfriendly critics this is again suggestive of the common jest about friars seeking sexual satisfaction with nuns—a jest that was notoriously exemplified in the case of the ex-friar Martin Luther and the ex-nun Katharina von Bora in 1525, much to the scandal of Sir Thomas More, who keeps returning to it in his works of controversy. At the end of the final scene we may note how the duke has to repeat his proposal to Isabella twice, without eliciting any reply from her. This leaves producers with the dilemma how to get the heroine to react on the stage, whether to imply acceptance or rejection. To this problem we may offer two solutions, according to the two levels of meaning in the play, while we may ignore the modern preference for a negative solution. On the surface of the play, as we expect a romantic comedy however problematic to have a happy ending in marriage, we may prefer Isabella, who hasn't yet entered the cloister or taken the religious vow of chastity, to accept the duke's offer with grace. At a deeper level, however, considering the moral and biblical implication in the play's title, the duke's identification in Angelo's repentant eyes with "power divine" (V i.370), and the above-mentioned incarnation of mercy in Isabella, we may recognize—in the teeth of the modern dogma of naturalism—a symbolic marriage of Justice (in Duke Vincentio) and Mercy (in Isabella). For so we read in Psalm 84(85), as mentioned above, that "Mercy shall spring out of the earth", as the earth mother, and "Justice shall look down from heaven", as the heavenly Father.

All's Well That Ends Well

The dating of *All's Well That Ends Well* is one of the most problematic among Shakespeare's plays. It has variously been assigned to dates between 1598, when it is seen as appearing in Meres's *Palladis Tamia* under the puzzling title of *Love's Labour's Won* (though this is more probably identified, as noted above, with *The Taming of the Shrew*), and 1605, when James I had long since succeeded Elizabeth I on the throne of England. The latter date is commonly chosen by those who emphasize the similarity between this play and *Measure for Measure*, as both being problem plays turning upon a bed-trick and both introduced with proverbial titles. This has even come to seem the most probable in view of the medical and religious background of the play, which would place it not before but after *Measure for Measure*. This background appears, first, in the medical controversies raging in London between the followers of Galen and those of Paracelsus (including Shakespeare's own son-in-law Dr. John Hall), owing to the serious outbreak of the plague that delayed the coronation of James I for almost a year, and secondly, in the religious controversies raging on either side of the Straits of Dover between Catholics and Protestants, owing to reports of miracles worked through the intercession of Our Lady at her two shrines of Montaigu in Brabant and of Halle to the south of Brussels from 1604 onwards.

In particular, the religious controversy directs our attention to the modest heroine of the play, Helena. For all the emphasis on her virginal modesty at the beginning, she stands out for her positive personality in the course of the play—in much the same way as Isabella does in *Measure for Measure*, in contrast to the nonentity of poor Ophelia and the wanton vanity of Cressida. Helena it is who, armed with a precious remedy left her by her deceased medical father, Gerard de Narbon, follows her master, the young Bertram, Count of Rousillon, to Paris. There she cures the king of a disease that has been given up as incurable by the royal physicians, or "congregated college" of "learned doctors" (II i.119), all of them no doubt orthodox followers of Galen, in what is given out to be a notable miracle. On this outcome the courtier Lord Lafeu comments, "They say miracles are past, and we have our philosophical persons to make modern and familiar things supernatural and causeless . . . when we should submit ourselves to an unknown fear" (II iii.1ff). His words seem to echo what Hamlet has said to Horatio on the occasion of the ghost's appearance: "There are more things in heaven and earth, Horatio,/ than are dreamt of in your philosophy" (I v.166). They also more significantly echo what the Archbishop of Canterbury has said about the cessation of miracles in *Henry V* (I i.67), in accordance with the Anglican teaching against the Catholics, and with a probable pun on "persons" with "parsons". In the mind of the dramatist, moreover, the words have an evident application to the controversy set afoot by the miracles claimed to have been worked through Mary's intercession by Philip Numan, town-clerk of Brussels, in a detailed account of them in his *Histoire des Miracles* in 1604, translated into English by the secular priest Robert Chambers in 1606. The well-known Catholic humanist Justus Lipsius also lent his support to the cause with two Latin works on the miracles worked at each of the Marian shrines, at Halle in 1604 and at Montaigu in 1605. For the Catholics, in contrast to the Anglicans, these miracles constituted proof of that holiness which was held to be one of the four marks of the true Church of Christ, as previously set forth by Richard Bristow in his classic *Motives* (1574).

As for Helena, though her miracle in curing the French king is provided by the dramatist with a natural explanation, in terms of the recipe left her by her father, she is characterized in this play, even more than Isabella in *Measure for Measure*, with reference to Our Lady. It is partly for this reason that *All's Well* has been presented by R. G. Hunter in his *Shakespeare and the Comedy of Forgiveness* (1965) as less a problem play than a precursor of the final romances and connected with the mediaeval miracle plays of the Virgin. Thus Helena, on coming into the presence of the French king, speaks in terms of Mary's hymn of praise, the *Magnificat* (Luke i.46ff), when proclaiming in a strangely incantatory tone, "He that of greatest works is finisher/ oft does them by the weakest minister" (II i.139). She goes on to invoke "the great'st grace lending grace" (II i.163), prompting the king to respond, "Methinks in thee some blessed spirit doth speak/ his powerful sound within an organ weak" (II i.178). And so she works her miracle, which Lafeu describes as "a showing of a heavenly effect in an earthly actor" and "in a most weak and debile minister, great power, great transcendence" (II iii.29, 40), to the confounding of the "philosophical persons" of the Anglican controversialists. It is as if the humble person of Helena is drawn up into the heavenly radiance of the Virgin Mary. This identification is subsequently hinted at by her patroness, the Countess of Rousillon, in commenting on the graceless behaviour of her son in turning his back on his newly wedded wife, Helena. "He cannot thrive," she says, "unless her prayers, whom heaven delights to hear/ and loves to grant, reprieve him from the wrath/ of greatest justice" (III iii.26).

At the same time, we may note that Helena's name recalls that of the most popular pilgrim of the Middle Ages, St. Helena, mother to the emperor Constantine, who went in search of the site of the holy sepulchre of Christ in Jerusalem. Here, too, when Helena finds that her recalcitrant husband has deserted her on her wedding night for wars in Florence, she decides to follow him in the guise of a pilgrim, not to Jerusalem but to the shrine of "Saint Jaques le Grand" at Compostela in Spain (III v.36). It seems somewhat strange for her, geographically speaking, to make her way from Rousillon to Compostela via Florence. But it is in Florence that she partly attains the end of her pilgrimage by means of a bed-trick, on learning that Bertram has been courting one Diana, the chaste daughter of the widow at whose house she is staying. Then, like the duke in *Measure for Measure* with Isabella and Mariana, she persuades Diana to feign acceptance of Bertram's lecherous advances, while she herself, as another Mariana, virtuously serves as Diana's substitute. Thus she fulfils the seemingly impossible condition laid upon her by her husband. As for Diana, she justifies their plan in words that strangely echo those of the duke in *Measure for Measure*—words that may also be interpreted as justifying the Jesuit theory of equivocation: "Only in this disguise I think't no sin/ to cozen him that would unjustly win" (IV ii.75).

Turning now to Bertram: He comes to the dramatist not only out of Boccaccio's *Decameron* or Painter's *Palace of*

Pleasure (1566–67), two works commonly invoked as sources of the play, but also from Shakespeare's favourite parable of the Prodigal Son (Luke xv). His relationship with Parolles (whose name implies worthlessness in word and deed) may, therefore, be compared to that of Prince Hal with Falstaff, though as a Vice of Prodigality Parolles is hardly comparable to Falstaff. At the same time, we may note that Shakespeare may also have in mind his former patron, the young Earl of Southampton, who despite his Catholic birth and upbringing went on in the reign of James I to forsake his profession of Catholicism. Then in Bertram's mother, the Countess of Rousillon, we may notice a further resemblance to Southampton's mother, Mary Browne, the dowager countess, who is thought to have commissioned the first series of Shakespeare's sonnets, urging the young man to marry and beget an heir. Unlike the Countess of Rousillon, however, Mary Browne was not content to remain a widow, but went on to marry two more husbands. As for her son, the third earl, he seems to be reflected more than once in Bertram. First, when the latter says of the French king that he is "now in ward" to him (I i.5), this may also be said of Southampton, whose fervently Catholic father died when he was only eight, leaving him to the care of Lord Burghley, who had since 1561 been Master of the Court of Wards. For his noble charges Burghley ran an academy at Cecil House in London, and among them at different times were the Earls of Essex and Rutland as well as Southampton. It was one of his chief aims to indoctrinate them in sound Protestant principles, but they became restless under his too sedulous care, rather as we see Bertram restless under the king's supervision. Secondly, both Bertram and the young earl may be implied in the king's derogatory words about "younger spirits, whose apprehensive senses/ all but new things disdain" (I ii.59). At least, if the young earl is the young man of the sonnets, we may notice in them how he inclines his ear rather to the "new-found methods" and "compounds strange" of the rival poet than to the relatively simple sonnets sent him by Shakespeare (Sonnet lxxvi). Thirdly, Bertram's complaints at court, that "I am commanded here and kept a coil with/ 'too young' and 'the next year' and ''tis too early' " (II i.27), were precisely those of Southampton concerning the queen's excessive solicitude for him and her reluctance to let him take part with Essex on the latter's expeditions to Spain. Fourthly, when Bertram is appointed "general of our horse" by the Duke of Florence (III iii.1), this is the very appointment received by Southampton from Essex on their ill-fated expedition to Ireland in 1599.

Now, we may ask, considering that so much of *All's Well That Ends Well* is on the Papist side, even in the case of the prodigal Count of Rousillon, what room is left for the Puritans, who figure so largely in *Measure for Measure* in the person of Lord Angelo? Here the only mention of Puritans as contrasted with Papists comes from the mouth of the clown Lavache, only to incur the instant rebuke of the Countess as "a foul-mouthed and calumnious knave" (I iii.61). He has just drawn a comic contrast between "young Charbon the Puritan" and "old Poysam the Papist", implying that in those days the Puritans were mostly young and hot-blooded (like Laertes in *Hamlet*), whereas the Papists, who abstained from fish (French *poisson*) on Fridays, not only adhered to the "old faith" but also tended to belong to the older generation after long years of repression and persecution. He further remarks, "Howsome'er their hearts are severed in religion, their heads are both one" (I iii.58), with the implication that both are liable (like every other husband) to grow horns on their heads as cuckolds, and this it is that no doubt earns him the Countess's rebuke. All the same, he goes on to say, "Though honesty be no Puritan, yet it will do no hurt. It will wear the surplice of humility over the black gown of a big heart" (I iii.98)—with reference to the hypocritical pride for which the Puritans were often taxed in those days, particularly in consequence of the vestiarian controversy of the 1560s, which continued as a thorn of contention in the side of the Anglican Church till the end of Elizabeth's reign. Lavache's mention of a "black gown" is reminiscent of Feste's remark in *Twelfth Night* when, as Sir Topas the curate, he dons such a gown for the baiting of Malvolio, adding, "I would I were the first that ever dissembled in such a gown" (IV ii.6).

Finally, we may note the words of the French king, "Our rasher faults/ make trivial price of serious things we have" (V iii.60), as both referring to Bertram's lack of appreciation for his new wife, Helena, and recalling the similar words spoken by Friar Francis in *Much Ado About Nothing*: "What we have we prize not to the worth/ while we enjoy it" (IV i.220). In either case we may note the implication of the high value Catholic recusants set on the ministration of priests, in contrast to their easier going ways in former times, when there had been no problem or danger attending the practice of their religion. We may therefore conclude that these two problem comedies are close to each other not least in their more daring reference to Catholic allegiance than might have seemed prudent in the days of Queen Elizabeth.

chapter 10
The Tragedy of Recusancy

Othello

AN INTERESTING triangular relationship appears among Shakespeare's plays about this time. Between *Othello* and *Measure for Measure* there is a common source in Cinthio's *Hecatommithi* (1565?) and a common outlet of first performance early in the new reign, probably in 1604. Moreover, between *Measure for Measure* and the earlier *Merchant of Venice* there is, as noted above, a common plea for mercy put into the mouths of their respective heroines, Isabella and Portia, with strong biblical overtones. Then between *Othello* and *The Merchant of Venice* there is a common setting in Venice for much of the play, besides the title, and a common characterization of a noble Moor—if we may consider the Prince of Morocco, though but a minor character in the earlier play, as a preliminary sketch for Othello, the noble Moor of Venice who claims "to fetch my life and being/ from men of royal siege" (I ii.21). Many of these similarities, such as plot sources, settings, and dates of production, may appear to be merely superficial, but others are more fundamental, such as that "quality of mercy" emphasized by the two heroines Portia and Isabella. In *Othello*, too, we may expect to find a corresponding "quality" and to find it in the heroine. And so we do, in Desdemona, in the special form of her intercession for Cassio.

First, what we find in Desdemona as heroine, as in so many of Shakespeare's heroines, is the general quality of "grace", recalling the words of the angel Gabriel to the Virgin Mary (Luke i.28). In fact, this quality is expressed more clearly in *Othello* than in any other of Shakespeare's plays, especially in the greeting with which the gallant Cassio welcomes "the divine Desdemona" (II i.73) on her safe arrival in Cyprus: "Hail to thee, lady! And the grace of heaven,/ before, behind thee, and on every hand,/ enwheel thee round!" (II i.85). These words of his almost uncannily echo those of the angel, as given only in the Catholic Rheims version of 1582, which translates the Greek *kecharitomene* via the Latin Vulgate *gratia plena* as "full of grace"—whereas the two Protestant versions chiefly available to Shakespeare at the time were the Genevan "freely beloved" and the Bishops' "in high favour". The words of the Rheims version are "Hail, full of grace, Our Lord is with thee, blessed art thou among women." Moreover, the second part of this greeting, echoed by Elizabeth in Luke i.42, recurs in words uttered first by Roderigo to Iago about Desdemona, "She is full of most blessed condition" (II i.256), then by Iago himself when he urges Cassio to seek Desdemona's intercession, "She is of so free, so kind, so apt, so blessed a disposition" (II iii.328).

In this way, the general fulness of grace applied to her from the angelic salutation of the "Hail Mary" comes to take on the more specific function of intercessor or advocate of sinners, as emphasized in two other traditional prayers of the Catholic Church to Our Lady. One is the *Salve Regina* of the eleventh century, attributed to Hermann the Cripple, and the other, the *Memorare* of the twelfth century, attributed to St. Bernard. In the first of these prayers Mary is hailed as "mother of mercy" and "most gracious advocate", while in the second she is asked to "remember that it is a thing unheard of that anyone ever had recourse to thy protection, implored thy help, or sought thy intercession, and was left forsaken". This theme of intercession is also emphasized by Dante in the climax of his *Paradiso* (canto xxxiii), where the words are put into the mouth of St. Bernard and addressed to Mary herself. These words were subsequently translated into English by Chaucer and used in his Prologue to "The Second Nun's Tale" of *The Canterbury Tales*. This is also what Iago tells Cassio in his above-quoted praise of Desdemona for the purpose of tempting Cassio: "She holds it a vice in her goodness not to do more than she is requested." (II iii.329) In this he may be compared to the "cunning enemy" mentioned by Angelo in *Measure for Measure*, who "to catch a saint" like Desdemona baits his hook with her own sanctity (II ii.180). This is also what Desdemona herself goes on to tell Othello in undertaking to intercede for Cassio: "I wonder in my soul/ what you could ask me that I should deny" (III iii.68). And Othello confirms her assumption, saying, "I will deny thee nothing" (III iii.76).

On his side, Othello professes to speak the unvarnished truth to the senators of Venice in terms of the Catholic sacrament of confession, "as truly as to heaven/ I do confess the vices of my blood" (I iii.122). He then recalls his conversations with Desdemona, in which he speaks of the varied adventures of his past life in terms of a "pilgrimage" (I iii.153), again using the Catholic metaphor already noted in the words of Romeo and Bassanio. But once Iago's temptation begins to work on his mind, he compares the pain he feels to the torture of the rack, shouting at Iago on the latter's return, "Avaunt! Be gone! Thou hast set me on the rack!"

(III iii.336). In his lurid imagination he goes on to connect the missing handkerchief he gave Desdemona, and the confessions attributed to her by Iago, with the form of death awaiting so many convicted recusants: "To confess, and be hanged for his labour. First, to be hanged, and then to confess. I tremble at it" (IV i.38). He is still Catholic in his thought when he turns on Desdemona's handmaid Emilia and charges her, "You, mistress,/ that have the office opposite to St. Peter" (who is said to be in charge of the gate of heaven), "and keep the gate of hell" (IV ii.89). On her side, Emilia, too, though wife to Iago, is evidently Catholic in her belief, as when she refers to "purgatory" in her subsequent conversation with Desdemona, even in her willingness to commit such a "small vice" as adultery, for which, she says, "I should venture purgatory" (IV iii.78). In fact, it seems as if the whole world of *Othello* is, for better or worse, deeply and instinctively Catholic. Of course, it is Venetian, and therefore Catholic, but it has evidently an atmosphere familiar to the dramatist from his childhood.

When we turn, however, from this world, which prevails so long as the ideal harmony between Othello and Desdemona continues, to the real world of Iago, we find a very different picture. Here, in the latter's temptation of Cassio, we come upon an implicit clash between two opposing heresies. On the one hand, there is the Pelagian doctrine of "free will", and on the other, the Calvinist doctrine of predestination, which could appeal to the authority of St. Augustine. The clash may be compared to the early Reformation controversy between Erasmus, with his *De Libero Arbitrio* (1524), in which the author comes dangerously close to Pelagianism, and Luther, with his flatly opposite *De Servo Arbitrio* (1525). To begin with, Iago's more cynical form of Pelagianism comes out in his conversation with

Roderigo, when he declares, "Virtue! A fig! 'Tis in ourselves that we are thus, or thus. Our bodies are our gardens, to the which our wills are gardeners." And again, "The power and corrigible authority of this lies in our wills." Love, however, is in his opinion, "merely a lust of the blood and a permission of the will" (I iii.323ff). By contrast, the Calvinist doctrine of predestination is echoed by Cassio, once he has become drunk as a result of Iago's persuasion, in his words "Well, God's above all, and there be souls must be saved, and there be souls must not be saved" (II iii.106). His opening premise, "God's above all," sounds suspiciously like Calvin's premise, *"Soli Deo Gloria"*—To God alone be glory. Then what follows is pure predestinationism. He himself hopes to be among the predestined for salvation, but once he is demoted by Othello for his drunken brawl with Montano, he falls into despair: "I have lost the immortal part of myself, and what remains is bestial" (II iii.265). But then, paradoxically at Iago's persuasion, he is as it were converted from his momentary Calvinism to a Catholic belief in the power of Desdemona's intercession, which is, as we have seen, implicitly related to that of the Virgin Mary.

Finally, considering the development of the play as a whole, we may note in it a Dantesque progression of thought, if in a sequence opposite to that of the *Divina Commedia*. Beginning with "the grace of heaven", seen by Cassio in "the divine Desdemona" (II i.85, 73), the play proceeds by way of the "purgatory" which Emilia would venture for the sake of a sin of adultery (IV iii.78), to "the gate of hell" of which Emilia is seen by Othello as "keeper" (IV ii.91), and that leads to Othello's own feeling of being "damn'd beneath all depth in hell" (V ii.135), in company with Judas and such traitors according to Dante's *Inferno*, for his betrayal of the Christ-like Desdemona. Yet in fact he has himself been betrayed, "ensnar'd" in "soul and body", by Iago (V ii.301). This feeling of his may be compared to that of not a few recusant victims in Elizabethan England, on finding themselves ensnared, or to use Bassanio's word, "entrapped" (*The Merchant of Venice*, III ii.101), by the cunning of their captors and induced by means of threats or blackmail to betray their priests and other recusants. Then behind all this Machiavellian blackmail stood the two Cecils, father and son, William, Lord Burghley till his death in 1598, and Sir Robert, subsequently Earl of Salisbury, who was soon to bring this elaborate scheming to an all too successful conclusion, with the "discovery" of the Gunpowder Plot in 1605.

Macbeth

Speaking of plays in pairs, we may note the impressive affinity between *Othello* and *Macbeth*. They are not just two of the "four great tragedies" as defined by A. C. Bradley in his great lectures on *Shakespearean Tragedy* (1904). That foursome is undermined by the removal, first of *Hamlet*, when considered as more of a problem play than a real tragedy, then of *King Lear*, when regarded (as remains to be seen) as looking away from "the dark backward and abysm" (cf. *The Tempest* I ii.50) of Shakespeare's tragic period to the ensuing tragi-comedies. Now what is common to the two remaining tragedies is the uniqueness and intensity of their tragic plots, in which we find hardly any of Shakespeare's customary comic variety to distract our attention from the main issue. To this feature of theirs we may well apply Othello's poetic comparison of his vengeful intent to "the Pontick Sea,/ whose icy current and compulsive course/ ne'er feels retiring ebb, but keeps due on/ to the Propontic and the Hellespont" (III iii.454ff). All the same, this similarity between the two tragedies may serve to emphasize their specific differences, as between not only revenge in one and ambition in the other, but also an atmosphere of light in one and darkness in the other. Thus if *Othello* may be called a tragedy of light, in view of its bright Mediterranean and Renaissance setting between the Italian mainland of Venice and the Greek island of Cyprus, *Macbeth* may conversely be called a tragedy of darkness, with its murky setting in early mediaeval Scotland, whose very name points to the Greek *skotia*, or place of darkness. We may add that, in terms of mediaeval drama, if *Othello* is seen as a morality play of salvation, in which the hero, despite his sense of being "damn'd beneath all depth in hell" (V ii.135) for his murder of Desdemona, is saved at the end by his loving embrace of her whom he has killed, then *Macbeth* is to be seen as a morality play of damnation, in which the "hero" is recognized even before his death as a "hell-hound" (V vii.32), and he goes on to die with no saving love, while the only heroine in the play is no less a villain than himself, and she has already died "with self and violent hands" (V vii.99). This pair, however much their love may be emphasized by starry-eyed critics, are justly characterized by Malcolm at the end of the play as "this dead butcher and his fiend-like queen" (V vii.98). In fact, their deaths are not just a culmination of tragedy, but from another point of view they constitute a happy ending for Scotland—and so the play is not so entirely tragic after all.

When, however, we abstract from this happy ending and see the play as a unique tragedy of darkness and damnation, we may notice how deeply the dramatist enters here into the problem of evil and the mystery of iniquity (cf. II Thess. ii.7). Nor is this unrelated to what he calls, in the words of Ulysses in *Troilus and Cressida*, the "mystery in the soul of state" (III iii.203). This darkness cannot, however, be explained only with reference to Shakespeare's dramatic imagination, as he gives it "a local habitation and a name" in Macbeth's Scotland. It has also to be explained, according to my present thesis, with reference to his religious and recusant background. This may be shown in relation to the probable dating of the play, with its two focal points in time and place. The first point, which is rarely noted, is Scotland in 1602, when in the aftermath of the Essex Rebellion of 1601, and the dramatist's presumed composition of *Hamlet*, Shakespeare and his company may have found it prudent—in spite of the dismissal of formal charges against them at the trial of Essex—to retire northwards, eventually to Edinburgh and even Aberdeen. As a result of this journey, for which the evidence remains murky, the dramatist may have drawn many of the details of his drama as well as its prevailing atmosphere, while at the same time winning the favour of the Scottish king, who was soon to become king of England and patron of the newly styled King's Men. The second point is London in 1606, in the aftermath of the Gunpowder Plot of November 5, 1605, and the subsequent trials of the few conspirators who had managed to evade a more sudden death. These trials were reported in what, apart from Holinshed and other Scottish chronicles, was a main source for *Macbeth*, the anonymous, government-sponsored *True and Perfect Relation of the Whole Proceedings* (1606). This came out in the early summer, hardly leaving time for the dramatist to draw upon it for his play, if *Macbeth* was indeed, according to most scholarly opinion, presented before the king at Hampton Court on August 7, 1606.

Moreover, what is too often overlooked by Shakespeare scholars and Elizabethan historians, yet what is common to both dates and both conspiracies, is the person of Shakespeare's Warwickshire cousin on his mother's side, Robert

Catesby. And behind the person of Robert Catesby, we may call to mind another Robert, Sir Robert Cecil, the secretary of state and successor to his father's genius for intrigue, whose spirits—as noted above, of Don John in *Much Ado About Nothing*—may well be described as ever toiling "in frame of villainies" (IV i.191). On both occasions Sir Robert was in supreme power, and it is not unlikely that he arranged the release of Catesby on the former occasion in order to make effective use of him for the latter. Such is the principle of Polonius in *Hamlet*: "Your bait of falsehood takes this carp of truth" (II i.63). It is also shown up as a Satanic principle by Banquo in his warning words to Macbeth: "Oftentimes to win us to our harm,/ the instruments of darkness tell us truths,/ win us with honest trifles to betray's/ in deepest consequence" (I iii.123ff). Both principles were evidently familiar to Sir Robert, who had doubtless learnt them from his father.

Thus we may see that one main source of the darkness in *Macbeth* is not just the northern climate of Scotland, nor just the foul crimes recorded of so many Scottish nobles by their chroniclers, nor yet the dramatic imagination of Shakespeare working on that remote country and period, but the London of his own time, with all the dark rumours spreading within the capital from the discovery of the plot in 1605 and swirling round the subsequent trials—centring as they did, according to the full title of the *Proceedings*, on "Garnet a Jesuit and his confederates". Garnet himself is commonly recognized in the speech of the drunken Porter, who refers both to "a farmer who hanged himself on the expectation of plenty" (II iii.5), since Farmer was an alias of Garnet, and to "an equivocator, that could swear in both the scales against either scale, who committed treason enough for God's sake, yet could not equivocate to heaven" (II iii.10ff), since Garnet himself admitted at the trial that he had resorted to equivocation—in accordance with the Jesuit theory. Here it may be added that so perceptive a critic as Coleridge was unwilling to accept Shakespeare's authorship of the Porter's speech but rather attributed it to the clown playing the Porter's part—like those fools criticized by Hamlet for their tendency to speak "more than is set down for them" (III ii.44). On the other hand, his friend De Quincey refuted that contention in his masterful essay "On the Knocking at the Gate in Macbeth" (1823), which has succeeded in convincing most scholars since then.

Anyhow, in this play the theme of equivocation is taken up not only by the Porter but also by Macbeth himself, as when he later complains of "the equivocation of the fiend/ that lies like truth" (V v.42). His use of the word is no chance phenomenon, as if it had already been in common use in Elizabethan English. Rather, at that time it had an almost exclusive connotation of Jesuit theory and practice, on the occasion first of the trial of Robert Southwell in 1595—from which it may have found its way into the mouth of Hamlet, speaking of the comic grave-digger in V i.148—then of this trial of Henry Garnet in 1606. It even looks, in the opinion of some scholars, as if the Jesuits were responsible not only (in the official mind) for the actual conspiracy in the Plot of 1605, but also (in the dramatist's mind) for the vein of indignation that seems to enter so deeply into the composition of *Macbeth*.

On the other hand, as Shakespeare himself is always warning us, not least in Bassanio's speech in *The Merchant of Venice*, we have to beware of "the seeming truth which cunning times put on/ to entrap the wisest" (III ii.99). Also, as he implies in Lucio's description of the duke in *Measure for Measure*, we have to interpret "his givings out" as being "of an infinite distance/ from his true-meant design" (I iv.54). We may also do well to remember that Shakespeare was no innocent bystander in all the events leading from the Essex Rebellion to the Gunpowder Plot, nor was he likely to have been deceived by the elaborate working of the government propaganda machine to cast discredit on the English Catholics. Not only was Robert Catesby (as noted above) his cousin on his mother's side, but it is also surprising to see how many as well of Essex's supporters as of the gunpowder plotters came from the same part of the English Midlands and met not infrequently at the same Mermaid Tavern in London. His friend Ben Jonson, too, was evidently implicated in the Gunpowder Plot, and it was no doubt to extricate himself from its toils that he renounced his recusancy (about which he had been imprudently more open than Shakespeare ever was) and turned state informer. So when it came to the Jesuit theory and practice of equivocation, we may safely say that not only did the dramatist feel no horror at it, but he even commended its use, even in terms beyond what the Jesuits themselves would have acknowledged, in the two problem comedies noticed above—in the strange incantatory chants of the duke-friar in *Measure for Measure* (III ii.302) and of the chaste Diana in *All's Well That Ends Well* (IV ii.75). So when he professes horror, with Macbeth, at "the equivocation of the fiend" (V v.42), he can hardly be thinking of the Jesuits, whom he would have known as innocent victims, but of their persecutors in those "cunning times", not least of their arch-persecutor, the crook-backed secretary of state, Sir Robert Cecil.

The most impressive utterance of horror, however, is put into the mouth not of Macbeth in his final despairing moments, still less of the drunken Porter, but of the man who becomes Macbeth's mortal enemy, Macduff, on his return from the scene of regicide in Duncan's bedchamber. Then he exclaims, "O horror! Horror! Horror! Tongue nor heart/ cannot conceive nor name thee!" (II iii.70). Also at this point we may notice more than one verbal echo from the *Proceedings* of 1606, both in the preliminary indictment, "The matter now to be offered is matter of treason, but of such horror and monstrous nature that before now the tongue of man never delivered, the ear of man never heard, the heart of man never conceived, nor the malice of hellish or earthly devil ever practised," and in Sir Edward Coke's speech for the prosecution, "Considering the monstrousness and continual horror of this so desperate a cause. . . . This offence is . . . without any name . . . sufficient to express it." Coke goes on to derive the Jesuit theory of equivocation from the devil himself, who "now draws the very grounds of equivocation concerning princes' lives out of the very scripture and by scholastic authority." We may notice the contrast between what Macduff has just seen with his eyes, a gory spectacle of regicide, and what the prosecutors of Father Garnet are imagining as the outcome of a plot that has fortunately been exposed by the government on the eve of its perpetration, and before they have offered any proof either of the reality of the plot or of Father Garnet's complicity in it. Rather, what they have to offer in the *Proceedings* is better described in Macbeth's words as "full of sound and fury,/ signifying nothing" (V v.27).

On the other hand, when Macduff goes on to speak of the "most sacrilegious murder" that "hath broke ope/ the Lord's anointed temple, and stole thence/ the life o' the building" (II iii.73), his words have a more concrete relevance than the mere possibility of the Parliament building being blown up by the hare-brained schemes of the conspirators. If we only cast our eyes back over the murky history of Tudor England, since the religious changes were brought in by the greed of Henry VIII, we may first pause at the certainly "sacrilegious murder" of Mary Queen of Scots at Fotheringay in 1587—considering that she was both lawful queen of Scotland and heir to the throne of England. This fact we may also compare with the odd remark of Lady Macbeth to her husband at the time of Duncan's murder, "Had he not resembled/ my father as he slept, I had done't" (II ii.14)—while recalling that Elizabeth Tudor and Mary Stuart were cousins by virtue of their common descent from Henry VII of England. Or we may cast our eyes further back to the suppression and destruction of so many holy shrines and monasteries up and down England during the "reformation" undertaken by Henry VIII with the aid of Thomas Cromwell and his henchmen. Of that event we may say, more than of any other event in the history of Christendom till the French Revolution, "Confusion now hath made his masterpiece!" (II iii.72). Of the abiding nature of this confusion Shakespeare himself was continually reminded, not by any mere chronicles, but by the evidence of the many old monastic ruins, such as those of Wroxhall Abbey in the Forest of Arden—mentioned by him in Sonnet lxxiii and *Titus Andronicus* (V i.21).

Out of all this confusion and its continuation under Elizabeth I and her "cruel ministers", for whom the maintenance of the Protestant Reformation was a necessary means of ensuring their hold on its practical advantages to themselves, there arose two consequences for those others who neither shared in the advantages nor could do so in conscience. First, they had to spend their lives oppressed by the continual need of secrecy and the accompanying fear of spies. Secondly, they couldn't but lament their own situation and that of their country. Both these consequences are amply illustrated in *Macbeth*, once the hero-villain has assassinated his king and replaced him on the throne of Scotland. Concerning spies, we have Macbeth's own statement, concerning the nobles of Scotland, "There's not a one of them but in his house/ I keep a servant fee'd" (III iv.131). As for the need of secrecy, we have the later conversation between Lennox and another lord. Lennox says, "My former speeches have but hit your thoughts, which can interpret further. Only I say,/ things have been strangely borne" (III vi.1). He fears to criticize Macbeth at all openly, in case his interlocutor turns out to be an informer. So he has to proceed "by indirections", so as to know from the other's response how far he may trust him. The same situation we find on a larger scale in the strangely protracted conversation between Macduff and Malcolm, a scene which many a producer feels tempted to cut but for the fact that Macbeth is already such a short play. Malcolm cannot easily put his trust in Macduff, who has after all abandoned his family in Scotland, possibly with the connivance of Macbeth. He later explains his reason for such hesitation—in view of a fact that is not shown in the play—that "devilish Macbeth/ by many of these trains hath sought to win me/ into his power" (IV iii.117). This again may remind us of Mary Queen of Scots, who was the object of continual plots by Sir Francis Walsingham and his spies to provide the English queen and her government with a sufficient excuse for getting rid of Mary.

As for the laments of those who had to live under the continual oppression of the "cruel ministers" of Queen Elizabeth for their loyalty to Rome and their conscience, they form the dominant background to Act IV, which centres on the personality and the family of Macduff. First, we hear Lady Macduff, when she cannot understand why her husband has undertaken such sudden flight from home, even going so far as to blame him with the words, "Our fears do make us traitors" (IV ii.4). Ross, however, defends him, pleading the cruelty of the times: "when we are traitors/ and do not know ourselves" (IV ii.18). Then her little boy pipes up, "Was my father a traitor, mother?" Sadly she replies, "Ay, that he was." But in his wise innocence he insists with the question, "What is a traitor?"—following it up with the perceptive remark, all too true in Elizabethan England, "There are liars and swearers enow to beat the honest men" (IV ii.44ff). Then he is killed by one of the murderers on stage, leaving his poor mother to reflect, "I am in this earthly world, where to do harm/ is often laudable, to do good sometime/ accounted dangerous folly" (IV ii.73).

The same vein, or strain, is continued in the following scene, between Macduff himself and Malcolm at the English court, in tones of even keener lamentation. First, we hear Macduff informing the prince, "Each new morn/ new widows howl, new orphans cry, new sorrows/ strike heaven on the face" (IV iii.4). Then, when he finds his words failing to produce the desired effect on Malcolm, he exclaims, "Bleed, bleed, poor country!" (IV iii.31). Yet Malcolm protests he does agree with him: "I think our country sinks beneath the yoke,/ it weeps, it bleeds, and each new day a gash/ is added to her wounds" (IV iii.39). But he doesn't see what he can do to remedy the situation. At length, Ross enters with fresh news from Scotland in such a way as to bring all their lamentation to a crescendo: "Alas, poor country,/ almost afraid to know itself. It cannot/ be call'd our mother, but our grave" (IV iii.164). Anyone who knows anything about the recusant background of Shakespeare's age—though there are all too few Shakespeare scholars or Elizabethan historians who show any real awareness of it or concern about it—cannot but recognize the relevance of these laments to the condition of English Catholics throughout the reigns of Elizabeth I and

James I. Needless to say, these laments are echoed in much of the recusant literature of the age, which was mostly printed abroad and smuggled into the country at the risk of the smugglers' lives. Such was, for example, the lament of Thomas Dorman, writing in the mid-1560s, before the oppression of the Catholics had developed into a full-scale persecution: "Behold, if you can, for tears, the miserable face of your native country" (*A Proof of Certain Articles*, 1564). His lament is taken up again and again by Robert Persons in his *Brief Discourse* (1580), by William Allen in his *Defence of English Catholics* (1584), and by Robert Southwell in his *Humble Supplication* (1600)—to mention but a few of the more notable titles.

Still, for all the evil done by "this dead butcher and his fiendish queen" and "their cruel ministers" (V vii.97)—who barely conceal the historical figures of Henry VIII and Elizabeth I, with their respective ministers, Thomas Cromwell and the two Cecils—and for all the sufferings inflicted by them on their innocent subjects, with all their laments as recorded in Act IV, Shakespeare's *Macbeth* has no really tragic ending—save for those romantic critics who persist in wasting their sympathy on the hero-villain and his partner in crime. For all his insistent exploration of the problems of human evil and innocent suffering, the dramatist has provided his tragedy with a paradoxically happy ending, not for Macbeth or his Lady, but for Scotland. This ending is brought about with the timely assistance of "gracious England" (IV iii.189), the pious English king, Edward the Confessor, whose shrine in Westminster Abbey was among the many despoiled by his impious successor Henry VIII. His "grace" is emphasized by the dramatist in the same scene of Act IV which is so full of lamentation, as if to suggest the truth of what St. Paul says to the Romans, "Where sin abounded, grace did much more abound" (Rom. v.20). It is even said of him that "sundry blessings hang about his throne/ that speak him full of grace" (IV iii.159). Still, as Malcolm emphasizes in the ending of the play, all has to be ascribed to "the grace of Grace" (V vii.101), to the gracious power of God from whom all blessings descend on men, by means of such saints as St. Edward of England and Malcolm's queen, St. Margaret of Scotland. Here it may further be noted that, whereas there is no heroine in this play worthy of the name of "grace", since all grace is fled from a fiend like Lady Macbeth once she has invoked the "murdering ministers" to "unsex" her (I v.42, 49), there are two kings who may deserve the name, "the gracious Duncan", as he is recognized even by Macbeth (III i.66), and St. Edward of England. It is as if in this play two kings have to take the place customarily reserved for heroines. And it is in this way that Malcolm with the aid of Macduff is able to restore law and order, with grace, to Macbeth's Scotland—though they have not yet, alas, been restored to Shakespeare's England.

chapter 11
Drama of Recusant Frustration

King Lear

"DECORUM", the word so dear to the heart of John Milton and the literary critics of the Renaissance, is a word (in its literary meaning) strange no less to the thought than to the practice of Shakespeare. The literary ideal is that a tragedy should be a tragedy, with no admixture of comedy, and a comedy should be a comedy, with no admixture of tragedy. Such is the serious ideal of Milton when in his Preface to *Samson Agonistes* he criticizes "the poets' error in intermixing comic stuff with tragic sadness and gravity". Thus indirectly, without naming him, he begs leave to differ from Shakespeare, in spite of the praise he has awarded his great predecessor in his poetic contribution to the Second Folio of 1632. So we may now beg leave, on behalf of Shakespeare, to differ from Milton. In almost all his plays Shakespeare shows himself unable, or unwilling, to restrict his genius to a single genre, whether comedy or history or tragedy or any of those other forms he satirizes through the mouth of Polonius in *Hamlet* (II ii.424). Rather, it is his aim in drama, as Hamlet says, "to hold as 'twere the mirror up to nature" (III ii.25). And in the world of nature there is no such clear division between the comic and the tragic as the Renaissance theorists maintained. Up to a point, no doubt, in his two tragedies of *Othello* and *Macbeth* the dramatist seems to go along with them. Yet even in them he is unable, or unwilling, to prevent comedy or common sense from breaking in, as in the drinking scene in *Othello*, where Iago appears for once as a jolly good fellow (II iii), or in the Porter scene in *Macbeth* (II iii). Now, however, we turn from those two tragedies to *King Lear*, and we note that, while it is also deservedly called "tragedy" and is indeed the most tragic of all the so-called "four great tragedies", it seems to defy both the name and the category. Its ending is indeed supremely sad, with the death of the poor old Lear following on that of the innocent Cordelia. Yet already a supremely happy ending has taken place, with the blissful reunion of Lear and Cordelia, the loving father and his dear daughter. As for the previous scenes showing the mad old king with his witless fool and the mad beggar, they are surely as crazy as anything in world comedy, whether human or divine. "Somewhere," says Chesterton, with reference to this play, "on that highest of all human towers there is a tile loose. There is something that rattles rather crazily in the high wind of the highest of mortal tragedies." From all this we cannot but conclude that *King Lear* belongs to no genre. It is its own genre, worthy of the claim made by one of Shakespeare's characters (Richard of Gloucester in Part III of *Henry VI* V vi.83), "I am myself alone."

For all that, or for that very reason, *King Lear* may well be regarded as the supreme masterpiece in the genre of what I would like to name "recusant drama". Nor is it surprising that it should have been chosen, with *Pericles*, to be presented by the Cholmeley Players to recusant audiences in the north of England during the winter of 1609–10. So it remains for us to consider in fuller detail how apt was their choice.

We may begin by recalling an instructive parallel between *King John* and *King Lear* in relation to their respective sources. In both cases the dramatist turns from his customary source for history plays in Holinshed's *Chronicles* to a previously existing dramatized version of that source. In both cases, too, he takes an obviously Protestant play and turns it into what may be interpreted as a Catholic, even a recusant, play. In the case of King John, whereas the dramatic source, *The Troublesome Reign of King John,* shows John as a Protestant hero before his time and as a precursor of Henry VIII in his defiance of the Pope and his spoliation of the monasteries, Shakespeare shows John as a usurper and a villain. In the case of *King Lear,* too, there is a source-play, *The True Chronicle History of King Leir and his Three Daughters,* which had already been performed in the mid-1590s but was not printed till 1605. Then its printing may have prompted Shakespeare to undertake a thorough revision of it in a different sense. In the earlier play the story is dramatized from a viewpoint that is not just piously Christian but recognizably Puritan—insofar as a good Puritan could have lent himself to the writing of plays for common players to perform on a public stage. The Puritanism appears, for example, when the heroine Cordella is scorned by her sister Gonorill as "sober, courteous, modest and precise"—that is, as a Puritan or "precisian". Similarly, her other sister Ragan says of her that "she were right fit to make a parson's wife". Gonorill in fact goes on to call her "Puritan" and "dissembling hypocrite", while betraying her own popery in warning Cordella, "I'll make you wish yourself in purgatory." Shakespeare, however, while recognizing the dramatic potential of the story, which had also been retold in poetic form by Spenser in *The Faery Queene*, may well have been riled at the pious anachronism of the Puritan play and resolved to put the story back in its pristine pagan setting, not without introducing a vein of biblical and recusant reference.

The vein of recusant reference we may notice from the outset, as soon as the misty, fairy-tale motif of an old king dividing his kingdom among his three daughters in accordance with their several professions of love is dissipated by the stark realism of Cordelia's "Nothing" (I i.89). It is out of this "Nothing" of her reply that the whole action of the play unfolds, as Lear responds to her with an appeal to the Aristotelian axiom, "Nothing will come of nothing" (I i.92), and banishes her together with the loyal Earl of Kent. Here already in this twofold sentence of banishment we may find *King Lear* joining those two previous recusant plays of banishment and disinheritance, the "history" of *Richard II* and the "comedy" of *As You Like It*. First, we may be reminded of Richard's advice to his poor queen Isabella, "Hie thee to France,/ and cloister thee in some religious house./ Our holy lives must win a new world's crown" (V i.22). Not that Cordelia goes to France to enter a religious house, but she does go there, as queen to the French king, who welcomes her in her new poverty with rich biblical overtones: "Fairest Cordelia, that art most rich, being poor,/ most choice, forsaken, and most lov'd, despis'd" (I i.253). Kent, too, while accompanying her into exile, echoes the words of Richard as he says of himself, "He'll shape his old course in a country new" (I i.190). He further declares, "Freedom lives hence, and banishment is here" (I i.184)—in words that echo Celia's similar declaration in *As You Like It*, "Now go we in content,/ to liberty and not to banishment" (I iii.140).

Turning now from the primary plot of Lear and his three daughters to the secondary plot of Gloucester and his two sons, borrowed by Shakespeare from Sidney's *Arcadia* for the combined purpose of seeming complication and deeper unification, we may notice a similar movement from "Nothing" to banishment and disinheritance—though here the "Nothing" is put into the mouth not of the good Edgar but of the bad Edmund. Here we are introduced to the old Earl of Gloucester, darkly ruminating on what has just occurred at court, which he sees as implying the general disorder attending on the day of doom. Then, he laments, "love cools, friendship falls off, brothers divide . . . and the bond cracked between father and son", adding in particular, "the king falls from bias of nature, there's father against child", and in his own case, "there's son against father"—though tragically he mistakes his loyal son for the traitor, and vice versa (I ii.118ff). This confusion is paralleled in the words of Albany to Oswald, that the latter "has turned the wrong side out" (IV ii.9), also echoing York's complaint in *Richard II*, "The traitor lives, the true man's put to death" (V iii.72). This is precisely the complaint of the Catholic recusants, who claimed to be loyal no less to the Queen of England in temporal affairs than to the Pope of Rome in spiritual affairs, while identifying the real traitor as Sir William Cecil, Lord Burghley, both in the earlier *Treatise of Treasons* (1572) and in the later *Declaration of the True Causes* (1592).

In the case of Edgar, now unjustly banished from his father's presence and obliged to resort to disguise as the mad beggar Tom o' Bedlam, we may further recognize the situation not just of a recusant but of a hunted priest. Thus, pretending to be his benefactor, Edmund warns him, "Intelligence is given where you are hid" (II i.23), as if to enable him to make his escape. Then Gloucester, coming on the scene, declares in Cornwall's name, "By his authority I will proclaim it," with a resolve to bar "all ports" (II i.62, 82). Not long afterwards, when we next see Edgar, we hear of the prompt effect of Gloucester's words, "I heard myself proclaim'd," and "No port is free, no place/ that guard, and most unusual vigilance,/ does not attend my taking." It is now that he decides to assume the disguise of a mad beggar and "to outface/ the winds and persecutions of the sky"—where we find the only use of the word "persecution" in all Shakespeare's plays. He concludes with significant words that associate him in his present predicament with Cordelia: "Edgar I nothing am" (II iii.1ff). In all these words of Edgar we may be reminded of the two royal proclamations, the one published on July 15, 1580, against "such rebels and traitors as do live in foreign parts", and the other on January 10, 1581, "for the revocation of students from beyond the seas, and against the retaining of Jesuits", which had special reference (without naming them) to the recent arrival in England of the first two Jesuits, Edmund Campion and Robert Persons, in July 1580. Theirs was the situation described by Campion in the letter he wrote to his general superior in Rome: "I cannot long escape the hands of the heretics, the enemy have so many eyes, so many tongues, so many scouts and crafts"; and he adds, concerning his disguise, "I am in apparel to myself very ridiculous, I often change it and myself also." Above all, he says with reference to the proclamations, "Threatening edicts come forth against us daily." Subsequently, Edgar exhorts himself to "lurk, lurk" (III vi.124), echoing the very language of Burghley in his *Execution of Justice* (1583) on "the secret lurkings of the priests."

From the way the dramatist goes on to characterize Edgar as the mad beggar, pursued by such fiends as Flibbertigibbet, Modo and Mahu, Frateretto, Nero, Hopdance, and Obidicut (III iv.118, 148, III vi.8, 33, IV i.60), he even seems to be thinking of one priest in particular, his own classmate from Shottery, Robert Dibdale. The latter had left Stratford with his master, Simon Hunt, for Douai in 1575; then he was ordained priest at Rheims in 1584 and sent to England in the same year, when he assisted the Jesuit William Weston (alias Edmunds) in the sensational exorcisms that took place in the mid-1580s at the recusant house of Edmund Peckham in Denham. (By the way, it seems ironical that Dibdale, if the original of Edgar, was associated with so many Edmunds—Edmund Campion, Father Edmunds, Edmund Peckham!) Already, as noted above, the dramatist had drawn upon those exorcisms in his *Comedy of Errors* for his presentation of the conjuring performed by Dr. Pinch on Antipholus of Ephesus. But now in *King Lear* he had a recently published document for his source, Samuel Harsnet's *Declaration of Egregious Popish Impostures* (1603). It may seem strange that Harsnet should have allowed such a long gap to intervene between those exorcisms of eighteen years before and his present refutation, but he had just come to the end of a controversy with the Puritan John Darrell (with his similar claim of exorcisms in the north of England) on behalf of the Bishop of London, Richard Bancroft (soon to succeed John Whitgift as Archbishop of Canterbury in 1604). Moreover, he could now make use of the recent discovery of an MS "Book of Miracles", recording the old Papist miracles, to show that the established Church was no less opposed to the Papists on this score than to the Puritans, in the name of reason. Then, too, his vivid dramatic style of writing, in which he showed some familiarity with the stage, may well have appealed to Shakespeare. Far more appealing to him, however, was the presence in its pages of Robert Dibdale, who was shortly to be executed at Tyburn in 1586 as well for his "conjuring" as for his priesthood, including a tenuous connection with the Babington Plot of that year.

Nor is Edgar the only representative of the hunted priests in *King Lear*. Another representative may be seen in Kent, who not only goes into banishment with Cordelia but also returns in disguise to help his master Lear. He comes before the king with a bluff demeanor, professing to seek service with him in view of the authority he recognizes in the king's countenance—reminding us of the old servant Adam in *As You Like It*, in whom his young master sees "the constant service of the antique world" (II iii.57). It is his aim to assist the old king in spiritual no less than in material matters, if in disguise—just as it was the aim of the seminary priests and Jesuits on returning to England to bring spiritual assistance to the beleaguered English Catholics, while seeming to be their servants, without any meddling in politics. At the same time, Kent is not unlike those English Jesuits, such as Persons, who found themselves practically forced into politics once they came to realize that without political, even military, intervention there was no hope for the Catholic cause in England. Thus we find Kent in the stocks, reading a letter from Cordelia by the light of the moon, while murmuring what might well be regarded as the motto of this play and those to come, "Nothing almost sees miracles/ but misery" (II ii.172). He also speaks of the presence of servants in noble houses, like those "fee'd" by Macbeth (III iv.132), "which are to France the spies and speculations,/ intelligent of our state". From them he learns that "from France there comes a power/ into this scatter'd kingdom", which is even now "at point/ to show their open banner" (III i.24ff). He is, moreover, instrumental, with Gloucester, in enabling Lear to make his way in safety to Dover, where he may meet Cordelia who has come over with an army for his rescue. But first, Gloucester has to suffer the loss of his eyes for being, as Regan calls him, a "filthy traitor" (III vii.32).

Now we may return from Edgar and Kent to Cordelia, whom we left in France. All this time they, with Lear's fool, may be seen as her representatives back home. She in turn may be seen as standing for the "old faith" as well as the "grace" and "wisdom" of her father. In her case, however, unlike most of Shakespeare's ideal heroines, there is no explicit mention of "grace", since in this play the word is mostly used in a titular sense for kings and princes. Still, in the opening scene we find her welcomed by the king of France as "this unpriz'd precious maid" (I i.262), and on her return home her tears, even before we see her, are described as "the holy water from her heavenly eyes" (IV iii.32). Then on her actual appearance, not alone but at the head of the French army, she shows herself chiefly concerned for the health of her father, saying—and echoing the first words uttered by the child Jesus on his finding in the temple (Luke ii.49)—"O dear father!/ It is thy business that I go about." (IV iv.23). She also adds, as if to forestall unfriendly criticism for her resort to arms, "No blown ambition doth our arms incite,/ but love, dear love, and our ag'd father's right" (IV iv.27). Such was also the motive emphasized by Allen and Persons in their support of the Spanish Armada in 1588, when their influence was discerned in the Bull of Pope Sixtus that had been prepared for publication in the event of success, while Allen added his own *Admonition to the Nobility and People of England* in the same year. Alas, however, the Armada was defeated as much by the elements of wind and water as by the smaller English fleet under Sir Francis Drake. In this connection Cordelia's words, uttered after her defeat by the British forces, "We are not the first/ who, with best meaning, have incurr'd the worst" (V iii.3), may be interpreted in the light of that other failure of the Spanish enterprise.

Turning again from Cordelia to Lear, we may pause a moment to reflect on the royal title in which he takes such pride, as in his response to Gloucester's recognition of him, "Ay, every inch a king!" (IV vi.110). There is a strange contrast, noted by all too few commentators, between the one fact everyone knows about him, that he is King of Britain, and the other fact that is largely ignored, that the name of "Britain" is never once mentioned in the play—though in the later play of *Cymbeline* the name recurs no less than twenty-seven times. Why is this? Several reasons may be offered. One is simply that the name is taken for granted. Everyone knows that Lear is King of Britain. But then why is the name repeated so often in *Cymbeline*? Another, more convincing reason is that in this play the dramatist wishes to emphasize its supra-national, metaphysical meaning, considering Lear not just as King of Britain but, in the old morality tradition, as *Rex Humanitas* or *Humanum Genus*. He is Man, who is fallen in the Fall of Adam, and this fall of his is indicated in the moment he banishes Cordelia, who stands (as we have noted) for his "grace" and the "old faith", as well as his heart—as *Coeur de Lear*. Then not only is the name of "Britain" unmentioned, but there are no other place names (for Cornwall and Albany, Kent and Gloucester, are but titles) apart from Dover. And Dover is the place where the powers on either side clash with each other as in an eschatological Armageddon—besides being the port of entry for many priests and Jesuits from the time of Campion and Persons onwards.

Yet another reason for the omission of "Britain" may be that Shakespeare sees himself as an Englishman, with a noble English ancestry going back on his mother's side to well before the Norman Conquest. From his viewpoint, therefore, the Welsh Tudors, no less than their henchmen the Dudleys, not to mention the Cromwells and the Cecils, would have seemed mere upstarts, to be despised and hated. So if Lear is a British king according to the chronicles, Shakespeare prefers to see him as transcending his narrow British (Welsh) limitations and to show his area of activity in southeast England not far from Dover. From the recusant viewpoint, moreover, the old nobility of England tended to support the "old faith", especially as personified in its female representative, Mary Queen of Scots, who was both rightful queen of Scotland and heir to the throne of England till her unjust execution in 1587. The Tudors had to rely on upstarts like themselves to push through their religious changes and to maintain them against Catholic opposition. The Tudors also, being Welsh, followed by the Stuarts, being Scottish, preferred the name of "Britain" to that of "England". It was, again, the Tudors who, from the time of Henry VII, cultivated the myth of their Welsh hero Arthur, as depicted in Sir Thomas Malory's *Le Morte Darthur*, which was first printed by William Caxton in the very year of the Tudor victory at Bosworth, 1485. On the other hand, in all Shakespeare's plays there is hardly a mention of Arthur—whom Spenser had made into a Protestant hero in his *Faery Queene*—apart from Mistress Quickly's comic description of Falstaff's death, showing him as now "in Arthur's bosom", instead of the biblical "Abraham's bosom" (*Henry V*, II iii.9, cf. Luke xvi.22).

All the same, in *King Lear* we do come upon a significant mention of Arthur's great magician Merlin, when the fool, professing to speak in Merlin's name, makes his prophecy concerning "the land of Albion" (III ii.93). This is an interesting prophecy, not only for its imaginary ascription to Merlin, but also as a quotation from "The Plowman's Tale", apocryphally attributed to Chaucer. What is particularly interesting about it is the fact that it recurs in two recent recusant publications, *A Letter by a Spanish Gentleman* (1589), whose anonymous author notes that this prophecy of "the future state of England" is now "the very lively portrait thereof", and *A Declaration of the True Causes* (1592), whose author (probably Persons's agent in the Low Countries, Richard Verstegan) describes his book as "a commentary upon Chaucer's prophecy", which he proceeds to quote in full. The relevant words in the fool's version are "When priests are more in word than matter" (implying the sermons, on which the Protestants laid more emphasis than on the sacrifice of the Mass), "No heretics burn'd, but wenches' suitors" (referring to the "fry of fornication" prophesied by the Porter in *Henry VIII* V iv.37, as the outcome of the king's divorce), "Then shall the realm of Albion/ come to great confusion" (III ii.92). Such words, taken by themselves, might well have seemed treasonous in Elizabethan England, especially as quoted from recusant writings. But when put into the mouth of an "all-licens'd fool", as Goneril calls him (I iv.223), in the context of Jacobean England, they might more easily escape both the censor's eye and the informer's ear.

Finally, turning back from the old king to his dear daughter, we may come to the climax of the play in their blissful reunion in the French camp at Dover, before the clash of the two armies and the victory of the British forces. Here, though the word "grace" is not used, Cordelia appears as the most heavenly of Shakespeare's heroines, and as the image not only of the Virgin Mary but also of Jesus Christ himself. Already we have heard her described by the Gentleman in the preceding scene, addressing the retreating figure of the mad Lear: "Thou hast one daughter,/ who redeems nature from the general curse/ which twain have brought her to" (IV vi.210). Who, we may ask, "redeems nature from the general curse"—terms used by St. Paul in his letter to the Galatians (iii.13)—but Jesus Christ with his divine grace? This is, moreover, a grace we find echoed by Cordelia when, in response to Lear's recognition of her as "my child Cordelia", she pronounces the name of God himself as revealed by God to Moses in Exodus iii.14, "And so I am, I am" (IV vii.70). In all the plays of Shakespeare there is no higher moment than this, in which we may well recognize the happy ending of *King Lear*—however excruciatingly sad may be the other ending that follows in Act V.

In this event, when Lear and Cordelia have been taken captive by Edmund and the British forces and sent to prison, and when Lear returns to the stage bearing the dead body of his innocent daughter in his arms with the cry, "Howl, howl, howl, howl!" (V iii.259), the stage is drowned not, as in *Hamlet*, with blood but with tears—and not only the stage but the whole theatre as well. Now Albany exclaims, "O see, see!" (V iii.306), while pointing to the tableau of Lear with Cordelia as another pietà—where it is impossible for anyone brought up in the Catholic liturgy of Holy Week not to hear an echo of the antiphon taken from Jeremiah's Lamentations (i.12), *"O vos omnes, qui transitis per viam, attendite et videte si est dolor sicut dolor meus"*—O all ye that pass by the way, attend and see if there be any sorrow like to my sorrow! Here the sorrow is that of the Virgin Mother as she receives into her arms the body of her innocent Son when it is taken down from the cross, but it may well be seen as that of the old father bearing the dead body of his innocent daughter. Then he too dies, not in an excess of sorrow (as emphasized by agnostic critics) but in a sudden access of joy when, as with Gloucester, whose end has just been related by his loyal son Edgar, "his flaw'd heart . . . 'twixt two extremes of passion, joy and grief,/ burst smilingly" (V iii.198). In this moment of death, Edgar urges the king, "Look up, my lord!" but Kent intervenes, almost angrily, "Vex not his ghost. He hates him/ that would upon the rack of this tough world/ stretch him out longer" (V iii.314ff). Indeed, Lear in his fallen condition has represented the people of England both in their rejection of the "old faith" (in his banishment of Cordelia) and in their consequent sufferings, not the least of which was the torture of the rack, on which so many innocent priests and laymen had been stretched to make them apostatize and betray their fellow Catholics. But now that he has passed to what the duke in *Measure for Measure* calls "a better life, past fearing death" (V i.398), he may expect to rejoice in another reunion with Cordelia, of which he has already experienced a foretaste in the happy ending of Act IV. It is, moreover, such a happy ending of reunion between father and daughter that Shakespeare goes on to repeat it, again and again, in his final romances, from *Pericles* and *Cymbeline* to *The Winter's Tale* and *The Tempest*—for the consolation of recusant audiences such as those for whom the Cholmeley Players offered their performances of *King Lear* and *Pericles* in the winter of 1609–10, in their recently printed quarto editions.

Timon of Athens

Three of Shakespeare's plays may be seen as sharing a common characteristic, in addition to the trivial fact that their titles all begin with a T—*Titus Andronicus, Troilus and Cressida,* and *Timon of Athens.* To put it bluntly, it is their triviality. On perusing them, we feel that Shakespeare, for all his genius, or because of it, ought to have been ashamed of himself! Shame on him! Fie on him! They are all unweeded gardens that have grown to seed. The best that can be said of them is that from time to time even Homer has to nod, and even Shakespeare has to let his genius fall asleep, leaving his dramatic fields to remain fallow and produce not sustaining corn but mere darnel. At least, we may forgive him his first apprentice attempt at drama in *Titus Andronicus*, on the supposition that he was following not his own inclination but the requirements of the time. In fact, we have to admit that it did at first enjoy some undeserved popularity both on the stage and in print, if only as a revenge play, or a parody of one, to satisfy the London rabble's thirst for blood. As for *Troilus and Cressida* and *Timon of Athens*, however, they have no such excuse. Both were written at the height of Shakespeare's dramatic career, the one in the immediate aftermath of *Hamlet*, the other (it seems) in the immediate aftermath of *King Lear*. Then why, we may ask, did the dramatist stoop to compose such inferior plays, considering that, unlike *Titus Andronicus*, neither of them was particularly apt for stage performance, and neither of them seems in fact to have been performed on the stage in Shakespeare's lifetime? Why did he let the greatness of *Hamlet* run to seed in *Troilus*? And why did he let the greatness of *King Lear* run to seed in *Timon*? All we find in *Troilus* is a continuing bitterness at the frailty of women and a consequent disillusionment in mankind. All we find in *Timon* is a continuing indignation at human ingratitude, with the negative feelings of a Lear unredeemed by a Cordelia. So Timon dies, without his death seeming in any way tragic, but merely as melancholic as himself, no longer Timon but "Misanthropos", the hater of mankind (IV iii.53).

Now, we may ask, what is the object of all this overflowing indignation, whether in *Lear* or in *Timon* or (as remains to be seen) in *Coriolanus*? What is the point of Shakespeare writing a play that is so unlikely to be performed on a stage?

It even seems as if he left *Timon* unfinished, and that is why it remained unperformed. And if he left it unfinished, it may be because he felt he had let his emotions get the better of him, and so he found himself unable or unwilling to complete his manuscript. Anyhow, we may further ask, what was the deeper reason, the "objective correlative", of all this indignation, if not within the limited context of the play, at least in the wider context of the world, not least in the dramatist's religious background? For there at least, if only on the assumption of Shakespeare's Catholicism or Catholic sympathies, we may find ample material for his indignation—not least against the politicians of the time, notably the two Cecils, father and son, for their unremitting, unrelenting persecution of the poor Catholics.

Certainly, of this kind of indignation there is abundant evidence in the text of the play—so much indeed that the dramatist might have regarded this fact alone as sufficient reason for not having brought his manuscript to completion or his play to performance. As it stood, the text may have struck him as offering too much scope for either the deleting pen of the censor or the accusing tongue of the informer.

To begin with, there is more than one indication in the first part of the play, while Timon is still in Athens (and Shakespeare was still in London), that the dramatist was deeply perturbed—as previously in his history plays of *Richard III* and *Richard II* and his tragedy of *Macbeth*—by the biblical memory of the betrayal of Jesus by Judas, especially in the episode of the Last Supper. Then, as we read, Jesus himself was perturbed by the thought that one of his disciples was about to betray him, and he said, "He that dips his hand in the dish with me, he shall betray me" (Matt. xxvi.23). This is recalled from the beginning of the play by the cynic philosopher Apemantus, who seems to recall the function of Thersites in *Troilus and Cressida*, as he remarks of Timon's flatterers, "It grieves me to see so many dip their meat/ in one man's blood" (I ii.42). He further underscores the relevance of these words to the Last Supper: "There's example for't. The fellow that/ sits next him now, parts bread with him . . ./ is the readiest man to kill him. 'T has been prov'd" (I ii.48). Nor is it just the jaundiced eye of Apemantus that perceives the biblical parallel. It is also noticed by the presumably impartial eye of the first Stranger in Act III: "Why, this is the world's soul, and just of the same piece/ is every flatterer's spirit. Who can call him/ his friend that dips in the same dish?" (III ii.71). The same stranger goes on to draw an explicit connection between such Judas-like treachery and the sin of ingratitude, which has so long rankled in the dramatist's mind, at least since the time of *Twelfth Night*, and has come to a climax in *King Lear*: "O see the monstrousness of man,/ when he looks out in an ungrateful shape!" (III ii.79).

This indignation at the ingratitude of others, as expressed first by such impartial lookers-on, then by Timon and the dramatist himself, is not just on a personal level, as in the case of Jesus and Judas, but on a supra-personal or national level. This appears in other comments made by the above-mentioned strangers. After the first has expressed his outrage at "the world's soul", betraying itself in such "monstrous ingratitude", the second adds, with explicit reference to the religious background of the age, "And religion groans at it", while the third is indignant that "men must learn now with pity to dispense,/ for policy sits above conscience" (III ii.72, 84, 93). In other words, the dramatist is evidently pointing at the way the politicians of his age, notably the two Cecils, have for their own political ends deliberately suppressed the consciences of a whole nation from the time Elizabeth I came to the throne of England in 1558. In the very next scene, moreover, it is a servant of Timon's who, commenting on the hypocrisy of Timon's flatterers, remarks, "The devil knew not what he did when he made men politic" (III iii.28). He even draws a paradoxical comparison between the cold, calculating Machiavellian politicians of the age and the Puritans "that under hot ardent zeal would set whole realms on fire" (III iii.33)—like Laertes in Hamlet (IV v.103) and "young Charbon the Puritan" in *All's Well That Ends Well* (I iii.57). That is to say, it is the former who have of set purpose, according to the author of *A Declaration of the True Causes* (1592), made cynical use of the latter to further their self-interest. And so, the servant concludes, with continuing reference to the politico-religious background of the age, no less than to the person of one of the flatterers, "of such a nature is his politic love" (III iii.35).

The climax to all this comment comes in Act IV in the contrast between the despairing lament of Timon's faithful steward, Flavius, and the misanthropic fury of Timon in his self-imposed exile. On the one hand, the words of Flavius, "We have seen better days" (IV ii.27), recall the nostalgia of the old duke in his reply to Orlando in *As You Like It* (II vii.120ff), and the general feeling of those who clung to the "old faith", whether at home or abroad in Elizabethan England. On the other, the words of Timon, enigmatically referring to the "sight of priests in holy vestments bleeding" (IV iii.126), can only point to the actual sufferings and martyrdom of Catholic priests that had been continuing throughout the dramatist's career. Not that the priests were actually wearing vestments while being tortured on the rack in the Tower or hanged, drawn, and quartered at Tyburn. But at the time of their capture in recusant houses, they were not infrequently caught by the pursuivants in "holy vestments" while offering the sacrifice of the Mass—a deed that was of itself declared to be a treasonable offence punishable by death, and so the prelude to the torture of the rack and the gallows.

Such is this play of indignant frustration, which is surely felt no less acutely by the dramatist than by his mouthpiece. First, we are shown scenes of his unreflecting prodigality. Then there are other scenes in which his prodigality catches up with him. Lastly, there are yet further scenes of indignation, both when he confronts his creditors at a mock banquet, at which all he has to give them is "nothing" (III vi.94), and when he goes off to dwell in misanthropic seclusion in a cave and woods by the seashore. Only in this anti-dramatic outcome of this anti-drama Timon seems, like Lear, to have learnt something precious for himself, partly from the triple "nothing" he has distributed among his creditors, partly from the loyalty of the "one honest man" he has found in his servant Flavius (IV iii.506). Such is the lesson of mystical enlightenment which is put into his mouth towards the end of the play, and close to the end of Shakespeare's own dramatic career: "Nothing brings me all things" (V i.193). So what we are left with at the end of the play—which, like *King Lear* but on a smaller scale, is neither comedy nor history nor tragedy, though with something of all three genres—is the lonely grave of Timon with its inscription (echoed by W. B. Yeats for the epitaph on his grave at the foot of Ben Bulben), "Pass by, and curse thy fill, but pass, and stay not here thy gait" (V iv.73).

For the dramatist, however, that is not yet the end. He must needs recall the ending of *Hamlet* to the accompaniment of the drums of Fortinbras, as Timon's friend Alcibiades accepts the apology of the Athenian senators, with the recognition that "all have not offended" (V iii.35), comes upon the grave of Timon, reads the inscription (for the benefit of the audience) and commands, "Let our drums strike!" (V iv.85). But in the sound of those drums, as in the ending of *Hamlet,* we may sense the dramatist's dissatisfaction coming after his spent utterance of frustration. And then "the rest is silence", as, unlike *Hamlet,* the play of *Timon* is consigned to the "formless ruin of oblivion" (*Troilus and Cressida*, IV vi.166).

chapter 12
Religion in the Roman Plays II

Antony and Cleopatra

IN THIS INVESTIGATION of the Catholic background of Shakespeare in his plays, sooner or later we have to face the basic question of how he envisaged the person of the great queen who gave her name to what is not unjustly called "the Elizabethan persecution". Even among recusant documents we may read a certain measure of flattery concerning the queen, as in Persons's dedication of his *Brief Discourse* (1580) and in the main part of Southwell's *Humble Supplication* (1600), where these Jesuits who had most reason to criticize her cruelty praise her clemency. There are also innumerable accounts of Elizabethan martyrs such as Campion, whose last words on the scaffold almost invariably include a profession of loyalty to the queen and a prayer for her good health and long life. On the other hand, there is also the less flattering and doubtlessly more sincere language of Allen's *Admonition to the Nobility and People of England*, which was printed in 1588 to be distributed with copies of the Bull of Pope Sixtus V in anticipation of a Spanish invasion of England. Here we find compressed into a small space many of the discontented feelings and terms of abuse no doubt current against the queen in the seminaries, from "bastard" to "Jezebel".

In the plays of Shakespeare, too, we may find both kinds of utterance, praise and blame. More openly, as in the above-mentioned writings of the Jesuits, we find words of praise. Thus in *A Midsummer Night's Dream* Elizabeth is evidently the "imperial votaress" mentioned by Oberon and described as lost in "maiden meditation" (II i.163), in a setting that recalls the famous entertainment prepared in her honour by the Earl of Leicester at Kenilworth Castle in 1575. In *Henry V* she is called "our gracious empress" in the Chorus to Act V (30), in connection with Essex's expedition to Ireland in 1599. In *Twelfth Night* she is identified with the Countess Olivia, who is adamant in rejecting the proposals of Duke Orsino in the name of "a brother's dead love" (I i.31), with reference to Edward VI, though that young king had died some forty years before the play was presented at court. On the other hand, at a deeper level we may find not a few implications of blame. Thus when the queen died in 1603, Shakespeare was rebuked by a fellow poet and dramatist, Henry Chettle, in *England's Mourning Garment* (1603), for his strange silence at a time when all other poets were loud in their lamentation. "Nor doth the silver-tongued Melicert," he complains, with evident reference to the "mellifluous" Shakespeare, "drop from his honeyed muse one sable tear/ to mourn her death." Already we have noted a probable portrayal of Elizabeth I in *Richard III*, in the depiction of another Elizabeth, queen to Edward IV, as a "poor shadow, painted queen" and a "shallow, changing woman" (IV iv.83, 432). The queen herself is further said, by her own courtier William Lambarde, to have recognized herself in Richard II, not only in the abdication scene of Act IV but also in its antecedent cause, the royal love of flattery—a cause that is also shown in *Julius Caesar* as Caesar's fatal weakness (II i.207). There is also the possibility that Elizabeth is implied in the "fiend-like queen" of Macbeth (V vii.98), while the reluctance the latter admits to taking up the dagger against Duncan, because he "resembled/ my father as he slept", recalls that of the English queen in signing the death-warrant against her royal cousin Mary Stuart. This in turn looks back to an earlier resemblance we have noted in *King John*, where John's blame of Hubert for having brought about Arthur's death is compared to Elizabeth's blame of her secretary William Davison for Mary's death.

So now, as we turn to the later Roman plays after the long gap from *Julius Caesar*, we meet with a perception not uncommon among critics and biographers that enshrined in *Antony and Cleopatra* is the tragic love affair between Essex and Elizabeth. From a historical viewpoint, this new Roman play may be seen as a sequel to *Julius Caesar*, and the dramatist's source-book remains *Plutarch's Lives*, as translated by Sir Thomas North in 1579. But from a dramatic and stylistic viewpoint, the dramatist seems to have changed out of all recognition during the interval of seven or eight years. From the sober, measured, rhetorical style of the earlier play, in a traditional Roman setting of black and white, the dramatist now offers us an almost orgiastic profusion of variety and colour, with a flamboyance of baroque imagery suited to the Egyptian background of Cleopatra. In the old Roman play the two women, Calphurnia and Portia, wives to Caesar and Brutus, remain minor characters in the background of events, neither of them worthy of being regarded as heroines, since the play as a whole is male-oriented. But now in this new play Antony himself plays a subordinate role to the glamorous Cleopatra, who is lavishly and memorably portrayed by his friend Enobarbus: "Age cannot wither her, nor custom stale/ her infinite variety" (II ii.243). It may even be said that of all Shakespeare's female characters Cleopatra is the most memorable, though not perhaps the most admirable, least of all the most reputable. What is so impressive about her characterization is, in fact, her duplicity or, to put it in more favourable terms, her ambivalence. On the one hand, she is no doubt, as Philo sees her from the beginning, a whore and a strumpet, while Antony is "a strumpet's fool" (I i.13). Antony himself recognizes his need to break "these strong Egyptian fetters" that bind him to his "dotage" (I ii.125), but he cannot bring himself to do so. Yet in yielding to her temptations of luxury, he and she both achieve a strange apotheosis that brings out the best in Shakespeare's powers of poetic description. We might even think that Shakespeare, no less than Antony, has fallen for the wiles of "this enchanting queen", who is "cunning past man's thought" (I ii.137, 155)—recalling the way he fell for the charms of the Dark Lady.

It is here, according to the opinions of the above-mentioned critics and biographers, that we may find the dramatist's mature reflection on the personality of the so-called Virgin Queen some four years after her passing and Chettle's mourning. And there at her side is, they add, the dramatist's other reflection on the personality of the deceased friend of his noble patron, the Earl of Essex, the queen's lover and victim, whose death warrant she is said to have signed with a reluctance (real or feigned) similar to that with which she had signed the death warrant for Mary Stuart. How then, we may now ask, does this comparison appear from a recusant viewpoint? It is, of course, only a probable comparison, but it is not improbable either. At least, granting its probability, what, we may ask, does the theory tell us about the dramatist's feelings with regard to Queen Elizabeth? Can we say that he approved of her on the whole, in spite of her religious policy? Or must we not rather say that, while fascinated by her, he had many misgivings about her—misgivings which may be seen mirrored in his attitude to the Dark Lady, who may have been (in the opinion of G. B. Shaw) the queen herself?

To begin with, we may say that Cleopatra is, like Elizabeth, imposing in outward splendour and inward strength of character. Wherever she comes, she instantly becomes the natural centre of interest and attention—unlike her clumsy successor, the Scottish James I. Whenever she appears, she wins the sympathy not only of those around her on the stage but also of those in the audience. As Enobarbus says of her, not without irony, "Vilest things/ become themselves in her, that holy priests/ bless her when she is riggish" (II ii.246). All the same, Shakespeare makes no attempt to disguise the fact that she is after all a strumpet, to be numbered on her own admission among those that "trade in love" (II v.2). This is also how Allen describes Elizabeth in his *Admonition* of 1588, as "an incestuous bastard, begotten and born in sin . . . the very shame of her sex and princely name, the chief spectacle of sin and abomination in this our age." Again, just as Cleopatra is said to be "cunning past man's thought" (I ii.155), in much the same way Elizabeth's own ministers, not excluding Burghley himself, noted and lamented the fact. To Cleopatra, with her easy conscience, lies are no obstacle to finding and embracing the appropriate means to keep "the ne'er lust-wearied Antony" (II i.38) in her "strong toil of grace" (V ii.349). In her ambivalent character bad and good, sin and grace, lust and love meet together without seeming discrepancy. Both aspects in her seem to lead herself and Antony to that apotheosis in which, as she proclaims in her final speech (comparable to that made by Elizabeth to her loving subjects at Tilbury on the eve of the

Armada), she becomes "fire and air" while giving her "other elements . . . to baser life" (V ii.291). And so, as "a lass unparallel'd" (V ii.318), she goes to rejoin Antony "where souls do couch on flowers" (IV xii.51). Her glowing words of eloquence are, however, undermined by Octavius Caesar, or rather "by her physician", with the information that "she hath pursued conclusions infinite of easy ways to die" (V ii.355). Thus right up to the end she is shown, no less than the Virgin Queen, as a coquette, ever conscious of playing her part on a stage and of the need to maintain her image in the sight of men, without caring how her servants or other underlings may suffer for it. We may therefore conclude that she is as empty and vain as Cressida, and that her "grace" is all in her toils, in the "seeming truth" she puts on "to entrap the wisest"—not only Antony but all who see or read or study the play.

This may lead up to a comparison between the two great plays Shakespeare presented to the world at this time, *King Lear* and *Antony and Cleopatra*. There can surely be little doubt as to which of them is the greater. Though some critics seem to favour the latter play, it is surely the former that has to be hailed as the dramatist's greatest masterpiece, reaching as it does both upwards to the height of human grandeur and downwards to the depths of human degradation. *King Lear* is the leaden casket chosen by Bassanio, within which alone is true happiness to be found, in the love of the lady Portia. The latter play, on the other hand, is all outward display and splendour, comparable to the gold casket chosen by the Prince of Morocco, who opens it only to find a skull grinning at him from within.

Now we may briefly turn from Cleopatra and Elizabeth to Antony and the Earl of Essex. In the course of this play Antony seems to have hardly any independent identity in himself. The undeniable poetic magnificence which the dramatist puts into his mouth seems to be drawn out of him by his dependence on Cleopatra. In himself he is a powerful man, a brave soldier, who, like the Earl of Essex, has won the loyalty of his followers, even if some of them turn to betray him—as Essex was betrayed by Sir Francis Bacon in his hour of need. But this aspect of his is not allowed full scope, so long as he remains in Egypt under Cleopatra's enchantments. She even betrays him in the end, in the sea battle at Actium, when, having insisted on accompanying him, she turns round and flees at a critical moment, leaving him to follow her with his ships. "I never saw an action of such shame" is the indignant comment of Scarus (III vii.31)—and many of Essex's followers may well have felt the same on their leader's abrupt desertion of his cause in Ireland. Moreover, from a recusant viewpoint, among those followers were not a few Catholic gentlemen like Robert Catesby, who saw in him and his cause a prospect of religious toleration. Also in Antony's mouth we may note the typical recusant reflection, already noted in the words of Friar Francis in *Much Ado About Nothing* (IV i.219) and of the French king in *All's Well That Ends Well* (V iii.60): "What our contempts do often hurl from us,/ we wish it ours again" (I ii.132). Interestingly, a similar reflection is also put into the mouth of his rival Octavius Caesar: "The ebb'd man, ne'er lov'd till ne'er worth love,/ comes dear'd by being lack'd" (I iv.43).

Such reflections, from seemingly opposing viewpoints, may serve to show how deep are the undercurrents of recusant thought flowing through a play seemingly dedicated to the memory of Queen Elizabeth. As Antony sadly comments, "Our terrene moon"—Cynthia, the commonly used poetic name for Elizabeth—"is now eclips'd" (III xi.153).

And as Cleopatra adds, "There is nothing left remarkable/ beneath the visiting moon" (IV xiii.67).

Coriolanus

The fierce indignation at human ingratitude so vividly dramatized in *King Lear* and so incoherently pursued in *Timon of Athens* spills over yet once more into the scenes of *Coriolanus*. Also in *Coriolanus*, as the third of the Roman plays, we look back to a similar if less intense manifestation of this feeling at the beginning of *Julius Caesar*, in the scene of the tribunes chiding the people for their fickleness in turning so readily from the dead Pompey to the living Caesar. This may prompt us to ask what it was that gave rise in the dramatist to such strong expressions of indignation over such a long period of time. Evidently, it did nothing to increase his popularity with his audiences or to improve his dramatic art. It was hardly the aesthetic consideration, proposed by the Roman satirist Juvenal, *"Facit indignatio versum"*—Out of indignation comes versification. Rather, the dramatist ought to have learnt the opposite lesson from his laborious composition of *Timon of Athens*—assuming that he composed it before *Coriolanus*—that indignation is an obstacle to versification, at least of the dramatic kind. Or was there something in his own life at the time, in the aftermath of the Gunpowder Plot, that induced him to turn on his London audience, like Coriolanus on the people of Rome, and berate them for their fickleness—as he had called them in Part II of *Henry IV*, "the blunt monster with uncounted heads,/ the still-discordant wavering multitude" (Ind.18)? Or was there something, as some commentators suggest, in the social and economic situation of the Midlands that had led to a confrontation between Shakespeare as landowner and the depressed people, which is somehow reflected in the background of the play? Or was it all an expression of his private concern over the declining health of his mother, Mary Arden, who was soon to die in the September of 1608, the very year when he is thought to have completed the play?

True, *Coriolanus* is endowed with more dramatic unity than *Timon of Athens*, and it is even praised by T. S. Eliot—in contrast to *Hamlet*—as a masterpiece of dramatic art. Yet for all its art, as I have suggested, *Coriolanus* may well be classified with *Troilus* and *Timon* among Shakespeare's dramatic failures. Whatever Eliot may say, there is something paradoxically frigid in the art of this play, for all the hot indignation felt by the hero against the people. It has to be confessed that the hero is antipathetic not only to his own people of Rome but to all people of all time. There is nothing in him to appeal to anyone, save to those who find romance in war. Coriolanus himself may be a successful hero in war, but he is a failure in peace—and it is his own fault. He is too proud to win anyone to his side, save only his fellow patricians, and even they get exasperated with him. So we cannot but consent to his banishment from Rome. It is what he deserves, and it is what he gets. He deserves no sympathy from the audience, and he wins it only insofar as we come to see him as the underdog—which is not exactly what might comfort a man of his pride! Insofar as in his banishment he joins company with Valentine and Romeo, Bolingbroke and Mowbray, Duke Senior and Orlando, Cordelia and Edgar, we may well feel pity for him. We may even see in him something of the recusant predicament. Particularly when, on being banished, he declares, "There is a world elsewhere" (III iii.133), he recalls Richard II's vision concerning a "new world" (V i.24) and Kent's in *King Lear* concerning "a country new", a theme common to recusant exiles. He even recurs to the typical recusant reflection noted above—in *Much Ado* IV i.219, in *All's*

Well V iii.60, and more recently in *Antony and Cleopatra* I ii.132, I iv.43—in his remark, "I shall be lov'd when I am lack'd" (IV i.15), though his words lose much of their force when applied by himself to himself.

Really, there is very little in *Coriolanus* to evoke our admiration. The play seems to be little more than yet another exercise in indignation which the dramatist feels he must vent on his unfortunate audience. So it is no wonder if he had no recorded audience in his own lifetime or for many years after his death. The people, as we say, vote with their feet. Whatever scholars may say in defence of the play, in their blind faith that whatever proceeds from Shakespeare's pen must be a work of genius, it has no form or comeliness that we should desire it. So why, we may ask—as with the above-mentioned three T's—did the dramatist choose to compose such an obviously unpopular play, so openly directed against the people as well of Jacobean England as of ancient Rome? We may suspect, in the first place, that it had something to do with his dying mother, especially considering that the central character of the play is not so much Coriolanus himself as his redoubtable mother, Volumnia. From her he has learnt both his prowess as a warrior and his pride in himself. He is, in short, his mother's boy, like so many of the great men in world history. Among the Romans he stands out for valour in battle, a valour that invariably spells victory, but in relation to his mother he remains the little Gaius Marcius. So when he is banished from Rome and returns with the Volscian army to avenge himself on the Romans, he is unable to resist his mother's pleading. He cannot but yield to her, and so his fate is sealed. Here we have the most memorable words, the only really memorable words, in the play, when he breaks down and exclaims, "O mother, mother,/ what have you done? . . . The gods look down and this unnatural scene/ they laugh at" (V iii.182). She may have won a victory for Rome, but her son has suffered a mortal defeat—which is still after all his own doing.

Now what, we may again ask from a recusant viewpoint, is the significance of these words concerning the ambivalence of "Rome" for Shakespeare and his contemporaries? Can we accept the interpretation (1) that Shakespeare was for a time composing his plays on behalf of the English Catholics, if in a seemingly non-committal manner; (2) that then, maybe on the occasion of the Gunpowder Plot, he became, like his friend Ben Jonson, disillusioned in the Catholic cause, even turning against it for a time, perhaps during his composition of *Timon of Athens* and *Antony and Cleopatra*; (3) that now, at the earnest plea of his dying mother, he gave up his disenchantment with the Catholic cause, only to foresee his days as a dramatist numbered and an early retirement to Stratford inevitable? Can we consider such an interpretation as at least feasible? It all depends on what kind of a woman Mary Arden was, and what were her relations with her husband John, not to mention her son William. Of course, we may conjecture that she lived and died a Catholic, true to the memory of both her Catholic father and her recusant husband, as well as her Arden ancestors. All we have to go on in Shakespeare's plays, however, is *Hamlet*, where the hero looks back to a golden age of childhood when his father was still alive and happily married to his mother, but now the father has become a ghost and his mother sadly married to his uncle, prompting him to exclaim against women in general, "Frailty, thy name is woman!" (I ii.146). Apart from these two mothers, Gertrude and Volumnia, not counting the mothers of Romeo and Juliet, we see few mothers in such close relation to their sons in the plays. We may even suspect that the relation between Shakespeare and his own mother was not such a close one, in contrast to that between him and his daughter Susanna, which is reflected in play after play of his final period. Needless to say, there is no question of Volumnia, or any of the other women connected with Coriolanus, his wife Virgilia and her friend Valeria, being described in terms of "grace". That epithet, which seems so out of place in a play like this, comes more naturally for the succession of ideal heroines who appear in the final romances. So I feel obliged to give it as my opinion that *Coriolanus* is, for whatever reason, the least recusant of Shakespeare's plays. And so I imagine, following the lines of Coriolanus's own imagination, the gods looking down from heaven and laughing at this play, in which the hero is himself—like Lear in his madness—playing the fool.

chapter 13
Recusant Romance

Pericles

In the winter of 1609–10 the Cholmeley Players, as noted above, presented two of Shakespeare's plays at recusant houses in Yorkshire, notably at that of Sir John Yorke, Gowthwaite Hall in Nidderdale—notably, because it was soon to become notorious as a case submitted to the court of Star Chamber in Westminster. One of the plays, which we have already considered at some length from a recusant viewpoint, was *King Lear*. The other, which we have now to consider, was *Pericles*, which we know was performed on the feast of Candlemas, February 2, 1610. So now we may ask, what would have been the appeal of this first of Shakespeare's last "romances" to such an audience?

First, it may be of interest to note how soon *Pericles* seems to have come upon the very heels of *Coriolanus*, that least recusant of Shakespeare's plays, seeing that both of them evidently belong to the same year, 1608. Yet apart from this common dating, the two plays seem to be opposed to each other in almost every respect. In point of popularity, *Coriolanus* is cold and forbidding, even or especially as a work of dramatic art, appealing to the fine discriminating taste of T. S. Eliot. There is nothing popular about it, even as its hero disdains the voices of the people. So not surprisingly, there is no record of any public performance of it in Shakespeare's lifetime, nor does it appear in any printed form till its inclusion in the First Folio of 1623. *Pericles*, however, for all its obvious imperfections, was evidently one of Shakespeare's most popular plays both on the stage and in a series of quarto editions—though it failed to achieve the canonization of appearing in a folio edition till 1664, in a second printing of the Third Folio.

Secondly, and more significantly, the climax of *Coriolanus* comes in Act IV, with the emotional appeal of the hero's mother Volumnia to her vengeful son on behalf of the city of Rome—an appeal that strangely coincides with the last illness and death of the dramatist's own mother, Mary Arden, in 1608. *Pericles*, however, leads up to the touching reunion between the grieving father and his long-lost daughter, and then to a further reunion between the grieving husband and his long-lost wife, the former having been born at sea and the latter seemingly lost at sea in the same tempest. Evidently, the people, whether in Shakespeare's time or our own, know what they want—not a proud hero bowing reluctantly to his mother's prayers and then turning away from her, persistent in his pride till the end, but a humbled hero reunited, like Lear with Cordelia, first with his graceful daughter and then, as a cumulation of grace, with his dear wife. Ben Jonson, in a significantly entitled "Ode to Himself", may have rebuked those audiences who preferred "some mouldy tale like Pericles" to his own works of dramatic art, but his criticism betrays more envy or self-love than judgment.

The imperfections of *Pericles*, summed up by Jonson as "mouldy", are there for all to see, especially in the first two acts, which were probably not of Shakespeare's composition. It seems as if the great dramatist has allowed some hack to work on the first two acts and then stepped in to show how dramatic success may be achieved out of the jaws of failure—though he himself had failed to do so in *Timon of Athens*, not to mention *Coriolanus*. Or it is as if he has been handed an unfinished, inferior play to revise and improve, and then, so far from disdaining it as inferior, he has discovered in it some interesting dramatic possibilities—as in his previous "problem" comedy of *Measure for Measure*. So he has developed it in such a way as to reveal a new dramatic vision of his own, at once unique among his previous plays and the starting point for a new genre of tragi-comic romance. Or again, it is as if he has found in the plot of the old play an exciting similarity with his previous tragi-comic masterpiece of *King Lear*, and has developed this similarity so as to atone for the sad ending of Cordelia's death followed by that of her poor father, by making Marina the occasion of a happy ending in new life for both her father and her mother. (Here we may also note the way Shakespeare likes to atone for faults in past plays, as we have already seen in *Much Ado About Nothing*.) It is, moreover, this kind of happy ending, consisting in a reunion of past with present, that the dramatist now goes on to present in the other plays of this new genre from *Cymbeline* through *The Winter's Tale* to *The Tempest*.

Nevertheless, even in the less than Shakespearian scene at the beginning of *Pericles* there is something that may have arrested Shakespeare's recusant attention. This is the strange case of incest between King Antiochus and his fair daughter, who remains no less nameless than the species of sin committed between them. It is indeed this that the king proposes to her prospective suitors, including Pericles, in the form of a riddle which they must solve on pain of death. Such, too, was the riddle in recent English history between King Henry VIII and his second wife Anne Boleyn, though at the time of their splendid wedding at court Henry's first lawful wife was living in retirement. It took the form of an ugly rumour, not unknown to Sir Thomas More and Thomas Cranmer, and handed down among the English Catholic exiles abroad, that Anne was not only Henry's second wife but also his daughter by her mother, Elizabeth, who had been one of Henry's mistresses. This rumour was first mentioned in print by the exiled Catholic theologian Nicholas Sanders, in his Latin history *De Origine ac Progressu Schismatis Anglicani*, which was not published till 1585, four years after his death. (In the first English translation, edited by David Lewis in 1877, the authenticity of the rumour is discussed in a long introduction of over one hundred pages.) This alone may suggest a recusant interpretation of Pericles' situation of perpetual exile, which is hard to explain in terms of the play alone.

Even before the master hand of Shakespeare becomes unmistakable from the beginning of Act III, there is one interesting scene, clearly Shakespearian, in which Pericles has suffered shipwreck and finds himself cast ashore on the unidentified coast of Pentapolis. Here he comes upon a group of allegorizing fishermen, not unlike the allegorizing gardeners in *Richard II* (IV iv). In their talk of "the poor men that were cast away" in the shipwreck, one of them seems to anticipate the pity of Miranda in *The Tempest* (I ii.9) with his lament, "Alas, poor souls! It grieved my heart to hear what pitiful cries they made to us" (II i.19). Then, in response to the question, "how the fishes live in the sea", he gives the satirically Shakespearian answer, "Why, as men do a-land, the great ones eat up the little ones" (II i.29)—recalling the precocious remarks made by Lady Macduff's son in *Macbeth* IV ii. This may be understood as referring to the "reformation" undertaken by Henry VIII and Elizabeth I with their Machiavellian ministers, or what has been more aptly termed "a revolution of the rich against the poor". So Pericles is left to wonder at the way "from the finny subject of the sea these fishers tell the infirmities of men" (II i.53)—not just in general, or with reference to that ancient time, but with precise reference to the dramatist's own time and that of his audience. There still follow two significant evocations of *Hamlet*, where the prince is in a Puritan mood. Thus in the second fisherman's hopes by craving (or praying) to " 'scape whipping" (II i.95), we may recall the very phrase used by Hamlet to Polonius concerning the universality of sin (II ii.562). Also in Pericles's comment on the conversation of the fishermen, "How well this honest mirth becomes their labour!" (II i.102), we may note a contrast to the scandal taken by Hamlet at the way the clown "sings at grave-making" (V i.72). Evidently, unlike Hamlet, Pericles is no Puritan!

Turning now to the second, more clearly Shakespearian, part of the play from Act III onwards, we note that what stands out is not so much the plight of the poor hero, who remains in the background till the last act, as the birth and growth to maidenhood of his daughter. She has been "born at sea" in the midst of a tempest, during which her mother dies in childbirth, and so she receives the name of Marina (III iii.13, V i.198). Her name may well have reminded a recusant audience, such as those who came for the performance at Gowthwaite Hall, of the folk etymology of Mary's name, derived by St. Bernard in the twelfth century from the Latin for sea, *mare*, in its neuter plural form, *maria*. From this comes the popular title of Mary as *Stella Maris*, or Star of the Sea, on which St. Bernard dwells in several of his sermons, notably in one for Advent, "Let me say something about this name, which is interpreted as meaning, 'Star of the Sea'." He goes on to exhort his hearers in significantly nautical imagery: "When tossed about by waves of pride, ambition, hatred or jealousy, look up to the star, call upon Mary." Secondly, it is not only the name of Marina that points to the Virgin Mary, but in the moving climax of the play, when Pericles recognizes his long-lost daughter and finds in her a new life, he greets her with the words, "Thou that begett'st him that did thee beget" (V i.197)—words that strangely echo those put by Dante into the mouth of St. Bernard on addressing the Virgin Mother in the climax of his *Paradiso* (canto xxxiii), "Virgin Mother, daughter of thy Son"—daughter as he is Son of God, mother as he is also son of man. In her, moreover, as a welcome relief from the series of "grace"-less plays—*Timon of Athens, Antony and Cleopatra,* and *Coriolanus*—we again meet with an ideal heroine associated with divine "grace", when the Chorus of old Gower, as it were anticipating the other Chorus of Time in *The Winter's Tale* (IV 24), hails in Marina "all the grace,/ which makes her both the heart and place/ of general wonder" (IV 10).

Another notable characteristic of this play, from the moment Shakespeare takes it over in Act III, is the accumulation of references to the goddess Diana. She is hailed as "bright Diana" (III iii.28), "celestial Dian, goddess argentine" (V i.251), and "immortal Dian" (V iii.37), and it is she who presides over the happy ending of the play both at Mitylene, where Pericles is reunited with his long-lost daughter, Marina, and at her temple in Ephesus, where he is reunited with his long-lost wife, Thaissa. The significance of all these references to Diana we may understand in view of the tendency in Florentine Neoplatonism from the late fourteenth century onwards to reinterpret pagan religion in the light of Christian theology. Then Diana, as goddess of chastity, was seen as foreshadowing the Virgin Mary, and while Christ was spoken of as the sun-god Apollo, Mary was symbolized by the moon, one of the three forms of Diana. So we have the liturgical hymn in which it is said of Mary, *"Pulchra ut luna, errantes collustrat"*—Fair as the moon, she shines on us wanderers. Even as early as the Book of Revelation, the last book of the New Testament, attributed to St. John "the Divine", Mary is recognized as the Woman in the strange vision of Rev. xii, clothed with the sun (in the glory of Christ) and standing on the moon (above the sphere of change). So when Pericles in the final scene prays to Diana in her temple at Ephesus, "Hail, Dian!" (V iii.1), it may sound in Catholic ears as an echo of the customary prayer to Our Lady, "Hail, Mary!"

With such abundant implication of the Virgin Mary, in the name of Marina, in her association with "grace", and in the patronage and intercession of Diana—where the name of Diana may be seen as protecting the dramatist from the penalties decreed in the Act of 1606 "in restraint of abuses of players"—we may well recognize in this play of *Pericles*, in contrast to the preceding Roman plays derived from Plutarch's *Lives*, a fully recusant play. We may even see it as no less recusant than *King Lear* and no less relevant to a recusant audience such as that which assembled at Gowthwaite Hall on February 2, 1610—namely, the feast of Candlemas, which used to be known in the Roman liturgy as the feast of Our Lady's Purification.

Cymbeline

Among the plays of Shakespeare there is an interesting contrast to be found in those that derive from two of his major sources, Holinshed's *Chronicles* and Plutarch's *Lives*, the former for his plays on England, the latter for his plays on

Rome. In particular, in his use of Holinshed's *Chronicles* we find the dramatist turning from plays on English history to plays of British prehistory in the successive tragi-comedies of *King Lear* and *Cymbeline*. Then in these plays of British prehistory we find the further contrast, noted above, between the strange absence of "Britain" from the former play (though the adjective "British" occurs three times) and the frequency of its mention (some twenty-seven times) in the latter. This may be because, on coming to *Cymbeline*, the dramatist is closer to recorded history, as opposed to legend, with the coming of the Roman legions to Britain and their demand for the tribute Cymbeline owed to Rome. We may also consider the awareness, mentioned by Holinshed and echoed by Shakespeare in the mysterious prophecy concerning Posthumus and Imogen, that the events in this reign are all contemporary with the birth of Christ in Bethlehem. Then, in the person of Cymbeline we may expect to find traces of Henry VIII, who, as a Welsh Tudor, preferred to think of himself as king rather of Britain than of England, not least in his devotion to King Arthur (the name given to his elder brother) and his knights of the round table, with elaborate feasts of jousting in special suits of knightly armour.

Here we may turn from the question of how Shakespeare may have regarded Queen Elizabeth, especially in the person of Cleopatra, to the related question of how he may have seen her father, King Henry, especially in the person of Cymbeline. After all, it was he who set afoot all the religious, as well as political and legal, social and economic, changes affecting the lives of all Englishmen in the sixteenth century. This is a question that is strangely relevant to almost all the plays of Shakespeare in the Jacobean age, as we may find something of Henry's known character in the persons of Othello and Macbeth and even Lear—though not in the Roman plays. But we may recognize his memory even more clearly in the tragi-comic romances from *Cymbeline* onwards, culminating in what may be termed the historical romance of *Henry VIII*—insofar as Shakespeare may be seen to have had a hand in its composition.

First, what we may note in *Cymbeline* is the contrast between the king's former payment of tribute to Rome, while he was married to his former queen, the mother of Imogen, and his termination of that tribute, owing to the influence of his present queen, the mother of Cloten. As we learn from Cymbeline himself only at the end of the play, it was because of this "wicked queen", now dead, that he was dissuaded from paying the tribute to Rome, but now in the happy outcome he decides to renew the tribute and with it the peace between Britain and Rome. Now if he is to be compared to Henry VIII, to whom may we more fitly compare his second queen than to Anne Boleyn, whose marriage with Henry led him to renounce his allegiance to Rome? And to whom may we more fitly compare Imogen than to the princess Mary, who was born to Henry's lawful wife Katharine of Aragon, and whose loyalty to Rome is here symbolized in Imogen's loyalty to her husband, Posthumus, though exiled to Rome? Then the anger expressed by Cymbeline against his daughter, in calling her such abusive names as "basest thing", "disloyal thing", "foolish thing", and "thou vile one" (I i.125, 131, 150, 143), may be seen as corresponding to the shameful treatment shown by Henry to Mary for her loyalty to both her mother and the Pope.

It is only, I would maintain, in the light of this Catholic background, with Catholic memories of the reign of Henry VIII, that we may understand why the patriotic sentiments uttered in the play concerning "Britain"—recalling as they do the similar sentiments concerning "England" put into the mouth of the Bastard in *King John* (V vii.112ff)—are put into the mouths of the "wicked queen" (V v.464) and her worthless son, Cloten. In the context of his rejection of the Roman general Lucius's demand for renewed payment of the tribute, Cymbeline is represented first by Cloten, who declares, "Britain is/ a world by itself" (III i.13), and then by his queen, who praises "the natural bravery of your isle, which stands/ as Neptune's park, ribb'd and paled in/ with rocks unscalable and roaring waters" (III i.18)—as though echoing the nostalgic speech of John of Gaunt on "this England" in *Richard II* (II i.40). Here we may find it strange that such sentiments, proceeding as they seem to do from the patriotic heart of the dramatist, are expressed by two such unsympathetic characters. Can it be, we wonder, that he is turning away from his early professions of patriotism to a rejection of his own country under the baleful influence of Papal Rome? Or isn't it rather that he is rejecting the new-born nationalism, misnamed "patriotism", fostered under Henry and Elizabeth as a means of justifying their breach with Rome and of stirring up in the hearts of their subjects a mistrust and even hatred of Rome? In this connection we may note how the good Belarius was originally banished from Cymbeline's court on the charge of being "confederate with the Romans" (III iii.168) and how he is accused by Cymbeline even in the final scene of being both "a banished man" and "a traitor" (V v.319)—though he hotly denies the latter accusation, as did many of the Catholic recusants. All the time of his banishment he has been living with the young princes, Guiderius and Arviragus, as exiles in rural Wales, like the exiled duke and his companions in *As You Like It.*

On the other hand, turning from the prehistoric court of Cymbeline in Britain to the cultural surroundings of

Posthumus in Renaissance Rome—as though moving from the atmosphere of Holinshed's *Chronicles* to that of Boccaccio's *Decameron*—we may be astonished to find Posthumus described by Iachimo in terms that are little short of papal. "He sits among men," says the villain to Imogen, as if to tickle her ears with exaggerated praise of her husband, "like a descended god", and "he hath a kind of honour sets him off/ more than a mortal seeming" (I vi.169). He goes on to call him "a sir so rare,/ which you know cannot err" (I vi.175)—as if assigning to Posthumus the attribute of infallibility recognized by Catholic theologians in the Pope when teaching the universal Church on matters of faith and morals. It is strange! Yet not so strange, when we further compare these words of Iachimo concerning Posthumus with other words of Leontes concerning Polixenes in *The Winter's Tale* (V i.170). Evidently, as remains to be seen in proceeding from the one to the other play, these two plays are both of a piece with *Henry VIII*.

Returning now to Imogen, in whom we have noted a historical parallel with the princess Mary, we also find her associated with "grace", if in the flattering words of Iachimo. He twice addresses her as "your grace" (I vi.181, 203), confusing her spiritual quality with the title due to her as princess. More sincerely, in the congenial rural surroundings of Wales, she is recognized by Belarius, even under her male disguise, as "an angel, or if not,/ an earthly paragon" (III vi.42). Later, when she is found seemingly dead, she is addressed by the prince Guiderius as "sweetest, fairest lily", and by Belarius, in contrast to her father's previous abuse of her, as "blessed thing" and "a most rare boy" (IV ii.201, 208). Her grace is, moreover, associated with prayer, as when she speaks of her prayers for her banished husband "at the sixth hour of morn, at noon, at midnight" as her times for "orisons", when "I am in heaven for him" (I iii.31). Here the three hours she mentions seem to correspond to the hours of the divine office known as "sext", "none", and "compline", or to the prayer of the Angelus, which is recited in Catholic countries three times a day, in the morning, at noon, and in the evening, in memory of Our Lady and the mystery of the Incarnation. Moreover, in her prayer on going to bed, "From fairies and the tempters of the night,/ guard me, beseech ye!" (II ii.9), Imogen echoes the liturgical hymn for Sunday Compline, *"Te lucis ante terminum, rerum Creator, poscimus,"* which continues, *"Procul recedant somnia et noctium phantasmata"*— Before the end of day we ask you, Creator of all things . . . that wicked dreams and phantasms of night may go far away. Thirdly, when Imogen mistakes the headless body of Cloten for that of her husband, Posthumus, she strews leaves and weeds over his grave, saying "a century of prayers" (IV ii.391), as it were the Catholic prayer of the Rosary, or what is called in the history plays "numbering Ave-Maries" on one's beads (*Henry VI*, Part II I iii.59, Part III II i.162).

Now we may go straight to the last scene of the play, in which so many plots have their unexpected dénouement— to the scandal of not a few scholars, but to the rejoicing of ordinary spectators. First, we are relieved to hear of the death of the wicked queen, as reported by the good doctor Cornelius—echoing the words of Seyton to Macbeth on reporting the death of his lady, "The queen, my lord, is dead" (V v.27). His further report on the manner of her death, "with horror, madly dying" (V v.31), is not only reminiscent of the suicide of Lady Macbeth "by self and violent hands" (V vii.99), but also accords with contemporary accounts of the deaths both of Anne Boleyn, who was beheaded after vain appeals to the king for mercy, and of her daughter Elizabeth, whose fearful end was described in detail by one of her ladies-in-waiting, Lady Southwell. As for Queen Elizabeth in particular, she may be implied in Posthumus's disillusioned words referring to all women, "They are not constant, but changing still" (II v.30)—which recall both Hamlet's "Frailty, thy name is woman!" (I ii.146) and Richard III's cynical dismissal of another Queen Elizabeth as "Relenting fool, and shallow, changing woman!" (IV iv.432). Thus it seems as if Cymbeline's queen may stand, in the dramatist's understanding of her, at once for mother and daughter, Anne Boleyn and Elizabeth I.

Secondly, when Imogen is at last revealed to her husband, Posthumus, and they embrace each other, she boldly tells him, "Think that you are upon a rock!" (V v.263). Again, what a strange thing for her to say! Yet it recalls at the end of the play the equally strange identification of Posthumus with the Pope at the beginning. For the word "rock" implicitly points to the original name of Peter, as the rock (Greek *petra*) on which Christ chose to build his Church, according to the Latin words round the dome of Michelangelo in St. Peter's, Rome, *"Tu es Petrus, et super hanc petram aedificabo ecclesiam meam"*—Thou art Peter, and upon this rock I will build my Church (Matt. xvi.18). Thus the reunion of Posthumus and Imogen, implying the reunion effected by Mary Tudor with Rome during her brief reign, may be seen as taking place "upon a rock". Also to Imogen, now revealed as his missing daughter, Cymbeline declares, in words that recall the tears of Cordelia in *King Lear* (IV ii.32), "My tears that fall/ prove holy water on thee" (V v.269).

Thirdly, and above all, even in his victory over Lucius and the Roman legions, Cymbeline, now that his "wicked queen" and worthless son are both dead, unexpectedly decides to "submit to Caesar, and to the Roman Empire" (V v.461). It is as if the rumoured intention of Henry VIII on his deathbed is realized, though he died too soon and was succeeded by his Protestant son, Edward. Then Cymbeline goes on to declare, "Let/ a Roman and a British ensign wave/ friendly together!" (V v.480). In this ending, which implies a desire on the dramatist's part for a reunion between Protestant England and Papal Rome, we may also recognize the known ideal of James I to act as mediator between Protestant and Catholic as another Constantine. This may seem all the more appropriate in view of the coincidence between the dating of *Cymbeline* in 1609–10 and the deaths of three major obstacles to such reunion—on the Anglican side, that of Richard Bancroft, Archbishop of Canterbury, and on the Catholic side, that of Robert Persons, the Jesuit and "arch-Papist", both in 1610, followed two years later by that of Sir Robert Cecil, Earl of Salisbury and arch-persecutor of the Papists.

The Winter's Tale

In comparing *The Winter's Tale* with its romantic source, Robert Greene's *Pandosto* (1588), we may notice a significant difference Shakespeare introduced into his treatment of the story. This is his strange switching of the two lands of Sicilia and Bohemia, and thereby providing the land-locked country of Bohemia with a coastline, so as to incur the ridicule of Ben Jonson. Few scholars, however, seem to have paid attention to Shakespeare's probable (recusant) reason for making this switch. Surely Sicilia, being a three-cornered island, or (as it was known in classical times) Trinacria, stands for England, while Bohemia becomes the Catholic continent. Then, if the events recorded by Greene as happening in Bohemia are transposed by Shakespeare to Sicilia, it may well be because the dramatist is thinking of similar events that have taken place in his native England, according to the principle enunciated by Hamlet that players are "the abstracts and brief chronicles of the time" (II ii.555).

Consequently, just as in *Cymbeline* we considered how Shakespeare looks through the ages of British history from the reign of Cymbeline to that of Henry VIII, so in *The Winter's Tale* we may consider how he looks across the seas and the continent of Europe from Leontes's Sicilia to Henry's England. Only, whereas in *Cymbeline* the "wicked queen", unnamed in the play, may stand for Henry's second wife, Anne Boleyn, in *The Winter's Tale* Leontes's queen, Hermione, may stand for Henry's first and lawful wife, Katharine of Aragon. Further, whereas in *Cymbeline* it was the influence of the wicked queen and her son Cloten that led the British king to withhold his promised tribute from Rome, in *The Winter's Tale*, when Hermione is put on trial for adultery, she makes her appeal to the shrine and oracle of Apollo at Delphos—just as Katharine of Aragon, in Shakespeare's final historical romance of *Henry VIII*, makes her appeal to Rome. Then, too, we may find a continuity of character between Imogen, as Cymbeline's daughter by his first wife, and Perdita, Leontes's true daughter by his wife, Hermione, with both pointing to the same historical parallel with Katharine's daughter, the princess Mary. There is yet another character from the reign of Henry VIII whose figure may be seen appearing in both plays, the king's loyal councillor, Sir Thomas More, who suffered for his primary loyalty to Rome. We may see him, first, in Belarius, who is charged by Cymbeline as having been "confederate with the Romans" (III iii.68), and secondly, in Camillo, who is called "priest-like" by Leontes and "clerk-like" by Polixenes in the same scene (I ii.237, 392).

Here is, moreover, an interesting analogy which, as noted above, links three of the final romances together, moving with increasing clarity from *Cymbeline* through *The Winter's Tale* to *Henry VIII*. Here, too, we may notice the charge of treason made by Leontes not just against Hermione but against all who support her. This may perhaps seem a point of difference between *The Winter's Tale* and *Henry VIII*, in that Katharine is never accused of adultery or treason, but her trial concerns only the validity of her marriage with Henry. Still, it may remind us of the extent to which the charge of treason was used by Henry, especially once the Act of Treason was passed by Parliament in 1535, allowing an almost indefinite extension of the meaning of "treason" according to the personal whim of the king, particularly against any who might call in question the validity of his second marriage, if only by refusing to take the oath in defence of it, as did Sir Thomas More and Bishop John Fisher. This is exemplified in *The Winter's Tale* by the dilemma of the good Camillo between the obedience he owes to his royal master and the recognition that the latter is "in rebellion with himself" and "will have all that are his so too" (I ii.254). Leontes also has the crazed conviction that not only is Hermione "a traitor, and Camillo is/ a federary with her" (II i.88), but he is among "a nest of traitors", when he sees they will not immediately obey his commands (II iii.81). Then there is Cleomenes's mention of "proclamations" as "forcing faults upon Hermione" (III i.15), in which we may recognize a reference to the royal proclamations of Elizabeth I against the seminary priests and Jesuits, in whom the cause of Katharine and More may be seen as continuing throughout the Tudor period.

On the other hand, just as in *Cymbeline* we noted a strange identification of Posthumus in his Roman exile with the Pope throned in honour and said to be infallible in his solemn decrees, so in *The Winter's Tale* we may also note in the oracle of Apollo at Delphos, to which Hermione makes her appeal, a reference to the similar decree expected by Katherine from Rome as a result of her appeal. Indeed, the wonder elicited in the minds of Dion and Cleomenes at the sight of "the temple" at Delphos, the solemnity of "the sacrifice" and "the ear-deafening voice of the oracle" (III i.2, 6, 9), seems to correspond not so much to anything the dramatist might have learnt from classical sources concerning either Delphi or Delos (two places he has confused in the one name of "Delphos") as to the sight of the newly built basilica of St. Peter's in Rome and the solemnity of a Papal High Mass celebrated there. Secondly, the description of Posthumus in Rome by Iachimo strangely foreshadows that of Polixenes by the repentant Leontes when he welcomes Prince Florizel to Sicilia, "You have a holy father,/ a graceful gentleman, against whose person,/ so sacred as it is, I have done sin" (V i.170). Here the words "holy" and "sacred", as well as "graceful", are hardly applicable to Polixenes as portrayed in this play, least of all in his anger against Florizel and his pursuit of his son with Perdita all the way to Sicilia. But they aptly apply to the Pope in Rome, the Holy Father, against whose person and the whole Catholic Church King Henry had committed the most flagrant sins of sacrilege in the highest degree, to say nothing of his disobedience to papal authority.

Above all, and behind all, we may notice in *The Winter's Tale,* more than in any other of Shakespeare's plays, the pervasive imagery and atmosphere of divine grace, which is so shamefully overlooked by Caroline Spurgeon in her famous study of *Shakespeare's Imagery* (1935). Needless to say, "grace" is, no less than "majesty", the customary title of royalty in Shakespeare's time, and in this play it is used of Leontes and Polixenes, and even little Mamillius, as well as of

Hermione and Perdita. But in the cases of Hermione and Perdita, mother and daughter, it is used with a more than titular meaning. Rather, it is imbued with a deep theological resonance, referring both to divine grace in general and in particular to her who was addressed by the angel as "full of grace" (Luke i.28). In Act I we find an abundance of "grace" on the lips of Hermione herself, as her husband Leontes shares memories of childhood innocence with Polixenes up to the time of meeting with their respective spouses. Then she exclaims, "Grace to boot!" (I ii.80). Their conversation next turns on the first good deed done by Hermione, in the opinion of Leontes, and she again exclaims, "O, would her name were Grace!" (I ii.99). Finally, when Leontes confesses it was the word by which she accepted his proposal, she fully agrees, " 'Tis grace indeed!" (I ii.105). It is this initial grace of Hermione which we find continually affirmed throughout the play, even in the teeth of Leontes's jealous accusations. So Camillo calls her "the gracious queen" (I ii.459), and Paulina, "a gracious innocent soul" (II iii.29). Such expressions are clearly more than merely titular. Rather, they emphasize the inner grace of the good queen, a grace that is inherited by her daughter Perdita, in whose very name we may recognize the theological term *perdita gratia*, the divine grace that was lost *(perdita)* for mankind by the original sin of Adam (or Man). This is symbolized by Leontes's rejection of grace in both his wife and his daughter—as we have already noticed in the case of Lear in relation to his daughter Cordelia.

Then in the Chorus of Time at the beginning of Act IV we are introduced to the maiden Perdita as "now grown in grace equal with wondering" (24), just as in *Pericles* we were introduced to Marina in the Chorus of Gower. Next, we are shown her offering flowers, notably those signifying "grace and remembrance", to the noble visitors at the sheep-shearing feast (IV iii.76). Later, Leontes welcomes her and Florizel, on their arrival in Sicilia, as "a gracious couple", even before he recognizes her as his long-lost daughter. Even without the word "grace", the supernatural reality is implied time and again—once when Florizel denies that the gods ever transformed themselves for a rarer "piece of beauty" (IV iii.32), again when his father Polixenes comments, "Nothing she does or seems/ but smacks of something greater than herself" (IV iii.157), and yet again when the Gentleman describes her to Leontes as "the most peerless piece of earth" and "the rarest of all women" (V i.94, 112)—as if recalling the words of Elizabeth to Mary in Luke i.42, "Blessed art thou among women." Above all, she is described as a source of wonder—first, on her arrival with Florizel in Sicilia, when Leontes hails them not only as a "gracious couple" but also as "begetting wonder" (V i.133), next, when the Gentleman speaks of "the passion of wonder" occasioned by the revelation of Perdita as Leontes's long-lost daughter (V ii.17), and lastly, when the same Gentleman adds that "such a deal of wonder is broken out within this hour", it seems as if "every wink of an eye some new grace will be born" (V ii.25, 124).

Finally, all this outpouring of grace and wonder comes to a climax in the last scene, when the statue is unveiled by the loyal Paulina and turns out to be the living reality of Hermione. Here it may be noted, first, that the sculptor's name is mentioned (contrary to the dramatist's custom) as "that rare Italian master, Julio Romano" (V ii.108). He is known as one of Raphael's disciples, and many of his paintings are to be seen in the Vatican Museum not far from the Sistine Chapel, amply justifying his surname of "Romano"—though he is not known as a sculptor. Secondly, before the statue Leontes recalls how the original Hermione was "as tender as infancy and grace" (V iii.26). Then Perdita falls to her knees, with an apology to Protestant members of the audience, "Do not say 'tis superstition that/ I kneel and then implore her blessing" (V iii.43)—as they would have said if this had been no more than a statue. Thirdly, when the time comes, Paulina tells the assembled guests, "It is required/ you do awake your faith" (V iii.94), presumably faith in miracles, before turning to address the statue, "Bequeath to death your numbness, for from him/ dear life redeems you" (V iii.102). Thus Hermione is restored by a "miracle"—comparable to that for Thaissa in *Pericles* (V ii) and that for Imogen in *Cymbeline*—to her husband Leontes and her daughter Perdita. Then for Perdita in particular she prays, "You gods, look down,/ and from your sacred vials pour your graces/ upon my daughter's head!" (V iii.121). So the play comes to its conclusion with a superabundance of divine grace, if in a seemingly polytheistic sense—for the sake of avoiding the penalty imposed on any "abuse" of the name of God.

The Tempest

There is something deeply, if not so obviously, recusant in the background of Shakespeare's last complete play, *The Tempest.* In its very title, referring only to what takes place in the opening scene, we may find implied all that has happened to the Catholic recusants during the reign of "the wicked queen" in the long years of her persecution. It is what Prospero calls "the dark backward and abysm of time" (I ii.50). Now, however, in spite of the aftermath of the Gunpowder Plot, their troubles seem to have passed with the passing of such an arch-enemy as Archbishop Bancroft in 1610, when the dramatist was presumably engaged on his composition of the play. The title also points to a real tempest that broke over the English fleet on their way to Virginia in 1609, when one of the ships, *The Sea-Venture,* was wrecked on the coast of "the still vex'd Bermoothes" (I ii.229). Various pamphlets on this event that were published in the course of the following year evidently inspired the dramatist to compose his play, which is mostly, if unusually, his own invention. From a recusant viewpoint, it is noteworthy that the Virginia Company, which sponsored the expedition, included not a few Catholics, including two noblemen, Shakespeare's former patron, the third Earl of Southampton, and the so-called "wizard earl", the ninth Earl of Northumberland, who was nephew to the seventh earl, Thomas Percy, now revered as a blessed martyr in the Catholic Church. Such ventures, they hoped, might bring them a measure of toleration, if only in exile, and eventually in the next reign of Charles I they did succeed for a time in establishing a Catholic colony in Maryland (named after the Catholic queen, Henrietta Maria) in 1632 under George Calvert, Lord Baltimore.

Another point of recusant interest in the background of *The Tempest* is the situation of exile which it shares with *As You Like It,* as well as with *Richard II* and *King Lear.* Here, too, in Prospero we see a banished duke, like Duke Senior, if with no other companion on his desert island than his daughter Miranda—not counting the spirit Ariel and the earthy Caliban. Here he has no old religious men, like those in the Forest of Arden, to keep him company, nor other exiled gentlemen. Yet Miranda alone, as another ideal heroine "full of grace", is a sufficient symbol of the recusant presence, standing as she does for the person of Our Lady. Her very name, parallel with that of Marina, suggests a combination of two titles under which Mary is invoked in the customary Litany of Loreto: *"Mater admirabilis"* and *"Virgo veneranda"*. This meaning of her name is specially emphasized by her lover Ferdinand, Prince of Naples, when he meets her soon after his safe arrival on the island. To him she is "the goddess/ on whom these airs attend" (I ii.418), whereas her father roughly pretends to treat him (like a recusant) as "a spy" and "a traitor" (I ii.452, 457). Subsequently, on learning her name, he exclaims, "Admir'd Miranda!/ Indeed, the top of admiration, worth/ what's dearest in the world!" (III i.37). He sees her, as Florizel sees Perdita, and as Orlando sees Rosalind (III ii.139), as "so perfect and so peerless" and "created/ of every creature's best" (III i.47). Again, like Perdita, Miranda is attended with "wonder"—from the outset, when she is addressed by Ferdinand as "O you wonder!" (I ii.423), to the outcome, when Prospero discloses the "wonder" of Ferdinand and Miranda at a game of chess (V i.170), and Miranda in turn finds "wonder" in the "many goodly creatures" so strangely gathered in her father's lonely cell, in the beauty of mankind, and in the "brave new world" she sees in them (V i.181). Yet again, she is the third heroine who is outstanding for the virtue of patience. The first was Viola in *Twelfth Night*, where she describes herself as "Patience on a monument,/ smiling at grief" (II iv.116). The second was Marina in *Pericles*, who is described by her father as "patience . . . smiling extremity out of act" (V i.140). Now we have Miranda described by her father partly as the abstract virtue of Patience, partly as the Virgin Mary, in his odd reply to Alonso, "I rather think/ you have not sought her help, of whose soft grace/ for the like loss I have her sovereign aid" (V i.141).

Also in the recusant background of *The Tempest* we may include the dramatist's personal memories of the days he spent in Lancashire as tutor in the household of Alexander Houghton before embarking on his dramatic career. This we may find in the scene where Prospero plays the part of "schoolmaster" to his dear Miranda, as he seeks to evoke in the Socratic manner her memories out of "the dark backward and abysm of time" (I ii.50). That was the time when the young Shakespeare was, as we have noticed, in a position to profit from the *Spiritual Exercises* of St. Ignatius under the direction of the Jesuit Edmund Campion. In this play he echoes one of those exercises, that on personal sin, in the words addressed by Ariel to the "three men of sin" (III iii.53), "The powers, delaying, not forgetting have/ incens'd the seas and shores, yea, all the creatures,/ against your peace" (III iii.73). In the *Exercises* what we actually find is the same language used in a contrary sense, as the exercitant is invited to wonder at the way all creatures have "permitted me to live and have sustained me in life", and the way the earth has not yet opened "to swallow me up and create new hells in which I should be tormented forever". The moral is, however, in either case the same, the need of "heart-sorrow/ and a clear life ensuing" (III iii.81). It was, moreover, in the same northern county of Lancashire a few years later that the young dramatist may have been introduced to his first noble patron, Ferdinando Stanley, Lord Strange, son and heir of the fourth Earl of Derby, and so entered the company of Strange's Men, who also performed on London stages. From this patron he may have taken the names of both the King of Navarre in his early comedy of *Love's Labour's Lost* and the Prince of Naples in *The Tempest*.

Apart from the pamphlets of 1610 on the expedition of the Virginia fleet and the wreck of *The Sea-Venture*, the one certain, if minor, source for this play, for Gonzalo's mock description of his ideal "commonwealth" (II i.154), is Montaigne's essay "On Cannibals" (1580), which was translated into English by Southampton's Italian tutor, John Florio, in 1603. All the same, by way of Montaigne, we may look further back in time to yet another connection between the dramatist and Sir Thomas More in the latter's *Utopia*

(1516). The actual words of Gonzalo are indeed taken almost verbatim from Montaigne's essay, but his humorous addition at the end of his description, that he has been indulging in a "kind of merry fooling" (II i.184), points rather to More, with his celebrated fondness for merry jests. Moreover, as the wise counsellor to King Alonso and as a "holy" and "honourable man" (V i.62), Gonzalo belongs to a succession of such counsellors in the final romances: Helicanus in *Pericles*, Belarius in *Cymbeline*, and Camillo in *The Winter's Tale*, all of whom may be taken to represent the treasured memory of Sir Thomas More in the mind of Shakespeare "the Papist".

Finally, as we approach the end of this last of Shakespeare's complete plays, we may notice a contrast of two seemingly opposite moods. One is the happy outcome in forgiveness and reconciliation, with a Catholic emphasis on "miracle" and "providence" as well as "wonder", notably in the prayer of the holy Gonzalo—recalling that of Hermione at the end of *The Winter's Tale*—for Ferdinand and Miranda: "Look down, you gods,/ and on this couple drop a blessed crown!" (V i.201). He goes on, in words that may recall to a Catholic mind the liturgical hymn for the Easter Vigil, the *Exultet*, "O rejoice/ beyond a common joy, and set it down/ with gold on lasting pillars!" (V i.206)—the hymn we have found recalled both in *Romeo and Juliet* (II ii.139) and in *The Merchant of Venice* (V i.1). On this Alonso makes the wondering comments "These are not natural events" and "There is in this business more than nature/ was ever conduct of" (V i.227, 243). So they all return happily to Naples to celebrate the wedding of hero and heroine, Ferdinand and Miranda, needless to say in a Catholic ceremony. On the other hand, the dramatist himself, through the mouthpiece of Prospero, is about to say farewell to the stage. Already at the abrupt ending of the masque, he warns the lovers, "Our revels now are ended," and then, "We are such stuff/ as dreams are made on, and our little life/ is rounded with a sleep" (IV i.148, 156). Such, it might seem, are the dramatist's final words on human life, and as such they are inscribed on the scroll he is holding in his statue in the Poets' Corner of Westminster Abbey. So while the lovers make their way to Naples for the celebration of their wedding, Prospero will return to Milan, where, he vows, "every third thought shall be my grave" (V i.311). Then he (or Shakespeare in him) goes on to speak the Epilogue, with no more "spirits to enforce" or "art to enchant", and his only "ending is despair,/ unless I be relieved by prayer" (14).

What a sad ending to Shakespeare's dramatic career! In these farewell words of Prospero, the dramatist seems to be speaking like an old man, weighed down by years of dramatic experience. Yet at the time Shakespeare was still, at the age of forty-seven, in the prime of his life—in contrast with (say) Lord Burghley, who had died in 1598 at the age of seventy-eight, and Queen Elizabeth, who had died in 1603 at the age of seventy. So why, we may ask, did Shakespeare feel that now, as Guiderius and Arviragus chant over the body of Imogen, "Thou thy worldly task hast done,/ home art gone and ta'en thy wages" (*Cymbeline* IV ii.261)? It may not yet have been the time for him to die—that was to come five years later. But now he may have felt that the time had come for him to leave the stage and retire to his home in Stratford, to enjoy his declining years in company with his wife, Anne, and his elder daughter, Susanna. Also at this time we may note two topical reasons that possibly prompted him to leave public life. One was his involvement with the recusant families in Yorkshire, at whose homes two of his plays had been presented in the winter of 1609–10; and the affair had been brought before the Court of Star Chamber in Westminster. The other was John Speed's mention of him in his *History of Great Britain* (1611), in conjunction with the Jesuit Robert Persons as "this papist and his poet". In the combination of these two events Shakespeare may have felt that, as we say of secret agents nowadays, "his cover was blown", and that in view of this double connection with recusancy he could hardly continue his work on the stage without danger. So now, he may have reasoned, was the time for farewell and prayer.

Henry VIII

Turning at last from Shakespeare's final romances, *Pericles, Cymbeline, The Winter's Tale,* and *The Tempest*, to his—insofar as it may be called his—final history play or historical romance, *Henry VIII*, we may find in the latter both an anti-climax and a conclusion to the series of romances. It comes as an anti-climax with its lack of plot structure and its weak characterization, not to mention its superabundance of feminine endings. It consists in little more than a procession of pageants, interspersed with the falls of princes, as one by one Buckingham, Wolsey, and Katharine lose the favour of the faceless tyrant and are replaced by Anne Boleyn, Cromwell, and Cranmer, culminating in the latter's glowing prophecy concerning the future reign of the newborn princess Elizabeth, when "God shall be truly known" (V v.37). Such a loose structure, with such feeble attempts at characterization, is rather to be attributed to the apprentice hand of John Fletcher, new to the King's Men, than to the master hand of William Shakespeare, already enjoying his retirement at Stratford. Those who do not admit Shakespeare's authorship of the play as a whole, from the time of James Spedding's influential study of it in 1850, agree in recognizing the hand of Fletcher in most of the scenes of Act V, those parts which are mainly indebted to Foxe's *Book of Martyrs* (1563). That was a book of which Shakespeare, for all its popularity in Elizabethan England, made very little use in his plays, evidently inclining to the critique made of it by Robert Persons in his three-volume treatise on *Three Conversions of England* (1603–04).

Considering *Henry VIII*, however, as the end in the line of Shakespeare's romances, and in the light of its historical subject matter, we may see it as making explicit in the person of Henry much of what has remained implicit in the line of such royal figures as Pericles, Cymbeline, Leontes, and Alonso. Yet the character of Henry himself, in spite of the many speeches put into his mouth, remains but dimly drawn. He bears the responsibility for the above-mentioned series of tragic downfalls, while remaining a faceless—and faithless—tyrant. At times he expresses anger, now at Buckingham, whom he spurns as "a traitor to the height" (I ii.214), now at Wolsey, on whom he frowns without speaking "as if ruin leap'd from his eyes" (III ii.206). Only Katharine, whose trial is for no fault of her own but for his doubt concerning the validity of their marriage, he professes to admire as "the queen of earthly queens" (II iv.139) and as "before the primest creature/ that's paragon'd o' the world" (II iv.227). These words of his, however, hardly accord with the cruelty he showed her in historical fact during the period of her retirement, when he refused to allow her daughter Mary any access to her even in her dying moments. At the same time, within the play we are shown his lust for Anne Boleyn, hinted at in the knowing conversation between two lords. When the Lord Chamberlain remarks, "It seems the marriage with his brother's wife"—meaning Katharine, who had been married to Prince

Arthur just before his death in 1502—"has crept too near his conscience", he is corrected by the Duke of Suffolk, "No, his conscience has crept too near another lady" (II ii.17).

As for this other lady, Anne Boleyn, we are shown the king's first infatuation with her in his exclamation, as if he were another Romeo, "O beauty, till now I never knew thee!" (I iv.75). His words are ironically taken out of St. Augustine's *Confessions*, where the saint is speaking to God: "Late have I known you, beauty of ancient days, yet ever new!" (X xxvii). Subsequently, we are presented with a whole scene, in which the hand of Shakespeare is generally recognized (like the above-quoted scene between the two lords), where Anne is subjected to the withering satire of an old court lady. The latter speaks slightingly of "this spice of your hypocrisy", "your mincing", and "your soft cheveril conscience" (II iii.2, 31), just before the Lord Chamberlain enters to inform Anne of her sudden ennobling as Marchioness of Pembroke—an honour which she, of course, readily accepts.

Concerning Katharine of Aragon, we have the comment of Dr. Johnson, writing in the eighteenth century, long before the critical study of James Spedding, that the scenes in which she appears—though some of them are ascribed by Spedding to Fletcher on stylistic grounds—are among "the greatest efforts of tragedy". Then he goes on to say, "The genius of Shakespeare comes in and goes out with Katharine." Otherwise, he notes, as if in anticipatory support of Spedding, "Every other part may be easily conceived and easily written." The scene in which Katharine is most deeply involved, that of her trial concerning the validity of her marriage with Henry, is both clearly Shakespearian and strangely parallel with Hermione's trial for adultery in *The Winter's Tale* (III ii). Here she speaks of herself as "a most poor woman" and yet "the daughter of a king", namely the King of Spain (II iv.13, 70), just as Hermione speaks of herself on that other occasion as "a great king's daughter", namely the emperor of Russia (III ii.40, 120), while Leontes on his side anticipates the words of Katharine in calling his wife "the daughter of a king" (III ii.3). Katharine goes on to make her "appeal to the Pope" (II iv.117), just as Hermione makes her appeal to the oracle of Apollo at Delphos. Further, in a recusant context we may add that Katharine appears in this play as yet another figure of Mary as "full of grace", though for the most part this word is used in a purely titular manner.

Also in *Henry VIII* we may see the lines of the future religious division being drawn, even in the words of Cardinal Wolsey at the time of his downfall. He may be a "proud priest" (III ii.252) and as such opposed by the good queen Katharine. Yet as a Catholic, he recognizes in Anne Boleyn "a spleeny Lutheran" (III ii.100), and in Thomas Cranmer, now "sprung up" in the royal favour, "a heretic, an arch one" (III ii.102). He further commends Sir Thomas More, who appears neither in this nor in any other of Shakespeare's official plays—apart from the detection of his hand in the unprinted, unperformed play of *Sir Thomas More*—as "a learned man" and one likely to "do justice/ for truth's sake and his conscience" (III ii.396). Then there is his famous speech to Cromwell, "Cromwell, I charge thee, fling away ambition" (III ii.441)—which is, however, not ascribed to Shakespeare. Finally, in the outcome of his downfall and death, Wolsey is movingly described by Griffith to Katharine in words that one might like to be Shakespeare's, though they are ascribed to Fletcher: "His overthrow heap'd happiness upon him,/ for then, and not till then, he felt himself,/ and found the blessedness of being little" (IV ii.64).

These lines of religious division come strangely from the mouth of Wolsey, who died in 1530, long before the division came into being, with the king's claim to be supreme head of the Church in England in 1534, his execution of More and Fisher in 1535, and his suppression of all shrines and monasteries in the realm from 1536 to 1540. These stirring events, for which the reign of Henry VIII has come to be chiefly remembered, are covered over with a strange silence in the play of *Henry VIII*. What is even more surprising is that the execution of Anne, though it took place at the same time as the death of Katharine, is also passed over in silence. Yet the dramatist, whoever he may be, hastens to go on to further events in Acts IV and V, from the solemnization of Henry's marriage with Anne in 1533 (IV i) to the christening of the baby princess Elizabeth in the same year (V v), while anachronistically presenting the plot of Gardiner against Cranmer, which did not take place till 1540. In that scene Gardiner points to Cranmer as "a most arch heretic, a pestilence/ that does infect the land" (V i.45), words that fall in Spedding's division among those he attributes to Shakespeare. In the outcome, however, Cranmer is protected by the king, and it is Gardiner who falls from grace.

In conclusion, we may well ask the reason for the abovementioned silence. Maybe even in the reign of James I, and even with the formal reinstatement of James's mother, Mary Queen of Scots, in a solemn tomb in Westminster Abbey (1612), Shakespeare may not have felt himself free to deal with such a delicate subject. So he wrote what he could, or allowed Fletcher to write, on the reign of Henry VIII, short of dealing with the religious changes that the king had set afoot. His emphasis is therefore rather on Henry's first queen, Katharine of Aragon, than on Henry himself, while he seems to have left much in the hands of his young collaborator. We also have to remember that we have no means of knowing how much he knew or approved of the play in its final version, particularly the anti-Catholic additions in Act V inspired by John Foxe. Perhaps he thought he had gone as far as he could, short of betraying his religious allegiance. And perhaps he thought, like Sir Thomas More in the Tower, that silence on such a matter as the impending religious "reformation" might speak louder than words.

Afterword

FROM THE TIME Roland Mushat Frye brought out his study of *Shakespeare and Christian Doctrine* in 1963, there has developed a certain prejudice in the world of Shakespearian scholarship against all attempts to find allegorical or theological "meanings" in the plays of Shakespeare. All such attempts Frye labelled "allegorizing" or "theologizing". Then, perceiving in some of them the influence of G. Wilson Knight, with his attribution of "Christ-figures" to certain characters, he classed them all together as "the school of Knight", with parodic reference to another school (of atheism) supposedly mentioned by Shakespeare in *Love's Labour's Lost*—in a disputed reading of the text—as "the school of night" (IV iii.255). His basic reason for rejecting such religious interpretations—though proposed by such eminent scholars as R. W. Chambers, Roy Battenhouse, Irving Ribner, and Paul Siegel, as well as Wilson Knight himself—was that with the Protestant Reformation there came in a resolutely secular approach to drama, with the full approval of Luther and Calvin, in opposition to the religious drama of the Catholic Middle Ages. It was, he argued, in accordance with this approach that Shakespeare would have written his plays in the Elizabethan age: and that, whatever his own religious convictions may have been, he had, in common with all his fellow dramatists, including a professed recusant like Ben Jonson, to cater to the tastes and expectations of a largely Protestant audience. In fact, it is undeniable that none of Shakespeare's plays are religious. They are no less secular than the other plays of his age. So there seems to be no reason—according to Frye, whether in the plays themselves or in the dramatic theory of the age, whether in the teaching of Renaissance humanists or of Reformation divines—to think otherwise and look for hidden meanings that are belied by the clear meaning of Shakespeare's text.

Such an argument, for all its seeming cogency, especially for those who already agree with its premises, is based on the supposition that Shakespeare himself either was a Protestant, in basic agreement with the teachings of Luther and/or Calvin, or was concerned to suppress any private religious opinions of his own in order to meet the expectations of his audiences. It overlooks the fact that, in the dramatic tradition of Shakespeare's time, there still remained strong Catholic tendencies, against which Puritan authors, such as Philip Stubbes in his *Anatomy of Abuses* (1583), were only too eager to warn their readers. Even the mystery and morality plays, which had been so popular up till the eve of the Reformation, retained much of their popularity in the teeth of continued episcopal hostility till well into the 1580s, and it is commonly admitted that the young Shakespeare may have seen performances of them in the nearby city of Coventry, which was a famous centre for them. As for the presence of hidden "meanings" in drama and literature, so far from being denied by Renaissance critics, at least those who were not Puritan, they were fostered by the theory and practice of such eminent poets as Dante and Spenser, as well as by the prevailing tendency of Florentine Neoplatonism, which spread from Italy to England not least during the Elizabethan age. Only the Puritans, in whose spirit Frye was writing, discouraged it, but they constituted a small minority of critical opinion, if we consider not only little England but also the learned world on the Catholic continent.

Shakespeare was, it is true, largely cut off from that wider world of learning in consequence of the so-called reformation in England—which might more accurately be called "secularization"—and the related marginalization of English Catholics, who now came to be regarded by the Elizabethan establishment as "recusants" for their refusal to swim with the current of religious fashion imposed by court and government. Hence, whatever his religious opinions may have been, Shakespeare had to observe the secular requirements of Elizabethan drama and to abstain from any religious profession in his plays, and so to produce the seemingly secular plays that have come down to us. Thus far I have no difficulty about agreeing with Frye. At the same time, we have to remember what he and his followers seem to have overlooked, namely, the ambiguity and ambivalence so deep in the language of Shakespeare and not a few of his contemporaries, such as John Donne—a quality that was fiercely opposed not only by the Puritans of the Elizabethan and succeeding ages but also by the philosophers and scientists of the "new age" from Sir Francis Bacon onwards. It is they who ultimately prevailed, with their insistence—stated explicitly by Thomas Sprat in his manifesto for the Royal Society in 1667—on the need of restricting one word to one meaning in the name of clarity. This is why, among other reasons, for all their admiration of Shakespeare's plays, the poets and critics of the Age of Reason—Dryden and Pope, Addison and Johnson—unite in condemnation of his addiction to puns, which they saw as a common literary vice of that age.

Even today, when Shakespeare's puns are receiving more scholarly appreciation, the variety of meanings with which he sprinkles his plays is less willingly tolerated by some who doubt if there is a "meaning" to be found in any of them, religious or otherwise.

Turning now to the age in which Shakespeare was composing his plays, it is all very well to say that he wisely suppressed his religious opinions to satisfy the expectations of his audiences, not to mention the more exacting requirements of the government, exercised through a rigorous censorship. Yet can we really expect such a lame subservience to authority on the part of so profound and versatile a genius? Had he held so lightly to his religious opinions, he might no less lightly have abandoned them in the face of determined official opposition, amounting even to persecution, such as we find in the English government of the time under the direction of the two Cecils, father and son. But if he was, like his father before him and his daughter after him, a Catholic and a recusant—though he managed to keep his name off the recusant lists—however much he had (like Hamlet) to hold his tongue, he could surely with all the versatility of his genius have found ways to express what he most wanted to say, even if (like Duke Vincentio) his givings out had to be an infinite distance from his true-meant design.

With all this in mind, it is not enough for us to indulge in ifs and maybes. We need some positive evidence to go on before seeking hidden recusant meanings in the plays. We need to weigh the historical facts of Shakespeare's birth and upbringing, not only with what may be gleaned from Stratford and other records, but also with what we know was taking place in England at the time of Shakespeare's growth to maturity. In this matter a certain consensus has been emerging among scholars both of English history and of Shakespearian biography, that Shakespeare was brought up in a traditional Catholic family and in an area, the Forest of Arden, where there were still many Catholic connections. These connections further point to a period in Shakespeare's youth, when he was living, teaching, and producing plays of his own for a Catholic gentleman's household in the largely Catholic county of Lancashire. This is the historical background which I have presented in summary form in my first chapter before going on to deal with the plays one by one, without omitting any of those included in the First Folio of 1623, but admitting one, *Pericles*, which only came to be included in a second printing of the Third Folio of 1664.

Still, we cannot say that Shakespeare was certainly a recusant. He was never, like his father John and his daughter Susanna, mentioned in any list of recusants that has come down to us. What is offered by the biographical facts amounts to no more than a strong probability, supported by much circumstantial evidence. But in passing from his biography to his plays, we have to examine each of them in turn, asking to what extent, given the probable recusancy of the dramatist and his need of disguising the fact, we may find in them signs of a lurking Catholic allegiance. Certain passages in certain plays may suggest doubts. One may point, for example, (1) to his portrayal of the pious Joan of Arc as a witch and a whore in the first Part of *Henry VI*, (2) to the denunciation of Rome by the king and the patriotic support given him by the Bastard in *King John*, (3) to the fact that *Measure for Measure*, with its sacrilegious presentation of the duke-friar pretending to have heard sacramental confession, was entirely deleted by the Jesuit censor for the Spanish Inquisition in the mid-seventeenth century, (4) to the implied ridicule in the Porter's speech in *Macbeth* of both the Jesuit theory of equivocation and its recent practitioner,

Father Henry Garnet, on trial for complicity in the Gunpowder Plot, and (5) to the prophecy of Cranmer at the end of *Henry VIII*, foretelling the glorious reign of Queen Elizabeth, when "God shall be truly known." Such problems for a recusant or Papist interpretation of the plays have to be faced and solved. The possibility has also to be admitted that there may have been times when Shakespeare was less strongly committed to the Catholic cause than at other times. This is what we see in the case of Ben Jonson, who became a Catholic recusant while in prison in 1598—when he was befriended by Shakespeare and introduced to the Chamberlain's Men—but went on to renounce his recusancy in the aftermath of the Gunpowder Plot, perhaps to save his skin. In Shakespeare, too, some decline in recusant reference has been noted in the series of Roman plays following on *King Lear* and preceding *Pericles*, as if he, too, was wavering in his religious allegiance till he was perhaps won back by his dying mother's prayers. So it may have been significant that, besides the fact that those two plays had recently been printed in quarto form, they were the ones chosen by the Cholmeley Players as most suited for performance before recusant audiences in Yorkshire.

All this is, I admit, a hypothesis, but it is a good working hypothesis, grounded on historical fact, for the purpose of examining the plays one by one. Indeed, I may claim that this is the first time this hypothesis has been tested by the plays, not just one or another but systematically, taking them all together in chronological order. In each case I ask the question, "In this play, insofar as we have it from Shakespeare's pen, what evidence is to be found in it of Catholic allegiance, or at least of Catholic sympathies?" In a book of this kind such words as "Recusant", "Papist", and "Catholic", as well as "Protestant" and "Puritan", inevitably recur in chapter headings and the text, and their repetition may get on the nerves even of sympathetic readers. But given my hypothesis, which has to be tested in play after play, I cannot see how this can be avoided. Then, too, there is an abundance of such cautious words as "may", "maybe", "may well", "perhaps", "possibly", and "probably" that may irritate the more factually or historically minded of my readers. But I have used such forms, instead of more positive forms, in the interests of historical truth, so as not to claim more for my hypothesis than the facts of Shakespeare's life or the text of his plays may warrant. Only, as I insist, what appears here and there in particular instances as no more than a possibility may join with other instances and thus, in the words of Hippolyta in *A Midsummer Night's Dream*, "grow to something of great constancy" (V i.26). Then for the perception of such joining what is needed is an open mind.

There still remains, however, one basic objection to my hypothesis, that in seeking to interpret the plays of Shakespeare from a Papist viewpoint I am incurring the charge of what is often called "reductionism"—that is to say, of restricting the much admired universality of Shakespeare's genius to one particular point of view. No, I have no intention of disputing or restricting Shakespeare's universality, or of denying what Ben Jonson says of him, that "he was not of an age, but for all time". But I do maintain two things which are not always noticed by those who are most ready to make this accusation of "reductionism". The first is that Shakespeare, while undoubtedly possessed of a universal genius, such that he might well be called a "citizen of the world", was none the less an Englishman of his own age, and proud to be so, though not necessarily well disposed to the queen and her ministers. And as an Englishman of his own age, claiming descent through his mother from the noble Warwickshire family of Arden, he could hardly have been indifferent to the religious issue of the time or to the fact that the "old faith" of his country from time immemorial was being systematically uprooted, for largely personal and political reasons, by the Welsh rulers of England, with the assistance of upstarts such as the Earl of Leicester and parvenus such as Cromwell and the two Cecils. Then, as poet and dramatist, he could hardly help giving expression, though necessarily in an indirect manner, to his deep feelings. Indeed, the very dilemma he must have felt between his inner desire and his inability to express it may well have been a principal source of his poetic and dramatic inspiration. On the other hand, those who, scandalized by such human particularity, emphasize the universality of the dramatist all too easily condemn themselves—like Harold Bloom—to the mouthing of commonplaces. As George Bernard Shaw wisely observes, in writing of *The Sanity of Art* (1908), "The writer who aims at producing the platitudes which are 'not for an age, but for all time', has his reward in being unreadable in all ages", whereas "The man who writes about himself and his own time is the only man who writes about all people and about all time."

The second point I wish to make is that the criticism of "reductionism" often has what I might call a boomerang effect. It all too easily returns to the hand and the head of the critic. Indeed, all criticism may be accused of "reductionism", especially in connection with an author of such universal breadth of mind as Shakespeare. Few critics, least of all academic critics when they are too concerned with the professional requirements of their discipline, can claim true universality of mind. Fewer still can claim a combination of such universality with the intimate knowledge required of all the particularities of Shakespeare's age and nation, especially when it comes to his religious background. Moreover, what I find strange in the accusation of "reductionism" in the mouths of modern critics is the way they often combine it with the latest theories of structuralism, post-structuralism, deconstructionism, new historicism, cultural relativism, and post-modernism, not to mention Darwinism, Freudianism, Marxism, and so many other modern -isms. Each by itself is enough to prevent any student from entering sympathetically into any human or personal connection with Shakespeare and his age. All are so many coloured spectacles, like the colours associated with various illnesses, revealing the dramatist not in his own light but in a perverted, distorted, inhuman obscurity. At least, I may claim that the particular viewpoint from which I approach the life and works of Shakespeare is neither mine alone, nor any modern fashion, but one that I may not unreasonably profess to share with him. Recusancy may not be a problem that faces me in today's world, but as an English Jesuit I have long been familiar with it as it existed in Elizabethan England, in Shakespeare's time, and as it affected my predecessors in the Society of Jesus from the time of Campion and Persons onwards. In fact, as I look at the plays of Shakespeare from this viewpoint, it amazes me how many of the problems connected with them find in it a convenient solution. Nor do I see them just as problems calling for a solution, but as words and sentences and whole speeches pointing away from themselves to a hidden source of inspiration. Thus the viewpoint is not so particular after all, but it is closely connected with something universal, encompassing all the plays of the great dramatist, while looking in and through them to "that within which passeth show"—and that is the heart of Shakespeare's mystery.

Bibliographical Notes

On General Reference

Two books that have always been close to my hand in the writing of this work are, first, *The Reader's Encyclopedia of Shakespeare* (1966), edited by O. J. Campbell, and supplemented by the two volumes of E. K. Chambers' *William Shakespeare* (1930) and secondly, the survey of *Shakespeare's Sources* (1959) by K. Muir, with occasional reference to the authoritative eight-volume *Narrative and Dramatic Sources of Shakespeare's Plays* (1957–75) by G. Bullough.

On Shakespeare's Biography

The standard book of reference, after the above-mentioned work of E. K. Chambers, is still S. Schoenbaum's *William Shakespeare, A Documentary Life* (1975)—for all the author's ingrained scepticism. It is, however, noteworthy how many attempts at replacing him have appeared recently, almost at the rate of one a year, two of them by professors of poetry at Oxford, Peter Levi's *The Life and Times of William Shakespeare* (1988) and Ted Hughes's *Shakespeare and the Goddess of Complete Being* (1992). In between them there appeared Gary O'Connor's *William Shakespeare, A Life* (1991) and—what I regard as the best biography of recent times—Ian Wilson's *Shakespeare, The Evidence* (1993). They were followed by

S. Wells's *Shakespeare, A Dramatic Life* (1994) and E. Sams's *The Real Shakespeare* (1995). Then came two biographies by novelists, A. Burgess's *Shakespeare* (1996) and his admirer A. Holden's *William Shakespeare* (1999). Then there were two notable interpretations by Jonathan Bate, *The Genius of Shakespeare* (1997), and by Harold Bloom, *Shakespeare, The Invention of the Human* (1998). Finally, there have been the difficult but competent biography by Park Honan, *Shakespeare, A Life* (1998), and K. Duncan-Jones's ungentle interpretation in *The Ungentle William Shakespeare* (2001), which harks back to S. Lee's earlier standard biography, *William Shakespeare* (1898).

On Shakespeare's Catholicism

The first account on this subject was H. S. Bowden's *The Religion of Shakespeare* (1899), based on notes left by the Victorian scholar Richard Simpson. Then came the Countess de Chambrun's *Shakespeare Rediscovered* (1938), J. H. de Groot's *The Shakespeares and 'The Old Faith'* (1946), and H. Mutschmann and K. Wentersdorf's *Shakespeare and Catholicism* (1952), which is summed up in an Appendix, "Was Shakespeare a Recusant?" to M. D. Parker's *The Slave of Life* (1955). Here I may add my own study of *Shakespeare's Religious Background* (1973), followed up by my two volumes on *The Religious Controversies of the Elizabethan Age* (1977) and *The Jacobean Age* (1978). Then came two Catholic biographies by R. Speaight, *Shakespeare, the Man and His Achievement* (1977), and Ian Wilson, *Shakespeare, the Evidence* (1993), mentioned above—to which I may add my recent Catholic interpretations, *The Catholicism of Shakespeare's Plays* (1997) and *Shakespeare's Apocalypse* (2000), as well as C. Enos's *Shakespeare and the Catholic Religion* (2000).

On Shakespeare and Religion

From an agnostic viewpoint, first to be mentioned is W. J. Birch's *Inquiry into the Philosophy and Religion of Shakespeare* (1846). Then from a Protestant viewpoint came R. M. Frye's *Shakespeare and Christian Doctrine* (1963), from a vaguely Christian viewpoint, M. Lings's *Shakespeare in the Light of Sacred Art* (1966), and from a spiritualist viewpoint, G. Wilson Knight's *Shakespeare and Religion* (1967). Two more came from a Protestant viewpoint, I. Morris's *Shakespeare's God* (1972)—echoing W. Empson's title, *Milton's God* (1961) and W. R. Elton's *King Lear and the Gods* (1965)—and R. G. Hunter's *Shakespeare and the Mystery of God's Judgments* (1976)—in turn echoing the title of R. H. West's *Shakespeare and the Outer Mystery* (1968). Then there came a notable anthology by Christian scholars edited by Roy Battenhouse and entitled *Shakespeare's Christian Dimension* (1994)—whose title may have come from my own *Shakespeare's Other Dimension* (1987), republished in America as *The Mediaeval Dimension of Shakespeare's Plays* (1990) and dedicated to Roy. Lastly, I may add the self-styled Gnostic approach of Harold Bloom in his above-mentioned *Shakespeare, The Invention of the Human* (1998).

On the Biblical Influence in Shakespeare

The first book calling for mention is C. Wordsworth's *Shakespeare's Knowledge and Use of the Bible* (1864), followed by detailed lists of biblical references in T. Carter's *Shakespeare and Holy Scripture* (1905) and R. Noble's *Shakespeare's Biblical Knowledge* (1935). Relying on these three books, I offered a discussion of *Biblical Themes in Shakespeare* (1975), and then with special reference to the four "great tragedies" I published *Biblical Influence in the Great Tragedies* (1985), which was republished in America as *Biblical Influences in Shakespeare's Great Tragedies* (1987). This coincided with N. Shaheen's *Biblical References in Shakespeare's Tragedies* (1987), followed by his companion volumes on *Shakespeare's History Plays* (1989) and *Shakespeare's Comedies* (1993). Lastly, there appeared S. Marx's compact handbook on *Shakespeare and the Bible* (2000).

On the "Shakeshafte" Theory

This theory goes back to O. Baker's *In Shakespeare's Warwickshire and the Unknown Years* (1937), followed by E. K. Chambers's *Shakespearean Gleanings* (1944) and L. Hotson's *Shakespeare's Sonnets Dated* (1949). It received much impetus from A. Keen and R. Lubbock's *The Annotator* (1954), concerning a copy of Hall's *Chronicle* with annotations attributable to the young Shakespeare, and from R. Stevenson's *Shakespeare's Religious Frontier* (1958). I devoted a few pages to the theory in my *Shakespeare's Religious Background* (1973), only to incur criticism from S. Schoenbaum in his *Shakespeare, A Documentary Life* (1975), followed by subsequent exoneration from E. A. J. Honigmann in his *Shakespeare, The 'Lost Years'* (1986). Two of the above-mentioned biographies pay special attention to this theory, those by Park Honan (1998) and Anthony Holden (1999), while a closer study of it has been undertaken by C. Enos in her *Shakespeare and the Catholic Religion* (2000).

On the Jesuit Background

The standard source is H. Foley's six-volume *Records of the English Province SJ* (1877–82), supplemented by J. Morris's three-volume compilation of *The Troubles of Our Catholic*

Forefathers (1872). From the political viewpoint, there is J. Gerard's *What Was the Gunpowder Plot?* (1897) and J. H. Pollen's articles on "The Politics of English Catholics during the Reign of Queen Elizabeth", in *The Month* (1902). On the spiritual testament of John Shakespeare, there are the two pioneering articles by H. Thurston, "The Spiritual Testament of John Shakespeare" in *The Month* (1911), and "A Controverted Shakespeare Document" in *The Dublin Review* (1923). Many Jesuit scholars have appeared in this field in the post-war years, led by L. Hicks with his book on the Babington Plot, *An Elizabethan Problem* (1964), and his edition of materials on the life of Persons, *The Letters and Memorials of Fr R. Persons SJ* (1942). After him came F. Edwards with his book on the Ridolphi Plot, *The Marvellous Chance* (1968), and a biography of Persons, *Robert Persons* (ca. 1990). Then P. Caraman translated the autobiographies (from Latin) of John Gerard (with an Introduction by G. Greene, 1952) and William Weston (1955), followed by *Henry Garnet and the Gunpowder Plot* (1964), and an anthology on Elizabethan Catholicism, *The Other Face* (1960). C. Devlin also published his *Life of Robert Southwell* (1956), with chapter 18, "Master W. S.", and a collection of essays on matters of Elizabethan and Shakespearian interest (originally appearing in *The Month*) under the title *Hamlet's Divinity* (1963). More general are T. Clancy's *Papist Pamphleteers* (1967), in which Persons's writings have pride of place, and B. Basset's *The English Jesuits* (1967), whose first few chapters are devoted to the heroic age of the Jesuits in England. The two major lives of Edmund Campion are not by Jesuits but by laymen, R. Simpson (1867) and E. Waugh (1935).

On Shakespeare's Comedies

For The *Comedy of Errors* I am particularly indebted to T. W. Baldwin's *Shakespeare Adapts a Hanging* (1931) and *On the Compositional Genetics of the Comedy of Errors* (1965). For *The Two Gentlemen of Verona*, in addition to *Romeo and Juliet*, to J. Vyvyan's *Shakespeare and the Rose of Love* (1960). For *A Midsummer Night's Dream*, in addition to *As You Like It*, to J. Vyvyan's other work, *Shakespeare and Platonic Beauty* (1961), also to G. K. Chesterton's essay on "A Midsummer Night's Dream" in *The Common Man* (1950), and N. Coghill's essay on "The Mediaeval Basis of Shakespearian Comedy" for *Essays and Studies* (1950). For *Much Ado About Nothing* to C. Prouty, *The Sources of Much Ado About Nothing* (1950). For *Twelfth Night* to L. Hotson's *The First Night of Twelfth Night* (1954).

On Shakespeare's Histories

Here I am particularly indebted to J. D. Wilson's *Fortunes of Falstaff* (1943) and his editions of the three Parts of *Henry VI* (1952) for the New Cambridge Shakespeare. Also to L. Campbell, *Shakespeare's Histories* (1947), and to A. L. Scoufos, *Shakespeare's Typological Satire* (1979).

On Shakespeare's Problem Comedies

For *Measure for Measure* I am particularly indebted to R. W. Chambers's Academy lecture on "The Jacobean Shakespeare and *Measure for Measure*", reprinted in his *Man's Unconquerable Mind* (1939), and to V. Whitaker's *Shakespeare's Use of Learning* (1953), showing the impact on Shakespeare's mind of Thomistic thought via Richard Hooker. Also for *All's Well That Ends Well* I must mention R. G. Hunter's *Shakespeare and the Comedy of Forgiveness*

(1965), supplemented by frequent conversations on the medical background of the play with my friend R. Stensgaard, at the Huntington Library.

On Shakespeare's "Great Tragedies"

In general I am indebted to J. Vyvyan, *The Shakespearian Ethic* (1959), to R. Battenhouse, *Shakespearean Tragedy, Its Art and Its Christian Premises* (1969), and to P. Siegel, *Shakespearean Tragedy and the Elizabethan Compromise* (1957). Then more specifically, for *Hamlet*, to J. D. Wilson's *What Happens in Hamlet?* (1935) and D. G. James's *The Dream of Learning* (1951), and for *King Lear*, to J. Danby's *Shakespeare's Doctrine of Nature* (1949), M. Mack's *King Lear in Our Time* (1965), and W. R. Elton's *King Lear and the Gods* (1966)—which I admire for its scholarship but reject for its agnostic interpretation.

On Shakespeare's Final Romances

Here I am indebted to two books by S. L. Bethell, *Shakespeare and the Popular Dramatic Tradition* (1944) and his particular study of *The Winter's Tale* (1947). Then there is G. Wilson Knight's *The Crown of Life* (1947), with an Introduction by T. S. Eliot. The editions by F. Kermode for the New Arden *Tempest* (1961) and by F. D. Hoeniger for the New Arden *Pericles* (1963) are each models of the kind. I must again mention R. G. Hunter's *Shakespeare and the Comedy of Forgiveness* (1965), showing how rooted are these plays in the late mediaeval miracle plays. Lastly, there is V. B. Richmond's *Shakespeare, Catholicism and Romance* (2000).

On the Particular Subject of the Cholmeley Plays

There is, first, C. J. Sisson's article on "Shakespeare's Quartos as Prompt Copies, with Some Account of Cholmeley's Players and a New Shakespeare Allusion" (in *Review of English Studies*, 1942), then H. Aveling's *Catholic Recusants of the West Riding of Yorkshire* (1963), C. W. Body's "Players of Interludes in North Yorkshire in the Early Seventeenth Century" (NY County Record Office Publ. 1976), J. L. Murphy, *Darkness and Devils—Exorcism and King Lear* (1984), and, more recently, M. Takenaka, "The Cholmeley Players and the Performance of *King Lear* in Yorkshire" (*Renaissance Bulletin*, Tokyo 2001).

Index

C

D

P

R

S

Y

About the Author

PETER MILWARD, SJ is Professor Emeritus of Sophia University in Tokyo. He entered the Society of Jesus at St. Beuno's College in North Wales in 1943 and then went on to study scholastic philosophy at Heythrop College, Oxon from 1947–50 and classical and English literature at Campion Hall, Oxford from 1950–54. He taught English literature, with special attention to Shakespearian drama, at Sophia University, Toyko from 1962–96, and then at Tokyo Junshin Women's College, as dean of the faculty of Modern Culture, from 1996–2002. Fr. Milward is the founder of the Renaissance Institute and Renaissance Centre at Sophia University, and also the Chesterton Society of Japan and Hopkins Society of Japan. He is the author of innumerable books and articles both in Japan and abroad, especially on Shakespeare, Hopkins, and Chesterton, including *A Lifetime with Hopkins* and *A Poetic Approach to Ecology* published by Sapientia Press of Ave Maria University.